D1555252

DIALECTICAL
READINGS

Stephen N. Dunning

DIALECTICAL READINGS

Three Types of Interpretation

The Pennsylvania State University Press
University Park, Pennsylvania

Library of Congress Cataloging-in-Publication Data

Dunning, Stephen N. (Stephen Northrop), 1941–

Dialectical readings: three types of interpretation / Stephen N. Dunning.

    p.   cm.

Includes bibliographical references and index.

ISBN 0-271-01647-7 (cloth: alk. paper)

ISBN 0-271-01648-5 (pbk.: alk. paper)

    1. Hermeneutics.   2. Dialectic.   I. Title.

BD241.D85   1997

121'.68—dc20   96-34938

                                          CIP

Copyright © 1997 The Pennsylvania State University

All rights reserved

Printed in the United States of America

Published by The Pennsylvania State University Press,

University Park, PA 16802-1003

It is the policy of The Pennsylvania State University Press to use acid-free paper for the first printing of all clothbound books. Publications on uncoated stock satisfy the minimum requirements of American National Standard for Information Sciences—Permanence of Paper for Printed Library Materials, ANSI Z39.48-1992.

Contents

Acknowledgments

This is a project that has evolved in the classroom over a period of ten years, with the result that there are literally dozens of students who have, whether knowingly or not, contributed to it. In particular, one person stands out, a poet who recognized the hermeneutical potential of the dialectical scheme I present in this book long before I was able to articulate its ramifications in anything like an adequate manner. Accordingly, I want to extend special thanks to Patrick Hartigan for his enthusiasm and encouragement at a very early and crucial stage of the project.

To those members of the New Haven Theological Discussion Group, the University of Pennsylvania Religious Studies Colloquium, and the Society of Christian Philosophers who participated in discussions devoted to this project, many thanks for comments that were often challenging and always helpful.

I am also grateful to Sanford Thatcher and Philip Winsor of Penn State Press for their willingness to give an admittedly hard-to-classify manuscript serious consideration. The comments of the readers engaged by them have also been unusually pertinent as I have gone about the task of revising the manuscript. Thanks also to Tirdad Derakhshani for preparing the index.

For the extended sabbatical leave necessary to write this book, I am grateful to the University of Pennsylvania School of Arts and Sciences; and for the grant necessary to extend the leave even further, I express my appreciation to the University Research Foundation.

As always, there is the matter of "collateral damage," and here I must mention my family, who often put up with strange talk or none at all during the writing of this book. I especially thank my wife, Roxy, for her editorial help as well as her unfailing patience and encouragement.

For Ben, Sarah, and David,
from whom I have learned
so much about interpretation

Introduction

A Question

The note has been staring at me for weeks now. A colleague—a scholar in the field of comparative literature—asks me if I have come across any essays that might effectively introduce students to "what we know about interpretation." Students, he finds, are so easily overwhelmed by the variety of interpretations they encounter. Naturally, their initial question is, which one is true? How can we initiate them into the complex world of conflicting understandings of texts and topics? How can we help them move beyond the assumption that only one interpretation can claim to be true, to see that differing readings of the same texts are often helpful, even when they are incompatible with one another? In short, how can we teach them to interpret the interpretations?

Some colleagues do not suffer over this problem. They offer students a method of reading that is, if not absolutely true, at least markedly superior to its competitors. Or so they say. And many students are grateful for the guidance. Although some may protest, perhaps silently, others will find themselves easily persuaded by the instructor—until they find themselves in another course where a contrary method is taught. Faced with this conflict, they either dismiss as a hopeless jumble of jargon any discussion about interpretation or they become real students again. In the process they also come to realize that their earlier enthrallment had been a bit like discipleship: sitting at the master's feet, they had apprenticed themselves to this person who had seemed so knowledgeable and articulate that they had not rigorously questioned what they were being taught.

I respect my colleague's refusal to turn his students into disciples. But I have no answer for him. I have not found any essay that sums up "what we know about interpretation," and I doubt that one could be written. There are so many important interpretations of interpretation that a small encyclopedia would be necessary to do justice to them all. Moreover, such a survey of all the options would not answer many students' primary question. In its effort to present each position fairly, it would scrupulously avoid any hint of privileging one of them over the others.

Yet the students continue to come, to question, to confront us with that question. They struggle on in their bewilderment over the variety of hermeneutical positions. Meanwhile, teachers (as opposed to masters) muddle on with the knowledge that, in presenting a variety of conflicting interpretations, we may inadvertently be encouraging a cynical hermeneutical relativism, the view that interpretation is nothing more than a personal and therefore arbitrary imposition of the reader's meaning on a text. Certainly relativistic and reader-response theories of interpretation abound, especially in our own time. So also do absolutistic assumptions, in particular the belief that it is possible to read a text directly, without the intervention of an interpretative lens. Let me say at the outset that I find both of these positions equally unsatisfactory.

As has often been pointed out, relativism is a self-contradictory position insofar as it claims truth for itself. If all interpretations are relative to culture, time, place, or personal bias of the interpreter, then so is that very interpretation of interpretation. If relativism is true, then belief in relativism is also relative, leaving consistent relativists trapped in a vicious circle. That we all interpret from different perspectives is obvious and should not be controversial. This fact in no way demands a devaluation of the entire enterprise. Indeed, the purpose of working to understand different perspectives is precisely to facilitate more-informed decisions about which is most adequate to the truth. Although hermeneutical relativism may seem like a plausible conclusion to those who are just discovering the diversity of interpretations, it is in fact internally incoherent and utterly opposed to what many of us wish to share with our students.

But that does not make us hermeneutical absolutists. The words of no less an advocate of absolute truth than Jesus remind us that conflicts in interpretation existed in his time as they do now, and are not to be dismissed. When challenged by an expert about a question of the Law, Jesus replied, "How do you read it?" (Luke 10:25–26). He clearly assumed that there exist many ways of reading a text, even (or especially) when that text has sacred authority. The challenge is not to avoid interpretation, but to interpret well. In a court of law or a religious dispute, that will mean coming to a clear decision about guilt or innocence, truth or falsehood. When considering poems or paintings, it may be possible to find incompatible interpretations equally valuable. Part of intelligent reading is being able to discern what is at stake in a particular text or question. The one option that is not available to us, however, is to avoid interpretation.

For purposes of the present discussion, I assume that all understanding presupposes interpretation and all interpretation requires some sort of particular understanding. This is an important point, since many readers think of understanding as a primary apprehension of a subject and interpretation as a secondary process by which we "put our own spin" upon that subject. In this view, understanding should be reliable, but interpretation rarely is. The one is objective and the other subjective. I thoroughly disagree with this way of construing the two activities. The understanding of any concept inexorably entails many prior acts of interpretation. Likewise, there can be no interpretation if there is no previous understanding of the concept to be interpreted. The experience of a new insight is invariably a new interpretation of a subject or concept that has previously been understood differently. In light of this hermeneutical circle, I use the terms "understanding" and "interpretation" interchangeably in the chapters that follow.

In this essay I propose a way to sort out some of the conflicts in understanding that we encounter in diverse interpretations of a half dozen subjects. What I provide is primarily a tool that readers may use to clarify the issues at stake in such conflicts. Although this tool certainly entails a theory of interpretation, my first hope is that readers will be able to appropriate and adapt what I discuss here to suit their own needs and the subjects of interest to them. I am encouraged in this hope by having seen it happen for many students in the courses I have taught during the ten years this project has been under development.

Indeed, the opening question concerning what we know about interpretation points toward the primary goal of this book. What we know about interpretation is that it generates innumerable conflicts, and that benighted readers and students are often bewildered by those conflicts. We also know that many respond by yielding to a relativistic viewpoint that undercuts the very purpose of trying to understand, while others retreat into a hermeneutical absolutism that ignores or denies those ambiguities and other difficulties in the text or subject to be interpreted. This book offers a way to grasp the contextual character of all interpretation without succumbing to relativism, and a way to sort out which interpretation of a text or subject seems to be most adequate without ignoring the genuine contributions of other understandings of that same text or subject.

Three Types of Interpretation

The central argument of this book is that interpretation can be construed in terms of three types, each characterized by the particular sort of dialectical understanding embedded in it, and that recognition of the dialectical character of each type will enable readers to understand more fully a rich variety of texts and topics. I call the three types theoretical, transactional, and transformational. After a preliminary definition of each type and some general reflections on typologies and the much misunderstood subject of dialectic, I outline a half dozen applications that illustrate how these types have helped me more adequately to grasp conflicting interpretations of diverse topics. Each of the following six chapters develops one of these applications in detail, for I believe that the usefulness of my typology is better expressed by illustration than by abstract formulation.

Theoretical interpretation begins and ends with a dialectic of contradiction. Its paradigm is a grid of binary oppositions, polarities in which the two poles are opposed to each other by definition, as in the binary relations of subject vs. object, positive vs. negative, high vs. low, good vs. bad, and rich vs. poor. Theoretical interpretation is driven by contradictions that may be explicit or implicit, but they never lose their mutually exclusive or opposed poles. Whether they involve such obvious contraries as winner vs. loser and oppressor vs. oppressed or more subtle polarities like nature vs. culture, human vs. divine, or male vs. female, the assumption prevails that some fundamental opposition is, so to speak, given. So long as such binaries are interpreted as contradictions, their opposition can be inverted but never subverted. For example, a clever analysis might reveal that the positions of winner and loser had somehow become reversed, so that the winner was now the loser and the loser had become the winner. But the fundamental opposition between winning and losing would not thereby collapse. In theoretical interpretation, the basic binary relation remains a dialectic of contradiction.[1]

---

1. Although those familiar with dialectical philosophy might expect the initial type to claim an immediate unity rather than an opposition, I treat the claim for immediate

I call this first type of interpretation theoretical because the posture of an inquiring subject over against the object being investigated is that of an observer or spectator, which is the original meaning of theory. The ancient Greek word *theōria* referred to ambassadors sent as spectators to oracles or games and, by extension, to any observation or contemplation of an event or object. Thus theoretical understanding dominates all efforts to arrive at objective knowledge, knowledge that resists being influenced by the subjective perspective of the knowing person.

Theoretical understanding can also move to the opposite extreme and reject the stance of the objective observer. When this happens, a subject may speak in the first person singular or be the object of intense scrutiny. The subject may even appear to be absent, except insofar as the author attacks or ignores objective criteria while asserting contrary views on his or her own authority, all the while assuming a binary opposition between objectivity and subjectivity. If the scientific mode is an objective theoretical understanding, then this reaction against it can be called subjective theoretical interpretation.

In addition to these objective and subjective extremes, some theoretical thinkers may vacillate between objective and subjective statements without taking sides, though never questioning the fundamental contradiction between the two poles. What all theoretical interpretations share is such a presupposition of some sort of contradiction, often that between object and subject or objectivity (self-denial) and subjectivity (self-absorption).

Examples of objective theoretical texts to be discussed below are provided by B. F. Skinner, Claude Lévi-Strauss, and Lee Benson. Examples of subjective theoretical works are drawn from Roland Barthes, Friedrich Nietzsche, and Michel Foucault. Because very careful exposition is necessary just to identify the dialectical type of a particular text, it is not possible to generalize responsibly about the type of an author's entire corpus on the basis of such short analyses. This is especially true of such subsets as the objective and subjective designations, where reversals and mixes are quite common. For example, Barthes's work on semiotics and Foucault's contributions to historiographical technique have strong objective elements, despite the fact

unity as one of many possible (binary) interpretations within the theoretical type. The reasons for this are too complex to explain adequately here. Suffice it to say that, in my view, dialectical unity is always an achievement and never a starting point, for it is the product of a process of reflection, and each type, representing distinct moments within that reflective process, is subject to the dichotomizing activity of all reflection.

that the works of theirs that I analyze below reveal a predominantly subjective theoretical character. Even on the level of the three types, writers
may seem to belong to different types in different works. Thus Nietzsche
might strike some readers an odd choice to represent theoretical interpretation, a choice that can be justified only by careful exposition of the
selected texts and then for those texts alone. If one of these six writers can
be nominated as a model of purely theoretical understanding, it is certainly
Lévi-Strauss.

Transactional interpretation understands itself as a critical response to
some form of the theoretical type. Here the dialectic is one of reciprocity:
a transactional interpreter asserts that each pole in the binary opposition
responds to and influences the other pole. Ideally, each also acknowledges
the proper role of the other in this interaction. Respect for and openness
to the other replaces mere opposition. Balance, harmony, and reconciliation subvert the tension of binary oppositions.

Transactional thinking is particularly adamant about the need to interpret human relations in a reciprocal manner. When the one to be known
is recognized as a knowing subject, a person who can choose whether to be
known, then what had been merely an object has become an "other," and
the other person's freedom and integrity must be respected. Here the opposition between subject, or self, on the one hand and object, or other, on the
other is at least partially reconciled. However, the distance between them
cannot be totally dissolved without threatening the very distinction between
self and other that reciprocity presupposes. If I cannot see any real difference between the other and myself, I can hardly engage in a relationship
of genuine mutuality.

Although a dialectic of reciprocity displaces the dialectic of contradiction in transactional interpretation, contradiction does not completely disappear. Rather, it resurfaces in the relation between the two dialectics now
in tension with each other. Reciprocity is a response to contradiction, a determination to overcome the stark binary opposition posited by theoretical
interpretation. As such, it presents itself as a critical response to the alleged
contradictory relation between the two poles. It is, to use a term popular
among dialectical thinkers, a negation; but like every negation, it must presuppose that which it negates in order to establish its own identity and task.
Reciprocity always assumes the very distinction that it moderates; it begins
with the binary opposition that it seeks to soften. This is particularly clear
in debates about theories of interpretation, where some of the major issues

pit binary against reciprocal thinkers in battles between theoretical and transactional interpretations.

Examples of transactional texts are drawn from the works of Jacques Ellul, Mary Douglas, E. H. Carr, Erich Fromm, Martin Buber, and E. D. Hirsch. Of these, Carr is the most intentional about maintaining a reciprocal dialectic, although he is not always consistent; and Buber writes of the truth of reciprocity with poetic passion, although he too employs other dialectical categories as he sees fit.

Transformational interpretation is a third type, which emerges out of this new opposition between the transactional and theoretical approaches. The dialectic of transformation is paradoxical through and through. It wants to have things both ways at once. Like theoretical interpretation, it acknowledges strong binary oppositions; but like transactional interpretation, it refuses to let contradiction have the last word, and so it seeks a union of the opposed poles. This union is achieved not by reciprocal interaction, however, but by a transformation that occurs in each pole and in their relation, a transformation that defies ordinary understanding. Rather than move each pole toward the other, a paradoxical dialectic asserts that they are united even as they remain opposed. It claims to see a higher or hidden unity of the two that is their truth, however much they may still appear to be in contradiction.

The plausibility of the transformational claim depends upon the possibility of a radical change in the way that both of the earlier dialectics—contradiction and reciprocity—are understood. Within a paradoxical perspective, contradiction is no longer a static opposition; it is a dynamic confrontation leading to mutual change in both of the poles. Likewise, within a paradoxical perspective unity goes beyond reciprocal interaction and compromise to reveal a new reality that embraces both poles in their creative tension. The unity is, as it were, manifest in the midst of radical difference. To put it differently, the transformational dialectic of paradox simultaneously affirms the theoretical dialectic of contradiction and the transactional dialectic of reciprocity. What it denies is the adequacy of either by itself and the negative relation that had set them utterly against each other.

Examples of transformational understanding are more difficult to find than their counterparts. In the following chapters I draw upon works by Thomas Kuhn, Joseph Campbell, Reinhold Niebuhr, Søren Kierkegaard, Paul Tillich, and Paul Ricoeur. Kierkegaard can serve as a paradigm case of a thoroughly paradoxical thinker, although the simplest and clearest statement of a paradoxical unity-of-opposites is provided by Campbell.

To sum up this brief introduction, *theoretical* interpretation presupposes a dialectic of contradiction and finds truth in clear distinctions. Even when it ironically and tactically exploits ambiguity, it continues to assume the validity of whatever fundamental binary oppositions it presupposes. It usually strives to be an objective method of explanation, but it can also take a subjective form in reaction against such objectivity. In either case, an active interpreting subject stands over against a passive object, text, or subject matter to be interpreted. *Transactional* interpretation involves give-and-take, contract, even covenant. It treats the two poles of the relation as two consenting parties to a hermeneutical transaction. It finds truth in interaction, harmony, and communication between subject and object as self and other. It is more concerned with dialogue than with method; it values mutual understanding over definitive explanation. *Transformational* interpretation is based upon a dialectic of paradox. It embraces both method and dialogue, both explanation and understanding. But it affirms them only as parts of a larger whole, a truth that cannot be equated with either binary oppositions or the reciprocal relations that moderate them. For transformational thinkers, the truth belongs to the subject matter that is the goal of all interpretation. It can be grasped by those who seek it only insofar as they realize that they have already been grasped by it.

Typologies

A few words about typological analysis in general may be helpful. There are many ways of constructing typologies. Biologists assign fauna and flora to taxonomic categories according to their distinguishing characteristics: mammals are different from reptiles, and conifers are not to be confused with leaf-bearing trees. Politicians polemicize about the evils perpetrated upon society by others who promote or oppose particular changes, whom they describe as either too liberal or too conservative. Psychologists analyze personality types according to key traits, such as how individuals perceive data and go about making decisions, and then use the results to help large organizations and small groups learn to cope better with their internal dynamics. We all habitually classify people and places and events according to one schema or another. Typologies pervade our textbooks, our news reports, and most of our thinking.

Yet typologies also incur a great deal of suspicion. Procrustes, a famous figure of ancient Greek myth, tied his guests to a bed and then stretched the short guests or surgically shortened the tall ones to make them fit the bed.[2] Critics of typologies honor his memory regularly by referring to this or that set of types as a Procrustean bed. There can be no doubt that those constructing typologies are often guilty as charged. For the sake of a classification system, many a writer's thought has been stretched or cut to fit a predefined category. But the difficulties inherent in constructing satisfactory typologies and employing them responsibly by no means justify rejecting them altogether. Such a negation is not even within our power. Just as thinking requires abstraction, classification is essential to the process of interpretation that is at the heart of all understanding. The challenge is to go beyond simplistic labels to the construction of types that identify genuinely important characteristics. To return to the political example, liberal and conservative are often employed as labels without a clear designation of meaning. But that does not undermine the legitimacy or importance of clarifying conflicting positions on issues, a task that necessarily involves the use of such typological rubrics.

One popular way of constructing a typology is to do an inventory of all the observed characteristics of a phenomenon and then to see how those characteristics cluster themselves around certain traits. These typologies have an ad hoc character. They can include anywhere from two to eight or more types of the phenomenon, depending upon the characteristics surveyed and the predilections of the investigator.

Other typologies are based upon the possibilities permitted by a linear spectrum. Thus left, right, and center are more or less exclusive spatial designations, as are higher and lower when we shift from a horizontal to a vertical axis. This linearity is intensified whenever statistics are introduced, for they segment the spectrum into ever more precise percentiles. However, what is thereby gained in mathematical precision may be lost in conceptual clarity. In order to be able to reduce the anticipated responses to quantifiable data, questions must often be constructed so simplistically that they perform Procrustes' operation before any answers have even been solicited.

Philosophers have explored the foundations of knowledge in ways that constitute, intentionally or not, a justification for typological analysis. As we shall see in the next chapter, Thomas Kuhn's famous essay on the role of paradigms in scientific investigation shows the extent to which the questions

---

2. Thomas Bulfinch, *Mythology of Greece and Rome* (New York: Collier Books, 1962), 151.

we ask are determined by the intellectual communities that have educated us.[3] Thinking is never done by a blank-slate mind (even the concept of a blank mind is dependent upon a particular paradigm). To shift the metaphor, paradigms are like maps of intellectual roadways, and thought will almost always follow a route that is clearly marked on the available map. New ways can certainly be found, but genuine revolutions occur in science only when a new map is constructed that presents the territory in a radically different way.[4] Kuhn's paradigms have much in common with Charles Taylor's concept of "inescapable frameworks." Although Taylor notes that the modern "naturalist temper" may be "suspicious of this talk of meaning and frameworks," he insists that there is a "moral ontology behind any person's views [that] can remain largely implicit."[5]

Typological analysis has often been employed to distinguish and analyze different approaches to interpretation. Northrop Frye classifies works of literary critics into four types: historical, ethical, archetypal, and rhetorical.[6] Robert Culley suggests that types be based upon who or what is thought to determine the meaning of a text: is it the author, the reader, or the text itself?[7] Roy Howard classifies types of hermeneutical theories as analytic, psychosocial, and ontological.[8] And Mark C. Taylor identifies one theme—the role of time and history in a theory—as a plumb line that he uses to differentiate romantic from structuralist and teleological types of interpretation.[9]

These are but a few of the many notable efforts to classify the diverse ways of interpretation according to a typological schema. Each offers a unique perspective and numerous insights of its own. Yet none of them is exhaustive or conclusive. No typology can be. The rationale for presenting yet another way of construing types of interpretation is that it can open up

3. Thomas Kuhn, *The Structure of Scientific Revolutions*, 2d ed. (Chicago: University of Chicago Press, 1970).

4. Kuhn himself extends the metaphor in a different direction: "[P]aradigms provide scientists not only with a map but also with some of the directions essential for mapmaking" (ibid., 109).

5. Charles Taylor, *Sources of the Self: The Making of the Modern Identity* (Cambridge: Harvard University Press, 1989): 19, 9.

6. Northrop Frye, *Anatomy of Criticism: Four Essays* (Princeton: Princeton University Press, 1957).

7. Robert C. Culley, "Structural Analysis: *Is It Done with Mirrors?*" *Interpretation: A Journal of Bible and Theology* 28, no. 2 (1974): 165–81.

8. Roy J. Howard, *Three Faces of Hermeneutics: An Introduction to Current Theories of Understanding* (Berkeley and Los Angeles: University of California Press, 1982).

9. Mark C. Taylor, "Interpreting Interpretation," in *Unfinished . . . . : Essays in Honor of Ray L. Hart*, ed. Mark C. Taylor, *JAAR Thematic Studies* 48, no. 1 (1981): 45–64.

previously unnoticed approaches to the subject, different ways of grasping the abundance of conflicting theories, and new criteria for assessing their value and truth. My purpose in this book is not to disprove or displace other typologies of interpretation, but to complement them.

Dialectics

The distinction I introduced in the last section, between ad hoc typologies, which include as many types as their creators happen to observe, and linear typologies, in which all types are sites in a space defined by two opposing poles or positions, is less innocent than it may appear. Ad hoc typologies are the least likely to be accused of Procrustean mutilation, but they are also unable to provide a compelling overview of how the various types are related to one another. With linear typologies, however, the space is conceived as a field of play, a field defined by positions and goals and sometimes clear borders. The expectation is that every type that belongs within a particular field can be situated in relation to all the other types located within that same field. Because such a field is defined by opposing goals or at least by the differing character of the two ends, it can be described as a dialectical field.

Although the term "dialectic" has had an extraordinarily complex history,[10] the binary or even contradictory relations mentioned above have always been key to the concept. In ancient Greek philosophy, dialectic was understood as the criticism of beliefs in order to discern any possible contradictions. It also often referred to a conversation devoted to the discovery of such contradictions. In tone, these conversations could smack of irony or sophistry, but the fundamental presuppositions were invariably binary: the logical binary relation of contradictory propositions, and the interpersonal binary relation of opponents in the debate. From this practice, the term dialectic came to be used loosely for all dialogues, all efforts to expose illusion, and even, among Stoics and early medieval thinkers, all logic. Modern thought has continued to use dialectic to characterize a variety of binary operations: the philosophical criticism of illusory notions and conceptual self-contradictions (Kant); the development of reason through a process of self-contradiction and the overcoming of that contradiction (Hegel); the

---

10. George J. Stack, "On the Notion of Dialectics," *Philosophy Today* 15 (1971): 276–90.

analysis of the struggle between classes for control of the means of material production (Marx); and the effort to clarify the complex relation between objectivity and subjectivity in thought and religious faith (Kierkegaard).

In all of these theories, dialectic refers to some sort of polarity or binary opposition, either a debate between two perspectives or a conflict between two realities. For all the diversity of usage, dialectic always deals with or presupposes such an opposition, two poles that stand over against one another.

Whereas an ad hoc typology claims no internal logical pattern, even a simple dialectical typology implies a certain logical necessity. If the field in question is defined by a binary opposition, like a playing field that has opposing goals at each end, then every type within that field is like a player who has a position in relation to the two goals. Proximity to one end will entail distance from the other. Moreover, both goal lines make sense only in relation to each other. Without two ends, there can be no dialectical playing field at all. To revisit the political analogy, neither liberalism nor conservatism can function without the other to oppose.

The fact that every type within a defined field can be located within that field by no means implies that the typology in question is comprehensive or exhaustive. There is much confusion about this matter. The ambition of some philosophers (preeminently Hegel) to portray their method as one that comprehends not only a particular field of dialectical possibilities but additionally every significant configuration of a phenomenon has not endeared dialectic to those on the lookout for Procrustean surgery. If all typologies risk presenting overly simple types, dialectical typologies multiply that risk exponentially when they claim comprehensiveness for their analysis. But Hegel's goal of systematic comprehensiveness is not the only path for dialectical analysis to follow. By carefully defining the typological traits that are to be dialectically related, and by limiting the inquiry to how those traits appear in relation to one another, it is possible to explore the dialectics of particular interpretations without making grandiose claims for either the method used or its results. I have tried to find strong examples of each of the types for each chapter in this book, but mixed types abound, and some interpretations may resist typological classification altogether.

That said, I must also admit to two views of dialectic that have had far-reaching influence on this book. One is the premise that some sort of dialectic lies, at least incipiently, at the heart of all understanding. If the mind can no more escape binary structures than it can think without concepts, then such binary relations are operative in all interpretation. Accordingly, even ad hoc typologies could in principle be probed to make visible the binary aspects that are both hidden within their particular types and embedded in the frameworks that relate the types to one another. In other words, while eschewing the comprehensive ambitions of Hegel, I do believe that my dialectical typology is applicable to a very wide range of material. What I present as types of interpretation are not simply ad hoc clusters of claims. Rather, they are analyzed according to how they view and employ binary oppositions. Interpretation, like all thinking, involves polarities, and the theory of interpretation I present in this book investigates conflicting understandings according to the dialectical manner in which they treat those polarities.

A second aspect of dialectic that has shaped this project is its teleological character. For this, the credit or blame must go to Hegel and his wayward disciple Kierkegaard (to whom I return shortly), who have persuaded me that dialectic unfolds, develops, and builds upon itself. Dialectic begins with binary opposition. For a theoretical thinker, it remains there. Transactional interpreters object to what strike them as sterile oppositions, and accordingly they try to bring about some sort of reciprocal reconciliation or balanced compromise. Beyond them both, transformational understanding claims to be able to do justice paradoxically to both theoretical polarities and transactional harmonies. Thus the three types of interpretation are arranged directionally, with theoretical at the beginning and transformational at the end. Although others might wish to rearrange the three, they could do so only by redefining the dialectical character of each type. Such a teleological direction formally privileges the transformational type of interpretation over the theoretical and transactional types, a relation that is evident in some of the chapters that follow.

However, it is equally true that transformational interpretation is not superior for every topic or in the hands of every interpreter. This is evident when a problem demands technical expertise or a question requires an immediate and practical answer. Transformational understanding is well suited to questions of meaning and truth, but its usefulness for, say, evaluating surgical techniques or adjudicating labor disputes, is going to be indirect, to say the least. For these matters theoretical or transactional types will offer more practical approaches. I shall reserve my evaluations of specific texts on particular issues for the chapters in which they are treated, but the reader should be aware that, despite the bias of this dialectical method of analysis toward paradox and transformational understanding, a particular transformational approach may be less helpful than one that is theoretical or transactional.

A note of caution is in order. The discussions of dialectical relations in the chapters that follow will have a formal character that might be confusing to some readers. By that I mean to indicate that the binary oppositions I identify in one text may share nothing more with those in another than the abstract or formal trait of polarity. Indeed, I find myself using terms such as "binary opposition," "polarity," and "contradiction" interchangeably. The point in each case is that something, call it X, is related to not-X. For theoretical interpretation, that relation remains one of opposition, no matter how greatly the content varies. For transactional thinkers, X and not-X must be understood in their reciprocal interdependence. Again, this mutual interaction can take many forms. It can be merely logical or dialogical or some sort of historical relationship. The one common point in all reciprocal dialectics is the rejection of both sheer contradiction on the one hand and of total union or identity on the other. The same indeterminacy characterizes my discussion of paradoxical dialectics. The unity-in-contradiction of paradox is, for purposes of this study, a purely formal one. Thus the paradoxes of one transformational thinker may appear to be quite different from those of another, and yet, upon closer inspection, they turn out to share that same dialectical character.

Finally, I want to emphasize that dialectical thinkers are, whatever their types, rarely self-conscious about their manner of thinking about polarities. In the chapters that follow, I am less interested in the intentions of the authors than in the dialectical disposition that is revealed in each text. This does not commit me to a dialectical determinism, according to which I might insist that every thinker must view every opposition through one and the same dialectical lens. That is not at all my belief. Neither would I agree that the dialectical types are choices that are made only with regard to the particular subject matter. I cannot resolve the age-old debate between radical determinists and defenders of total freedom here, but I do need to clarify that neither position expresses my own understanding of the subtle and often obscure ways in which we arrive at our various dialectical interpretations of a range of subjects.

Something About Kierkegaard

This project was initially conceived as an application of Søren Kierkegaard's theory of three stages in the development of human consciousness, published by the Danish philosopher in a series of remarkable books in the 1840s. Readers who are familiar with Kierkegaard's writings—and especially with my study of them, *Kierkegaard's Dialectic of Inwardness*[11]—may be able to recognize my debt to him in what I have written here. In the earlier book I argue that Kierkegaard's three stages on life's way, which he calls aesthetic, ethical, and religious, are forms of consciousness that can be understood in terms of three dialectical patterns embedded in them: contradiction characterizes aesthetic consciousness; reciprocity is apparent in ethical understanding; and paradox can be discerned in religious, or at least Christian, thought. I also examine Kierkegaard's interest in showing how consciousness develops from the aesthetic through the ethical to culminate in the religious stage, or sphere, a developmental dialectic like Hegel's but without Hegel's comprehensive and systematic ambitions.

Following Kierkegaard, in this book I explore the three dialectical types of understanding as they appear in interpretations of a variety of topics. This entails transposing Kierkegaard's aesthetic, ethical, and religious stages into my theoretical, transactional, and transformational types, a transposition that is in some respects so great that those who are familiar with Kierkegaard's stages and expect me to spell out their hermeneutical implications faithfully may be disappointed. However, this book is not about Kierkegaard, and he bears no responsibility for the use to which I have put his theory of stages. Accordingly, I do not discuss him further except in the chapter on love, where he appears as a representative of transformational interpretation. Those readers who are interested in considering further the relation between his thought and this project are welcome to consult my earlier book.

Applications

The chapters that follow are examples of how this typology can illuminate conflicting understandings of the same topic, both individually and in relation to one another. The essays do not presuppose either previous knowledge of the topics discussed or familiarity with current debates over the nature of interpretation, although I do hope that my expository and typological

---

11. Stephen N. Dunning, *Kierkegaard's Dialectic of Inwardness: A Structural Analysis of the Theory of Stages* (Princeton: Princeton University Press, 1985).

discussions will be of interest to those who are familiar with the relevant literatures as well as to those who are not. Moreover, in spite of frequent references to authors treated in previous chapters, each chapter stands as a self-contained essay in dialectical analysis and an illustration of the three types of understanding. Some readers may prefer to begin with whichever topic most interests them, and then return to the chapters on other topics. I especially hope that additional applications will occur to readers, and that they will work out ways in which this typology can illuminate debates about other issues.

It is important to underscore that most of the writings to be examined below are not *about* interpretation as such; they *are* interpretations of a particular subject. That is why my project can be characterized as an interpretation of interpretations. But this book is not a comprehensive overview of theories of interpretation or of theories about any of the other topics treated, or even of any of the authors analyzed. The materials chosen for analysis have been selected because they illustrate characteristic aspects of the three types. The primary point of this project is to offer a new and different way of understanding interpretation, not to argue for one or another position on the subjects that serve as examples. Some of the authors discussed are leading authorities on their subjects; some are not. Some of the texts chosen are recent, but others are decades or more than a century old. In every case I have limited my analysis to a small selection of the literature produced by an author, since my intention is to demonstrate my typological method of analysis, not to explore an author's entire intellectual output.

I hope I have selected the texts well and succeeded in showing how the typology can promote new and interesting readings. This is crucial, for the value of a typology is not that it labels writers but that it illuminates their writings. My effort in the chapters that follow is to discuss selected works in such a way as to show how they are representative of one of the three types. I do not attempt to offer complete summaries or condensations of those works, for to discuss each chapter and theme in them is both unnecessary for my task and potentially burdensome for readers. Many aspects of the writings are ignored. The analyses I offer are close expository readings of the texts in order to illuminate their dialectical character, and thereby to develop my typology by showing how the types appear in a variety of texts. Moreover, I do not attempt to address the scholarly literature that deals with the texts under consideration. To do so responsibly would so lengthen each chapter that I would have to cut drastically the number of chapters I can include. Again, my hope is that those readers who are familiar with that literature will easily see where the readings afforded by my typological framework are distinctive, while those who are not will be spared the burden of wading through the abstruse debates that scholarly discussions often engender.

In the first chapter, I discuss texts dealing with the topic of science and technology in relation to human life and values. As a representative of a theoretical perspective, I have chosen B. F. Skinner's *Beyond Freedom and Dignity,* a succinct and powerful call for a science and technology of human behavior as the only way to solve the massive problems, such as overpopulation, that confront modern society. *The Technological Society,* by Jacques Ellul, is a transactional examination of the human costs of modern technology. Although Thomas Kuhn does not discuss the effects of science upon society in *The Structure of Scientific Revolutions,* his analysis of paradigm shifts in the history of science provides a transformational alternative to the dilemma posed by the conflict between the theoretical position of Skinner and the transactional approach of Ellul.

A chapter on texts illustrating various approaches to myth follows. It opens with a few essays by Claude Lévi-Strauss, no doubt the preeminent structuralist engaged in the interpretation of myth. His brilliant, if sometimes eccentric, method of analysis has been a major influence on my conception of the theoretical type of interpretation. Mary Douglas is also an anthropologist, and her system of classification of societies according to grid and group has been helpful to many scholars in diverse fields. Although in *Cultural Bias* her approach to myth is embedded in a discussion of cosmology, the conceptual framework she provides there is a good example of a transactional perspective on the subject. Finally, the late Joseph Campbell may well be the most famous interpreter of myth at present, due to his enormously popular televised interviews with Bill Moyers. His early work, *The Hero with a Thousand Faces,* reveals the transformational character of his way of understanding myth.

From myth we move on to texts about history and historiography, where I begin with the theoretical work of Lee Benson. In *Toward the Scientific Study of History,* Benson argues that methods for establishing the truth of causal claims in historical analysis are available and ought to be generally employed. For a transactional type, I turn to E. H. Carr's witty series of lectures, *What Is History?* Carr affirms individual freedom of choice in the manner typical of many transactional thinkers, and his analysis of historical interpretation is clearly driven by a dialectic of reciprocity. Finally, Reinhold Niebuhr's fusion of social analysis with theological meaning in *Beyond*

Tragedy demonstrates a transformational type of historical interpretation rooted in paradox.

Texts reflecting conflicting understandings of love can also be illuminated by the three types of interpretation. In Roland Barthes's *Lover's Discourse*, it appears that this discourse is less a dialogue than the internal monologue of a single individual who is engaged in a struggle with his beloved. Erich Fromm's *Art of Loving* is a classic exploration of love as an interpersonal transaction that has a reciprocal and ethical character. For a transformational interpretation, I examine Søren Kierkegaard's *Works of Love*. Kierkegaard's religious vision of love manifests the same paradoxical pattern of thinking that is at the center of his earlier books on the religious stage.[12]

From Kierkegaard, the preeminent religious existentialist, it is both a long and a short step to Friedrich Nietzsche, the greatest of atheist existentialist writers, who opens the next chapter. Nietzsche's *Twilight of the Idols* and *The Anti-Christ* offer an emphatic theoretical affirmation of the idea that personal identity must embrace contradictions. In contrast, Martin Buber's *I and Thou* blends existential philosophy with religious poetry to proclaim reciprocal relations as the meaning and truth of human identity. It is a striking example of transactional thinking. Finally, Paul Tillich's *Courage To Be* explores the way in which identity is complete in a faith that paradoxically unites anxiety with the courage to be.

The sixth and final set of texts to be treated takes us directly to the center of contemporary hermeneutical discussions. I open my analysis of theories of interpretation with Michel Foucault's *Archaeology of Knowledge*, a postmodern manifesto that calls for a radical decentering of understanding and is governed from start to finish by a dialectic of binary opposition. For a reciprocal theory of interpretation, I examine E. D. Hirsch's *Validity in Interpretation* and *The Aims of Interpretation*, two works that argue that text interpretation is fundamentally a transaction in which an author expresses a meaning that a reader is duty-bound to try to grasp. This relation is implicitly dialogical: the author writes *for* the reader, just as the reader respects the meaning of the text *for* the author. A major transformational theory of interpretation is available in Paul Ricoeur's *Hermeneutics and the Human Sciences*. Ricoeur does not emphasize a paradoxical dialectic as such, yet his

---

12. The expected course of action might have been to analyze the paradoxical notions of faith and God in books by Kierkegaard that are much better known. But I have already done that in my book on Kierkegaard's theory of stages (note 11 above), which readers are welcome to consult if they wish. See *Kierkegaard's Dialectic of Inwardness*, especially 112–25 on *Fear and Trembling*, 166–80 on *Philosophical Fragments*, and 181–213 on *Concluding Unscientific Postscript*.

entire way of thinking makes it inescapable. For him, interpretation is neither a decentering by the reader nor a centering on the author's intended
meaning; it is an opening to the world that is revealed through the text.

Readers may have noticed that I routinely refer to "texts" and "topics" in
the preceding discussion as if they were interchangeable. Within the context
of my dialectical typology, the distinction between them blurs. Generally,
topics are specific subject matters, such as science, myth, and history, and
texts are understood as writings about topics. Here, however, the topic of
the chapter on theories of interpretation is precisely the nature of textu-
ality. Conversely, topics that are not "texts" in the conventional sense can
certainly be treated as if they were. The different dialectics that I discern in
the texts analyzed below are the same dialectics that those texts' authors see
in the topics they examine (whether or not they consciously think about
dialectic as such). Dialectic is a characteristic of thought and meaning, so
anything that qualifies as human thinking or as a meaningful object or
action can potentially be "read" as a "text."

In the conclusion I clarify and briefly develop one of the primary argu-
ments of this study, a point that is made by transformational interpreters
and often misunderstood or disputed by theoretical and transactional
thinkers. Every interpretation is an expression of the subject matter that
it interprets. This implies that the methods and results of each approach to
interpretation are inseparable from what is being interpreted. This can be
applied to and also discerned in each of the three dialectical types of interpretation. Theoretical explanation is the pursuit of knowledge, whether
of an external object or of the interpreting subject, and always on the
assumption that the object and subject stand over against one another.
Transactional understanding focuses upon relations that are reciprocal,
whether between individuals or groups. And transformational interpretation is a response to a paradoxical revelation of a new world, or at least a
radically new understanding of a subject matter that had previously been
seen in a very different way.

1

Paradigms of Science and Technology

If any single development characterizes contemporary culture, it is the extent to which science and technology have come to dominate our thinking and our lives. Scientists are assumed to be experts whose authority outstrips that of all other professionals. They stipulate the methods that must be followed in order to attain reliable knowledge; they determine what is or is not a fact; and, for most educated people, their theories define the reality in which we live. Technology is often assumed to be the practical application of the findings of science in order to improve our tools for living. Entire societies are categorized by their position on a technological scale that runs from agrarian to postindustrial, from dirt tracks traveled by bullock carts to the information superhighway.

Not everyone shares such a sanguine view of science and technology. Many doubt the methodological claim that scientists engage in research in a value-free manner. Others question specific accomplishments, whether nuclear power, audiovisual surveillance devices, or chemical additives in prepared foods. Behind all these debates, however, there lurks a deeper question: How do science and technology affect human life? More precisely, what is the impact of science and technology upon the way in which we think and arrive at knowledge of ourselves and our world?

The three works I examine in this chapter address this question from different perspectives. In *Beyond Freedom and Dignity*, B. F. Skinner issues a behaviorist manifesto calling for a scientifically grounded technology of human behavior. Although Skinner never mentions dialectics or even his own assumption of binary oppositions, careful analysis of his text demonstrates the objective theoretical character of his thought. Jacques Ellul's *Technological Society* is a passionate protest against the very sort of program that Skinner advocates. Ellul's objections can be shown to presuppose a dialectic of reciprocity that structures his sociological reflection in a transactional manner. Whereas Ellul's focus is on technology, with just a glance at science, Thomas Kuhn's *Structure of Scientific Revolutions* is an account of how major changes occur in science, with some attention paid to the role of technology in those changes. The paradoxically circular character of Kuhn's argument demonstrates the transformational nature of his understanding. Even Kuhn's famous and controversial concept of paradigm, which has strongly influenced my conception of how the three types of interpretation function, implies a dialectic of paradox.

A Science and Technology of Human Behavior

The title of B. F. Skinner's *Beyond Freedom and Dignity*[1] is calculated to shock the unsuspecting reader, and so it does. No values are more central to human thought in general and modern thinking in particular than freedom and dignity. At first we might suppose that Skinner simply wants to add another value to them, to go beyond them without in any way displacing them. But we are soon disabused of that assumption. Skinner proposes nothing less than a scientific revolution in how we think about every aspect of life, and especially in how we understand the nature of human thought itself.

Skinner's term for the ideal of freedom is "autonomous man," a concept that carries several important implications for how we understand human thinking. The first of these is the most obvious, namely, that autonomous man is believed to behave in accordance with his own intentions rather

1. B. F. Skinner, *Beyond Freedom and Dignity* (New York: Bantam Books, 1972).

than any external causes, to control his environment rather than to be controlled by it (17). Skinner develops his argument by means of an analysis of what he calls "the literature of freedom," which he describes as "designed to induce people to act to free themselves from various kinds of intentional control" (28). This is a literature of enormous substance and impact in the areas of religion and politics, produced by such enlightened philosophers as Leibnitz, Voltaire, and Mill, but they consistently made the mistake of identifying freedom with a subjective feeling. As Mill put it, "'Liberty consists in doing what one desires'" (29). Skinner grants that this subjective feeling of freedom may have to suffice for those in bondage, such as slaves who must work to escape punishment. For them, freedom is the ability to avoid or reduce pain. It may also account for freedom as a positive condition, such as occurs when a person labors for a wage. But to posit freedom as a subjective feeling fails to address long-term results. For example, Skinner suggests that a piecework system of compensation has short-term benefits but later produces negative consequences. It is this sort of situation that the literature of freedom fails to explain.

Skinner's attack on the literature of freedom is not limited to protesting the confusion of liberty with subjective states. His primary concern is that this literature inculcates a suspicion of all forms of control, even positive controllers. It does so by stressing negative reinforcement with such maxims as "It is better to be a conscious slave than a happy one" or by advising teachers to inculcate the illusion of freedom among pupils, as does Rousseau in *Émile* (37). These ways of thinking assume that freedom is simply the negation of reality. Skinner does not reply by paradoxically claiming that freedom lies in submitting to control. He agrees with the logical assumption that control and freedom stand in contradiction to each other, but not with the subsequent inference that all control is bad: "What is overlooked is control which does not have aversive [negatively reinforcing] consequences at any time" (38). The literature of freedom subtly stigmatizes all forms of control, so that we are not able to "deal with the social environment as simply as we deal with the nonsocial" (39).

This attack upon thought that treats subjective feelings as causes and not just by-products is a clear indication of Skinner's tendency to polarize the issue he is addressing. The literature of freedom, he believes, propagates subjectivism, pure and simple. True to this binary vision, the alternative that Skinner proposes is to strip desire of this subjective character (that is, feelings) and redefine it in completely objective terms: "A person wants something if he acts to get it when the occasion arises. . . . Wanting is not, however, a feeling, nor is a feeling the reason a person acts to get what he wants. Certain contingencies have raised the probability of behavior and at the same time have created conditions which may be felt. Freedom is a matter of contingencies of reinforcement, not of the feelings the contingencies generate" (34–35).

Desire is evident, then, not as feelings (which actually follow from it) but in the behavior it causes. Such behavior is as objective as feelings are subjective, for behavior can be scientifically observed, whereas feelings cannot. The freedom to fulfill one's desire consists not in gratifying feelings but in behaving in such a way as to get what one wants, that is, to produce those "contingencies" or direct consequences that will satisfy one's need or desire. Skinner recalls William James's famous statement that "we do not run away because we are afraid but are afraid because we run away" (10–11). Behavior causes feelings, not the other way around. But Skinner wants to go beyond James to explain why we run away in the first place. This is the challenge that a rigorous science of behavior must address. Such analysis will ignore mental states and personal purposes in order to determine the actual causes of behavior in terms of anticipated environmental results.

Thus Skinner pits objective analysis of causes against the appeal to subjective feelings, and then proceeds to build his philosophy upon that binary opposition. He emphasizes the urgency of this matter by pointing out that modern science and technology have provided medical resources that save many lives, but this very progress has resulted in a population crisis of gigantic proportions. We now have better means of birth control, but not the methods to influence people to use them. Skinner proclaims that "our strength is science and technology" (1), but he also laments that we lack both "a science of human behavior" and "a technology of behavior" (3).

Not one for false modesty, Skinner informs the reader that his scientific revolution will be on the order of those started by Copernicus, Darwin, and Freud (202). All four have undercut the human-centered thinking of prescientific times: Copernicus showed that our earth revolves around the sun, not vice versa. Darwin shattered the illusion of anything uniquely human in the process of evolution. Freud proved that our conscious thinking is governed by dark unconscious repressions. And Skinner is showing that the causes of human behavior are to be found scientifically in the anticipated results of that behavior, not in subjective feelings that precede or accompany it. If we wish to improve human behavior, we need a technology based upon a science of behavior: "It is science or nothing" (153).

The first thrust of Skinner's attack on the myth of autonomous man is, then, a critique of a subjective view of thinking and a defense of objective and scientific thought. The second thrust takes aim on dignity, for there Skinner sees a concept that is both deeply embedded in our culture and utterly opposed to scientific method and analysis. The literature of freedom may be wrong when it attributes causal power to feelings, but the literature of dignity actually perverts the scientific analysis of causes when it tries to establish an "inverse relation between credit and the conspicuousness of causes" (44). This is a reference to the fact that occupations that bring less remuneration often earn their practitioners greater credit or respect. Artistic activity is more valued when less commercial, and may even be valued most of all if it is appreciated only by a small group. Greater honor accrues to an actor who memorizes the part than to one who depends upon a prompter. In other words, the belief in dignity is grounded firmly in a devaluation of visible causes, the very causes that can be analyzed by behavioral science. The literature of dignity may extol the inexplicable and mysterious behavior attributed to autonomous man (49), but science "naturally seeks a fuller explanation of that behavior; its goal is the destruction of mystery" (54). The opposition that Skinner had discerned between subjective freedom and objective thinking here emerges into full light, and full-scale warfare.

Interestingly, Skinner manages to exploit the complex relation between the literatures of freedom and dignity. He notes that "[f]reedom is an issue raised by the aversive consequences of behavior, but dignity concerns positive reinforcement" (41), meaning that freedom tries to avoid negative results, while dignity thrives on positive feedback. So, although freedom and dignity are thought to support one another, in fact they can conflict: a behavior such as natural childbirth may diminish a woman's freedom at the same time that it enhances her dignity. Although dignity sometimes prevails over freedom, as when soldiers march into battle for honor and glory, Skinner believes that "freedom usually wins out over dignity" (53). His example is the popularity of calculators, which free their users from burdensome work even though they bring less credit than using only one's mathematical skill (54). But a more important point has also been made: even the literatures of freedom and dignity must acknowledge the power of consequences, and the positive value of being controlled, even aversively, by one's environment. Autonomy is neither scientifically true nor socially beneficial to human development.

In addition to freedom and dignity, Skinner has a third target in view in his critique of the prevailing understanding of the nature and power of thinking. It is self-control, the extent to which autonomous man trusts in his own ability to choose and pursue one lifestyle or another, one set of values or its opposite. Skinner asserts that behavioral analysis shows that "whether or not a person obeys the norm 'Thou shalt not steal' depends upon supporting contingencies" (108). People do not refrain from stealing in order to be virtuous but because they are avoiding punishment. Those who choose to be religious do so not out of devotion but due to the contingencies that religions offer. Feelings of ambivalence are not inner struggles but "conflicts between contingencies of reinforcement" (111). All questions of values and norms are really objective matters of reinforcement, which require behavioral analysis rather than subjective ethical reflection.

Although Skinner never claims that scientists are exempt from being environmentally determined, he believes that they alone are qualified to carry out the behavioral analysis upon which the new technology of behavior must be based. Scientists must study the workings of "operant behavior," which is any action upon the environment that produces consequences. In working to identify these "contingencies," scientists can also experimentally arrange environments in order to ascertain "which specific consequences are contingent upon [a behavior]" (16). Indeed, behavior always manipulates the environment. Unlike changes in genetic makeup, which is the only other significant cause of human behavior, changes in the environment occur rapidly, so a "technology of operant behavior" is feasible. This technology will exploit the process of "operant conditioning" (24–25), by which the consequences of a behavior become reinforcers of that behavior. If a consequence is welcome, it is a positive reinforcer, as when food satisfies a hungry person. If it is unpleasant, such as a bad sunburn, then it is a negative ("aversive") reinforcer of the behavior (25). The guiding behaviorist principle of all this research will be "Whatever we do, and hence however we perceive it, the fact remains that it is the environment which acts upon the perceiving person, not the perceiving person who acts upon the environment" (179).

Skinner's understanding of this environmental determinism is complicated by his admission that it often acts indirectly. Rather than passively respond to human actions or aggressively coerce them, "the environment acts in an inconspicuous way: it does not push or pull, it *selects*" (14). Skinner prefers this Darwinian way of thinking to the Pavlovian stimulus-response theory, which still requires some concept of conscious intention in order to account for how stimuli are converted into responses. According to Darwin's theory of natural selection, traits that promote survival are neither planned nor chosen; they occur by chance, succeed by environmental circumstance, and propagate themselves simply because they have succeeded at a greater rate than other traits. The selected individuals do not exercise any choice in the matter.[2] The web of causes is within nature and fully available to scientific inspection.

Consistent with this Darwinian perspective, Skinner asserts that "[s]urvival is the only value according to which a culture is eventually to be judged" (130). However much some individuals may work to help a culture survive, the simple fact is that it will survive only "if those who carry it survive" (128). By implication, acts of self-sacrifice for the survival of the culture are self-defeating, since they destroy the very persons who could transmit that culture to future generations. But if self-sacrifice earns an increase in dignity, it might serve as a positive reinforcer to those who also carry that culture. Still, culture is not a matter of maintaining customs or living up to ideals: "If there is any purpose or direction in the evolution of a culture, it has to do with bringing people under the control of more and more of the consequences of their behavior" (137).

It is important to realize that Skinner does not see himself as repudiating either consciousness or rational thought, despite his attack on the myth of autonomous man and his explicit rejection of feelings in the determination of behavior. He does insist that reinforcers, whether positive or negative, are always objective things rather than subjective feelings. Feelings are merely "by-products of the contingencies" (105), that is, incidental responses to the behavioral results of environmental causes. But consciousness is not identical with feelings, for it is a direct, rather than an incidental, product of the environment. Aggressiveness, for example, is a real state of consciousness, but it is not a cause of behavior; it is the result of an anticipated reinforcement such as the hope of acquiring additional goods (176–77). As Skinner puts it: "Rather than ignore consciousness, an experimental analysis of behavior has stressed certain crucial issues. The question is not whether a man can know himself but what he knows when he does so" (181). Mental activity is explained in terms of behavioral and environmental causes. Introspection, like all consciousness, is a social product whose only failing is its inaccuracy (183).

Skinner understands that "the last stronghold of autonomous man is that

2. "To use a well-worn example, the giraffe does not stretch its neck to reach food which is otherwise out of reach and then pass on a longer neck to its offspring; instead, those giraffes in whom mutation has produced longer necks are more likely to reach available food and transmit the mutation" (ibid., 124).

complex 'cognitive' activity called thinking" (184). He is perfectly happy to abolish that man, whom he decries as "the inner man, the homunculus, the possessing demon, the man defended by the literatures of freedom and dignity" (191). This abolition does not destroy thinking; it restores it to the whole person, that is, to the body and the behavior that demonstrate who the person really is (190). Nor does it undermine human control. By understanding how we are controlled by the environment, the possibility arises for scientifically informed operant behavior, that is, for influencing the environment to our advantage: "As the individual controls himself by manipulating the world in which he lives, so the human species has constructed an environment in which its members behave in a highly effective way" (197). We cannot control the ultimate results of such changes, but behavioral analysis increases the chances that our operant behavior will be more adaptive in relation to our environment: "A scientific view of man offers exciting possibilities. We have not yet seen what man can make of man" (206).

Although Skinner does not mention binary oppositions or a dialectic of contradiction in *Beyond Freedom and Dignity,* this brief exposition of the text has shown that his argument is based upon the assumption that subjective mental states are utterly opposed to objective scientific knowledge. This contradiction is taken to be the foundation of all rigorous scientific method and behavioral research, and it shapes Skinner's objective theoretical interpretations of philosophical and moral issues also. He believes that science must analyze environmental and genetic controllers to be able to control and manipulate the subjective feelings of people. A rational science of behavior can lead to an effective technology of behavior, on the assumption that technology is simply applied science (5).

Since subjective intentions and feelings have no causal power, Skinner does not urge individuals to promote better communication concerning personal goals and preferences. Such dialogical and reciprocal relations are absent from his technology of behavior, although he does occasionally use the term "reciprocal" in a different way, for example, to describe the relation between an experimenter and the pigeon in the experiment (161). Certainly such an asymmetrical relation based upon manipulation and observation of a passive object by an active investigator is an odd example of reciprocity. Skinner further demonstrates the distance between his concept of reciprocity and mine when he writes that "[r]eciprocal control is not necessarily intentional in either direction, but it becomes so when the consequences make themselves felt" (162). For reciprocity that does entail human choosing, we must turn to a transactional exploration of the way in which science and technology influence human thought.

The Tyranny of Technology

Whereas Skinner writes as a psychologist who believes that the only hope for society lies in a technology of human behavior, Jacques Ellul is a sociologist who discerns in modern history a growing tyranny of technology. *The Technological Society*,[3] published in French in 1954, runs to 436 pages in the 1964 English translation, and often reads more like a Luddite tract than an academic treatise. But its pages contain a complex and probing analysis of the consequences and implications of the influence of technology on modern thought. To distinguish his treatment of technology as a way of thinking from the more common practice of identifying technology with current technical achievements, Ellul refers to it as technique.

A brief survey of the history of techniques provides a backdrop for Ellul's definition of technique. Early societies balanced techniques for making and using tools with magic as a technique of a "more or less spiritual order" (24). Ancient Greece made an effort "to economize on means and to reduce the sphere of influence of technique" (29). Roman law also strove to use minimal means, and to achieve "an equilibrium between the purely technical factor and the human factor" (30). For different reasons, both Christianity and the Enlightenment slowed the development of technique. Only with the Industrial Revolution does modern technique, as defined by Ellul, make its debut: "[T]echnique is the translation into action of man's concern to master things by means of reason, to account for what is subconscious, make quantitative what is qualitative, make clear and precise the outlines of nature, take hold of chaos and put order into it" (43). In other words, technique replaces the goal of equilibrium with the quest for mastery. Whereas technical and human factors had been held harmoniously in a reciprocal relation, now they are opposed to one another in a clear contradiction.

3. Jacques Ellul, *The Technological Society*, trans. John Wilkinson (New York: Vintage Books, 1964). In 1990 Ellul wrote of his earlier work: "With no false modesty I can say that social, economic and technical developments have confirmed in its entirety what I said thirty years ago. I have no need to correct or modify anything." See Jacques Ellul, *The Technological Bluff*, trans. Geoffrey W. Bromiley (Grand Rapids, Mich.: William B. Eerdmans, 1990), xii.

Ellul insists that his purpose is not to criticize: "We are registering a fact and not nostalgia for the old whole-wheat bread of our ancestors" (327). Yet his rhetoric gives the appearance of a passionate transactional attack upon theoretical interpretation. He asserts that modern technique has changed the way we think in important ways. Wherever dominant, it "brings its own ideology" (323) to justify both technique itself and those who serve it. The primary example of this pattern is the Tennessee Valley Authority (TVA), which started out as a plan to harness water power for electricity and to control flooding, but soon developed into a major experiment in regional comprehensive planning of matters affecting the environment and community life. Technique has also altered the space and time in which we live and work. Machines now fill our homes as well as our factories, and they serve to increase the pace of every aspect of life. Thus the temporal and spatial framework for all our thinking has been radically altered. A major change is occurring in society, and its ultimate effects are still unknown.

One result of the triumph of technique is known, however, and that is the way that traditional communities have been displaced by a mass society. Modern technique homogenizes everyone with the technical environment, so that individuals no longer participate in groups: they become mere elements of the group (335). "Social plasticity" is Ellul's term for the disappearance from our thinking of both social taboos and natural social groups (49). This first occurred in England, was violently implemented in France during the Revolution, and came about more peacefully in nineteenth-century America, which had the "exceptional flexibility" to begin to change itself into a fully technological society (59).

The resulting loss of equilibrium leads to a final development, the effort to discover techniques that will change human beings so that they can adjust more easily to the new world of technique. Some, such as psychoanalysis, aim to provide a freedom from technique through knowledge or inner experience. Others employ technique to try to restore to human beings a sense of unity or equilibrium. There are also those who hope that technique will find a way to create a new, superior human being. But the most important of all such efforts is the goal of humanizing technique itself, of "making the interests of technique and man correspond, [and] thus rendering technique flexible" (337). Ellul denounces this project as hypocritical hocus-pocus: "Today's technique may respect man because it is in its interest and part of its normal course of development to do so. . . . Tomorrow it might be in technique's interest to exploit man brutally, to mutilate and suppress him. . . . To me, therefore, it seems impossible to speak of a technical humanism" (340).

Ellul reviews the ways in which technique has already instilled a "lower threshold of consciousness" (403) in such diverse human activities as work, education, sports, amusement, and medicine. He views advertising as "the application of psychoanalytic mass techniques" to create a homogeneous mass society, one in which critical thinking has been suppressed (370). Ultimately we arrive at "the phenomenon of technical convergence," that is, the way in which vast systems of techniques have all converged upon individuals and produced "an operational totalitarianism; no longer is any part of man free and independent of these techniques" (391). Pervasive technique, including even human techniques, has led to a thoroughly technical human. Human life is now a matter of technique. This is not a new essentialism; it is simply the recognition that "technique permeates everything human" (393). The final state is "technical anesthesia," in which the disadvantages of technique have been obscured so successfully that individuals no longer wish to escape from machine techniques or from human techniques (412–13).

Although Ellul frequently disavows any polemical intent, the thrust of his book is clear: modern life is in the grip of technique, and this grip threatens to squeeze out of it everything that previously made it human. Freedom and responsibility, individuality and community, workplace and home: every aspect of life is now so dominated by technique that women and men necessarily become its pawns. Technicians may believe that they can preserve a sacred human center in the midst of technique, or that they can employ human techniques to combat the deleterious effects of machine techniques. But they delude themselves. Technique enslaves all equally and inexorably. Ellul must respect Skinner's bold insistence that a technology of behavior based upon deterministic behavioral science will necessarily leave the illusions of freedom and dignity as mental realities behind.[4] On this they are in agreement: subjective freedom and dignity are incompatible with the assumptions, methods, and goals of a technology of human behavior.

---

4. The translator of *The Technological Society*, John Wilkinson, considers Skinner one of the "technolaters" against whom the book is directed. He adds that Skinner is "the familiar type of the American intellectual caught in an ecstatic technical vertigo and seldom proceeding beyond certain vague meditations on isolated problem areas such as 'the population explosion,' if indeed he considers the real problems posed by technology at all" (xi).

Even Ellul's attempt to analyze the character traits of technique has the ring of a polemic against objective theoretical thinking. He barely mentions either the rationality of technique—meaning that it strives to be systematic, to organize or divide labor according to tasks (specialization), and to define and maintain certain standards or production norms—or the artificiality of technique, manifest in that it actually "destroys, eliminates, or subordinates the natural world" (79), for both have been the subject of much discussion. Ellul focuses instead upon characteristics of technique that seem to him to impinge upon human freedom. The fact of its automatism denies personal choice to those who participate in it. When choosing from competing techniques, personal preferences are superfluous. The most efficient means will always win out. The automatic character of technique also inevitably displaces nontechnical activities whenever a confrontation between them occurs: "Technical activity automatically eliminates every nontechnical activity or transforms it into technical activity. This does not mean, however, that there is any conscious effort or directive will" (83). Technique is a blind force that simply propels itself forward, conquering or converting whatever stands in its way. For all their freedom and dignity, individuals cannot resist its onslaught. Technicians affirm its victory only by becoming its slaves (84).

Another trait that shows how technique has usurped human freedom is self-augmentation, which is defined as the way in which technique "is being transformed and is progressing almost without decisive intervention by man" (85). Technique propagates itself both irreversibly and in a geometric progression (89). Humans are powerless to alter its course. The same consequence follows from the monism of technique, by which Ellul means that it presents, "everywhere and essentially, the same characteristics" (94). Differences are merely secondary. Ellul sees a connection between monism and moral paralysis. As he sees it, technique abolishes all moral considerations, rendering ludicrous the common opinion that technique can be separated from the use to which it is put. Thus the monism against which Ellul inveighs is not just the homogeneity of technique, it is also the way in which technique dissolves the dualism of moral reflection.

Closely related to the amoral monism of technique is its geographical universalism. Here Ellul cites many examples of traditional cultures that are threatened by the invasion of Western technique. Again the problem of the destruction of equilibrium arises, for technique "does not, of itself, carry its own equilibrium. The opposite is nearer the truth" (122). The fruits of technical civilization are social plasticity and technical consciousness, resulting in the rupture of economic from social life and "the dissolution of the entire group" (126). The technical "preoccupation with 'objectivity'" obliterates the significant differences among individuals and cultures (129, 131).

In the context of this chapter, there is a certain irony in the final characteristic that Ellul sees in technique: autonomy. Whereas Skinner attacks the myth of autonomous man, Ellul decries the autonomy of technique. Technique is free of all moral constraints, "beyond good and evil," a "new morality" based upon the principle of self-interest (134). Technical autonomy forces individuals to adapt their goals to the means offered by technique. It displaces other values: it undermines the gods who have been worshiped, and declares itself to be the one sacred mystery worthy of worship (142–43). The autonomy of technique is nothing more (or less) than its freedom from all the values and beliefs of traditional cultures.

Given this no-holds-barred attack upon modern technique, it might appear that Ellul is really nothing more than a subjective theoretical thinker who is opposing precisely the objective sort of theoretical understanding we found in Skinner. But that is not the case. What Ellul opposes in not technique as such but only technique that is no longer in equilibrium with other aspects of human life.

The heart of Ellul's argument is that the advances of modern science have enabled technique to "become a reality in itself. It is no longer merely a means and an intermediary. It is an object in itself, an independent reality with which we must reckon" (63). This contrasts sharply with the limited ways technique functioned in traditional societies, where it appeared only as an amalgam of various techniques employed for specific purposes. According to Ellul, traditional societies were more interested in such nontechnical matters as religion, and when they joined together for work, it was as much to be together as to use their techniques. "Society was free of technique" (65) as a way of thinking; it remained restricted to particular tasks and situations.

Traditional societies were also committed to perfecting old techniques rather than inventing new ones. The focus was upon improving one's use of the tool, not forever devising new tools. Ellul acknowledges that these two orientations overlap, and that skillful persons in traditional societies would often try to improve their tools. "But traditionally the accent was on the human being who used the tool and not on the tool he used" (68).

This was reflected in the local character of traditional technique. Societies did not rush to borrow techniques from their neighbors, for "technique was not some anonymous piece of merchandise but rather bore the stamp of the whole culture. . . . technique was not objective, but subjective in relation to its own culture" (69). The results were social equilibrium within each society, a very slow pace of change, a great deal of technological diversity among different societies, and a clear sense that, in the relation between humans and their techniques, the techniques were subordinate (72). Ellul claims that this diversity allowed stability within each culture and also choice for those individuals who were exposed to other cultures. Although he may be exaggerating the degree of personal freedom enjoyed in traditional societies, his point about technique is worth noting: people could choose among the available techniques according to their own values, without any compulsion to employ the one most efficient method (76; cf. 20–21).

Ellul's obvious commitments to personal choice and moral responsibility certainly qualify him as a transactional thinker, as I defined it in the Introduction. As is so often the case with this type of interpretation, it is presented as a protest against a theoretical position, a position that it considers inimical both to individual freedom and to a humanistic ethic. The extent to which Ellul also understands these matters in terms of a dialectic of reciprocity, which is central to transactional interpretation, requires elaboration.

The most obvious reciprocal element in Ellul's thinking is his frequent return to an ideal of equilibrium, a trait that can be destroyed but not created by technique. This equilibrium must be more than just stability, for almost any tyranny is capable of maintaining the status quo. Indeed, equilibrium is seen by Ellul as a dynamic relation between the impersonal forces at work in a society and the persons who are its members. Throughout *The Technological Society,* he draws attention to the way technique dominates lives without any reciprocal counterinfluence whatsoever. What is most frightening about modern technique is its totalitarian character, the fact that it is impervious to the needs and desires of those under its sway. It shapes them, but they have no control over it. Ellul's concept of equilibrium presupposes a dialectic of reciprocity similar to the relation between the technical and the human factors that he attributes to Roman law (30).

Ellul also seems to understand the relation between science and technology in a reciprocal manner. Whereas Skinner expresses the conventional view that technology is applied science, Ellul denounces that opinion as "radically false" except "for the physical sciences and for the nineteenth century" (7). He believes that technology precedes science historically, and ideally should always yield to it. Technology lacks the prudence and patience of science. But modern technique has made science its instrument

(10, 21), abolishing the reciprocal relation between them. Technique precedes and produces science, and should be informed by it. Science arises out of techniques, and must never ignore the technological consequences of its own endeavors.

Finally, a presupposition of reciprocity is also discernible in Ellul's brief references to objectivity. On the one hand, he insists that his book is an objective sociological analysis of the facts. Whether or not we agree with that claim, it clearly indicates a commitment to objective analysis. On the other, he accuses technique of treating human beings as mere objects, and of inculcating a "preoccupation with 'objectivity'" (127, 129). What technique destroys most fundamentally is human subjectivity. Although Ellul does not articulate the proper relation between objectivity and subjectivity, it is clear that, in his view, neither should exist is isolation from the other. Objective social forces should respect and foster human subjectivity, just as subjective individuals must adapt to objective reality. Thus Ellul's understanding of the dialectic of objectivity and subjectivity is at least implicitly reciprocal. Each needs the other, for neither can function properly alone. Objectivity alone degenerates into social plasticity, while mere subjectivity lacks a foundation in social reality and sociological fact.

A Paradoxical Paradigm for Science

Ellul's notions of equilibrium between technical and human factors within society, between technology and science, and between objectivity and subjectivity, stand in sharp contrast to Skinner's tendency to explain all relations in terms of a theory of causal connections. Rather than reciprocity in social relations, Skinner sees a behavioral determinism that redefines freedom and repudiates dignity. Instead of a complex interaction between science and technology, he perceives technology as the application of advances in scientific knowledge. And rather than a balance of objectivity and subjectivity, Skinner's binary view is that society must support a purely objective scientific analysis of human behavior that can provide guidelines for reforming the behavior of individuals, which in turn will alter their subjective feelings. Thus Skinner looks to science and technology to reform human thinking, whereas Ellul would like to see us resist the domination of technique over our thought.

Although Thomas Kuhn does not side with either position in *The Structure of Scientific Revolutions,*[5] his careful analysis of how scientific changes impact on our thinking has startling implications for this debate. We might have expected Kuhn to agree with Skinner, for his background in logical positivist philosophy[6] has much in common with the objective theoretical position of Skinner's behaviorism. At times Kuhn writes about interpretation as if it were merely a subjective reading of the data that goes beyond what can be established by scientific consensus. This is a common use of the term among logical positivists and other thinkers for whom interpretation is secondary to the observation of a fixed reality (120, 123). It shows the extent to which Kuhn shares important aspects of a logical positivist perspective. As he puts it in his 1969 postscript, interpretation is "a deliberative process by which we choose among alternatives as we do not in perception itself" (194). Kuhn opposes the modern belief ("traditional since Descartes") that we unconsciously choose among possible perceptions in much the same way that we consciously choose among possible interpretations, so that it is legitimate "to analyze perception as an interpretive process" (195). With the logical positivists, he maintains a sharp distinction between perception and interpretation.

But Kuhn also develops a concept of paradigm in his book that seems to undermine that sharp distinction. To the dismay of logical positivists and other objectivists, Kuhn argues that paradigms precede and shape all the operations of rational thinking: methodology, theory building, the determination of facts, and even perception itself. He does this while embracing a definition of the term that dates back to the fifteenth century, when "paradigm" came to signify an exemplary pattern or model. Usage has included a broad spectrum, from the exemplary behavior of a "paradigm of virtue" to linguistic paradigms in which one noun or verb was used to illustrate the morphology of an entire declension or conjugation. Kuhn emphasizes this aspect of the term: a paradigm is a conceptual configuration that is demonstrated and learned by example rather than by discursive elaboration.

The radical aspect of Kuhn's understanding of paradigms is his claim that they are prior to all other mental operations. Methods are based upon paradigms. They implement a paradigm and direct the scientist toward

5. Thomas S. Kuhn, *The Structure of Scientific Revolutions,* 2d ed. (Chicago: University of Chicago Press, 1970).

6. Kuhn published the 1962 edition of *The Structure of Scientific Revolutions* as part of the *International Encyclopedia of Unified Science,* edited by Rudolf Carnap and other prominent logical positivists, despite the fact that his book is in some ways a sweeping criticism of the methods and assumptions of logical positivism.

answers to the questions that it poses, but methods can never solve problems that arise outside the categories of that particular paradigm (3). The same can be said for theories, at least for most theories. Unlike paradigms, theories do not normally conflict with their predecessors (95). Since they explain only a part of a defined whole, they can easily coexist with different theories that explain other parts of the same whole. They can also modify previous theories about the same part of the whole without totally displacing them. All such theories are referred to by Kuhn as "paradigm theories," that is, theories that operate entirely within an established paradigm.

The priority of paradigms extends beyond methods and theories to the establishment of fundamental facts, for it is the paradigm that identifies for scientists which facts are significant and worthy of study (25). It also promotes investigation of factual predictions made on the basis of its own guidelines, and gathers those facts that will aid in articulation of the paradigm. Finally, the belief that paradigms precede and make possible perception is where Kuhn departs most radically from logical positivists. He agrees with them that perception precedes interpretation, but then he adds that paradigms precede perception. In his view, paradigms are what determine both the shape of perception and the range of possible interpretations.

When Kuhn argues that paradigms precede and govern all scientific thought, he departs from a positivist position. Yet the tension in his thinking remains prominent, for he also subscribes to the notion that "pre-paradigm" science is possible: "[N]ot all theories are paradigm theories. Both during pre-paradigm periods and during the crises that lead to large-scale changes of paradigm, scientists usually develop many speculative and unarticulated theories that can themselves point the way to discovery" (61).

This reference to pre-paradigm periods raises an interesting question: is science possible without paradigms? Many would answer in the affirmative only because they do not accept Kuhn's understanding of paradigms. When scientists accept a particular paradigm, they tend to identify that paradigm with nature. When that happens, they become convinced that they can engage in scientific work with no constraints other than those imposed by the nature of whatever they are studying. Methods and theories are assumed to correspond as fully as possible with reality. Progress in science is understood as a linear process in which new findings correct old errors, as cumulative rather than as a series of ruptures. This view of scientific change is the primary target of Kuhn's book, and with it the "prevalent image of the scientist" as a researcher who works without a paradigm (87).

In Kuhn's view, pre-paradigm science is a time of "frequent and deep debates over legitimate methods, problems, and standards of solution, though these serve rather to define schools than to produce agreement" (47–48). It would appear from this that his use of the term "pre-paradigm" is misleading, for a period in which different schools are competing is not one without any paradigm at all; it is one in which each school is defending and articulating a different paradigm. In relation to a discipline or specialization that results from the victory of one paradigm over its competitors, such a period is really preparatory to the victory of the soon-to-be-normative paradigm. Thus a pre-paradigm period is best understood as a time of rival paradigms. The very idea of a time without any paradigms whatsoever is implausible, given Kuhn's assertion that "something like a paradigm is prerequisite to perception itself" (113).

Every "normal" or established science is, according to Kuhn, governed by a particular paradigm. Normal science does not employ paradigms as instruments: it is based upon them. It cannot step outside of its own paradigm to correct the assumptions and methods by which it operates. According to Kuhn, normal science has "two essential characteristics." First is that each paradigm illustrates an "unprecedented" scientific achievement, just as each religious or linguistic paradigm is also distinctive of a particular configuration. Second, every paradigm is "open-ended," for they all encourage further research in science or additional applications in religion and language (10). This second characteristic deserves emphasis, since the popular understanding of paradigms often construes them as a set of boundaries that limit creative activity.[7] Paradigms, according to Kuhn, are what make mature science possible, for they provide the "rules and standards" that are essential to all research in every established discipline (11).

One of the most important aspects of paradigms for Kuhn's argument is implicit in that first characteristic, their distinctive or unprecedented character. To be distinctive means that old paradigms cannot gradually evolve into new paradigms. They are not subject to reform. Tinkering certainly occurs, but it must always be conducted within the fundamental parameters of the existing paradigm, which no doubt accounts for the failure to distinguish paradigms from boundaries as such. Kuhn makes this point with respect to the shift from Newtonian to Einsteinian mechanics, which he says "illustrates with particular clarity the scientific revolution as a displacement of the conceptual network through which scientists view the world" (102).

7. For example, Joel Barker, *Discovering the Future: The Business of Paradigms,* as reported in *Benchmark,* fall 1989, 2–7.

The relation between successive paradigms is one of displacement, not development. The differences between them are "both necessary and irreconcilable"; they are "not only incompatible but incommensurable" (103).

The description of a paradigm as a conceptual network is especially relevant to the way the term is used in the humanities and in my typology. Kuhn's reference to this network as that "through which scientists view the world" alludes to the metaphor of a lens. Not only is a paradigm like a lens, but a scientist who adopts a new paradigm is like a person looking at the world through "inverted lenses" (122). Kuhn also employs the metaphor of a map. A paradigm shows the scientist how to identify the routes that will facilitate further research. Beyond this, a paradigm also guides the scientist in the activity of mapmaking (109). This does not mean that one paradigm enables scientists to spin off brand new paradigms at will. Rather, every paradigm provides the theory and methods necessary for its own further development. Kuhn refers to this activity as "paradigm articulation," which involves "resolving some of its residual ambiguities and permitting the solution of problems to which it had previously only drawn attention" (27).

Normal science may be limited by its paradigm, but it can certainly recognize data that it cannot explain within that paradigm, and it can also realize that these data have become so plentiful that a crisis exists. When the end of such a crisis finally arrives, it seems to come quickly and inexplicably, "not by deliberation and interpretation [within the existing paradigm], but by a relatively sudden and unstructured event like the gestalt switch. Scientists often speak of the 'scales falling from the eyes' or of the 'lightning flash' that 'inundates' a previously obscure puzzle, enabling its components to be seen in a new way that for the first time permits its solution. On other occasions the relevant illumination comes in sleep. No ordinary sense of the term 'interpretation' fits these flashes of intuition through which a new paradigm is born" (122–23).

The language of this passage—"illumination" and "flashes of intuition"—reflects Kuhn's description of the discovery of new paradigms in terms that we would expect more in discussions of religion than in analyses of scientific progress. It also points toward the paradoxical character of his understanding of scientific paradigms and revolutions. He writes that scientific education is similar to theological education in important ways (136, 166), and that "neither proof nor error is at issue" in the scientist's commitment to a paradigm: "The transfer of allegiance from paradigm to paradigm is a conversion experience that cannot be forced" (151). Such an experience comes at the end of a long and agonizing period of doubt. Scientists do not immediately abandon an old paradigm just because it fails to account for all the data, nor do they reject it before they have a new one to replace it. They go through an extended period in which they gradually "lose faith" in the old paradigm and consider possible new ones. The culmination of this struggle comes as a conversion that is paradoxically the result of a long and gradual process of reflection and also a sudden decision: "The decision to reject one paradigm is always simultaneously the decision to accept another" (77).

All this paradoxical talk about conversion and faith raises the question of the objectivity of science itself. Kuhn gives what appear to be two quite different responses to this question. On the one hand, he points out that the belief that nature is fixed, while scientific interpretations of it are subject to change, is itself "an essential part of a philosophical paradigm initiated by Descartes and developed at the same time as Newtonian dynamics. That paradigm has served both science and philosophy well" (121), but is now being challenged by new research in a number of disciplines. On the other hand, perception is capable of objective cognition. Kuhn never disputes the claim of science to provide reliable knowledge based upon valid perceptions.

If paradigms are lenses that make valid perceptions possible even as they filter them, then Kuhn's concept of paradigm implicitly undercuts the entire debate over objectivity and subjectivity. No longer do they oppose one another or cooperate in a reciprocal relation of equilibrium. Both are reconceived as moments or aspects within a particular paradigm, which is itself a conceptual network within which knowledge is established, whether that knowledge is construed objectively as direct cognition of reality or subjectively as paradigm-dependent. In Kuhn's concept of paradigm, the contradiction between the poles of this traditional modern dichotomy is overcome even while the opposition between perception and interpretation is maintained. In this way Kuhn presents a paradoxical epistemology of science that supports the appeal to paradox in his analysis of scientific revolution as a conversion by scientists from one paradigm to another.

That Kuhn is aware of the paradoxical character of his own understanding of paradigms is demonstrated by his comments on the circularity of scientific inquiry and debate. The philosophy of science may be armed with an "entire arsenal of dichotomies" (description vs. interpretation, discovery vs. justification), but Kuhn counters that all such "methodological distinctions, which would thus be prior to the analysis of scientific knowledge, . . . now seem integral parts of a traditional set of substantive answers to the very questions upon which they have been deployed" (8–9). That means: the answers are already entailed in the questions. Kuhn adds that such "circularity does not at all invalidate them," but it certainly does undermine the positivist assumption that a linear progression from question to answer prevails. Question and answer are simultaneous moments or revelations of a shared paradigm. This circularity is also evident in scientific revolutions. During the phase of intense debate between schools adhering to competing paradigms, they cannot help but talk past each other, since each is appealing to irreconcilable structures of question and answer: "When paradigms enter, as they must, into a debate about paradigm choice, their role is necessarily circular. Each group uses its own paradigm to argue in that paradigm's defense" (94).

Kuhn's dialectic of paradox reaches its most intense pitch when he tries to explain more fully the relation between scientific knowledge and nature itself. As he puts it, the goal is to show that paradigms are "constitutive" not only of science but "of nature as well" (110). He comments frequently on the "different world" in which scientists seem to live after a paradigm shift (111, 117, 118, 121). The data are not stable, for they are dependent upon the paradigm by which they are established. Yet "the scientist after a revolution is still looking at the same world" (129). There certainly exists a real objective world, in Kuhn's view, but there does not seem to be any unmediated access to it. This is why he must resort to paradox in describing a paradigm shift such as the one that occurred when scientists adopted Dalton's chemical atomic theory: "But it is hard to make nature fit a paradigm. . . . even after accepting the theory, they still had to beat nature into line, a process which, in the event, took almost another generation. When it was done, even the percentage composition of well-known compounds was different. The data themselves had changed. . . . we may say that after a revolution scientists work in a different world" (135).

Paradox is present in the disintegration of paradigms as well as in their establishment. Kuhn describes as "anomalies" any data that conflict with the prevailing paradigm, and that eventually lead to its collapse. It is tempting to describe the conflicts that arise from such anomalous data as simply differing interpretations of identical perceptions. Did not Priestley see as dephlogisticated air the same thing that Lavoisier came to see as oxygen? Kuhn is uncomfortable with this effort to flatten out the paradox by appeal to a fixed nature: "Scientists do not simply see something *as* something else; instead, they simply see it. . . . the scientist does not preserve the gestalt subject's freedom to switch back and forth between ways of seeing" (85). In gestalt psychological experiments, the subject can see the same drawing as a duck or as a rabbit. But for scientists, new views displace old understandings (114–15). Kuhn makes this point in another reference to Lavoisier: "At the very least, as a result of discovering oxygen, Lavoisier saw nature differently. And in the absence of some recourse to that hypothetical fixed nature that he 'saw differently,' the principle of economy will urge us to say that after discovering oxygen Lavoisier worked in a different world" (118).

A further paradox can be seen in the fact that anomalies are normally the result of research that is inspired and guided by the same paradigm that they threaten: normal science "prepares the way for its own change" (65). This tendency of normal science to produce research instruments that in turn provide anomalous data is one of the few points at which Kuhn touches directly on the subject of technology: "Without the special apparatus that is constructed mainly for anticipated functions, the results that lead ultimately to novelty could not occur" (65). Thus "technology has often played a vital role in the emergence of new sciences" (15–16).

· · ·

Contrasting the views of Skinner, Ellul, and Kuhn on technology is instructive. For Skinner, technology is the straightforward application of science to the world. Ellul sees science and technology as reciprocally influencing one another. Kuhn's understanding introduces a paradox: science produces a technology to further its own agenda, but that very technology often undermines the science that produced it. This is more than an interesting irony, for it illustrates that the agent of change is neither science alone (Skinner) nor the interaction between science and technology (Ellul). Change comes from beyond, as it were, from a source outside of the circle of the existing paradigm. It is the effect of something that enters existence through science and technology, but is not part of any existing science or technology at the moment of its inception.

In addition to forcing upon human thinking paradoxes that are never intended and rarely even acknowledged, scientific paradigms also influence the emergence and self-definition of scientific communities. Normal science is a community activity, a commitment to a common paradigm that unites all who share it in a community of scientists (167–69). One of the reasons it is so difficult to bring about revolutions in science is the social pressure that discourages individuals from breaking with the accepted way of doing science: "Like the choice between competing political institutions, that between competing paradigms proves to be a choice between incompatible modes of community life" (94). Educational methods, and especially textbooks, present the reigning normal science as though it were the inevitable outcome of centuries of progressive development toward a goal, rather than the result of mistakes, misunderstandings, lucky guesses, and the zigzagging that characterizes actual science. An individual practitioner who refuses to be converted to a generally accepted new paradigm "has *ipso facto* ceased to be a scientist" (159).

Kuhn's understanding of paradigms and scientific revolutions also implies a paradoxical response to the choice between Skinner's belief in environmental control of people through a technology of behavior and Ellul's alarm at the loss of equilibrium between techniques and those who use them. Kuhn does not believe that we can ever have complete conscious control over our own science and technology, for they are the products of paradigms that we inherit. However, it is equally true that, apart from the rigorous methods of ordinary research within a normal science, science and technology in no way control us. In the opposition between old paradigms that are threatened by anomalies and new ones that have not yet managed to convert sufficient numbers to qualify as normal science, creative energies are unleashed and new communities are born. This is a process of "perceptual transformations" (112) in which novelties emerge that have not been planned by anyone. It is a paradoxical process in that it unites destruction with creation, both in scientific developments and in the communities that resist, promote, and are affected by them. If this is to be believed, then Skinner's technology of behavior is impossible to achieve or sustain, and Ellul's harmonious equilibrium between technique and social forces is equally beyond human control. The one certainty is that science, technology, and society will all continue to change each other and to be changed beyond our wildest imagination.

When I first conceived of a chapter on science and technology, I assumed that the subject matter alone would privilege objective theoretical interpretations. Certainly science is based upon observation, like all theoretical activity, and rigorous scientific method requires striving for the utmost objectivity. But this chapter grew beyond science and technology alone. It became a chapter on the relation between them on the one hand and human thinking on the other. And there our theoretical thinker has seemed to be out of his depth. Skinner is extremely lucid about how to engage in a behavioral analysis of human thoughts, feelings, and actions. He is always honest about his commitment to a rigid environmental determinism and the implications of that commitment for such concepts as freedom and dignity. But lucidity and honesty cannot mask the fact that Skinner's behaviorism sacrifices humanity on the altar of control. He is totally committed to the ideal of complete control over knowledge, feelings, social forces, and people. He is committed to that very totalitarianism of method that Ellul detects in all technique.

But does Ellul offer anything more than a protest? If technique is as autonomous and as inexorably self-augmenting as Ellul thinks, then the days of social, intellectual, or moral equilibrium are long gone, and his diatribe—for that is what it is—takes on the apocalyptic quality of a vision of the imminent end of the world. Indeed, if Ellul's diagnosis is correct, the patient (human life and thought as we have known it) is terminally ill. But if Ellul's values are true, if nature abhors imbalance as much as a vacuum, then there are ample grounds for hope. The very power of technique seems to engender its own counterforce, and novel developments, from flextime in the workplace to accommodation for "special" students in schools to the contemporary commitment to affirming and protecting diversity within society, witness to a concern for transactional values that I cannot dismiss as little more than camouflage for further enslavement.

This may mean that we are witnessing a major paradigm shift in the way in which we understand science and technology in relation to human thinking. It is difficult to see paradoxes in social relations. Paradox is such a conceptual term that it, like Kuhn's entire book, deals primarily with modes of thinking and only peripherally with communities in process. But even the most ardent futurist has to admit that the one thing we can be sure of is that no one can be sure of the future, that it will surprise us, and that whatever new paradigm displaces the old will not be one that was predictable on the basis of the old. It would be comforting to think that the wide popularity of Kuhn's book means that the age of "two cultures" is passing away, that the sciences and the humanities are at a point where they can realize not only their need for each other but, more deeply, their inseparability in the midst of all the tensions between them. As is so often the case with transformational visions, however, this one may never become more than a dream. Nevertheless, like many dreams before it, it has a ring of truth that more mundane renderings of the actual world lack.

2

Myths and Their Meanings

Of all the expressions of human imagination, few are as fascinating and yet bewildering as mythology. Some myths mirror the lives of the cultures that created them, while others seem to present a counterpoint to what is known and ordinary. Myths can be deceptive in their simplicity and exasperating in their complexity. Rich in local detail, they resound with universal themes. The lush imagery and often fantastic narratives of myths are a source of inspiration and instruction, although one that is often inaccessible to those who think of myths simply as bizarre stories that are not historically true. Romanticism bequeathed to us both a love for mythology and a modern historical consciousness, but the language of myth and the reason of history are often at war within our minds. We sense that the myths of distant cultures have many secrets to reveal, but we find it impossible to probe their meanings in the terms that our modern rational and historical ways of thinking provide.

Of the many ways of understanding myth that modern anthropologists have proposed, the writings of Claude Lévi-Strauss provide the best example of theoretical interpretation. For five decades Lévi-Strauss has applied his structuralist method of binary analysis to myths, kinship systems, and other expressions of human thought. I focus here upon a few of the essays collected in *Structural Anthropology* and the radio interviews first heard on the CBC and later published as *Myth and Meaning*. For a transactional type I then turn to Mary Douglas, an anthropologist whose influential grid-group analysis of types of societies offers a way of understanding why different groups think as they do. Although Douglas does not discuss myths directly in *Cultural Bias,* her general analysis and specific comments on cosmology provide clear guidelines for how to interpret myths in a reciprocal manner. I conclude with a look at Joseph Campbell's reading of myths. Shortly before his death in 1987, Campbell was interviewed by Bill Moyers for what became a very popular PBS television series, *The Power of Myth.* I will limit my discussion, however, to the transformational interpretation of myth spelled out in *The Hero with a Thousand Faces,* the book that first established Campbell's reputation and remains one of his most widely read statements about the paradoxical meaning of myth.

The Structuralist Sorcerer

Lévi-Strauss is a philosopher of contradictions. He has done more than almost any other writer to make a structuralist method of analysis seem plausible, and yet he seems to delight in presenting particular interpretations that are frankly implausible. His application of the method to the Oedipus myth is one of his most influential writings, despite his disclaimer at the beginning that its "use is probably not legitimate in this particular instance."[1] It is not surprising that Lévi-Strauss has many critics, yet even they acknowledge the brilliance with which he waves his structuralist wand over the most intractable subjects, turning up connections and correlations that elude less intrepid interpreters. The cautious reader will often wonder if one bold claim or another is not more an expression of the fertile yet idiosyncratic imagination of Lévi-Strauss than a result of sound scholarship and careful analysis. Yet nothing could be further from his stated intentions

---

1. Claude Lévi-Strauss, "The Structural Study of Myth," in *Structural Anthropology,* trans. Claire Jacobson and Brooke Grundfest Schoepf (Garden City, N.Y.: Basic Books, 1963), 213; hereafter cited as SSM.

than idiosyncrasy.[2] In *Myth and Meaning*,[3] Lévi-Strauss insists that his writings are in no way merely an expression of his personal ego:

> I don't have the feeling that I write my books. I have the feeling that my books get written through me. . . .
>
> I never had, and still do not have, the perception of feeling my personal identity. I appear to myself as the place where something is going on, but there is no "I," no "me." Each of us is a kind of crossroads where things happen. The crossroads is purely passive; something happens there. A different thing, equally valid, happens elsewhere. There is no choice, it is just a matter of chance. (*M&M*, 3–4)

This sense of the self as a passive crossroads where things just happen, events that are not subject to the self's choice or control, is a fitting expression of a structuralist approach to interpretation. Simply put, structuralism is the theory that the shape and often the contents of human consciousness are determined not by the intended meanings of the humans themselves but by structures of which they remain largely unaware: structures embedded in language dictate what speech is possible; class structures govern social and political relations; psychological structures shape learning and development; and structures in the mind account for all forms of thought and knowledge, including myth.

As an erstwhile philosopher whose primary interest is in the intellectual rather than the material aspects of culture, Lévi-Strauss is preoccupied with these mental structures. Just as he thinks of a person as a passive crossroads—an empty intersection where things happen by chance—so also all human thinking occurs within the formal structures of the mind. Fundamental among these is the structure of binary opposition. According to Lévi-Strauss, we are bifurcating creatures. Our consciousness is forever struggling with contradiction and opposition. We live with dualities that our own minds have created, however much we may try to overcome or deny them.

Foremost among the devices we employ to come to terms with contradictions in our lives and thought is myth. As Lévi-Strauss puts it: "[T]he

---

2. If the method is not idiosyncratic, then imitation should not be too difficult. See the interesting effort by Eugene A. Hammel, "The Myth of Structural Analysis: Lévi-Strauss and the Three Bears," Addison-Wesley Modular Publications, no. 25 (1972): 1–29.

3. Claude Lévi-Strauss, *Myth and Meaning* (New York: Schocken Books, 1979); hereafter cited as *M&M*.

purpose of myth is to provide a logical model capable of overcoming a contradiction (an impossible achievement if, as it happens, the contradiction is real)" (SSM, 229). The logical model provided by myth always conforms to the binary structure of the mind. Every myth presents a polarity, an opposition that the mind wants to overcome but cannot, unless the initial impression of opposition was mistaken. The futility of myth, however, does not render it useless. Although it fails to overcome contradictions in real life, it does help us to accept them as consistent with the structure of existence.

Even if it is not a "legitimate" example of how this method works, Lévi-Strauss's analysis of the myth of Oedipus is certainly one of his most brilliant performances. He believes that myths are like musical scores: they must be "read" vertically as well as horizontally (SSM, 212–13; M&M, 44–54). To follow the horizontal diachronic dimension (the literal narrative of a myth or the sequential melody of a musical score) by itself is to miss the vertical synchronic correlations that give the myth or the music its meaning. In the case of music, those correlations consist in chords, harmonies, and dissonances that occur by virtue of the simultaneous playing of different notes or a variety of instruments. The synchronic correlations in myths are what Lévi-Strauss calls "bundles" of relations among the narrative elements, relations that constitute core meanings, or "mythemes" (SSM, 211).

In the Oedipus myth, Lévi-Strauss finds four such synchronic correlations, which he arranges in vertical columns (SSM, 214–15): (1) blood relationships sometimes result in ignoring moral or civil laws (e.g., Oedipus marries his mother, and Antigone buries her rebel brother, Polynices, both acts considered crimes); (2) blood relationships can also be violated (e.g., Oedipus kills his father, Laios, and Polynices is killed by his brother); (3) monsters are slain (e.g., Oedipus kills the Sphinx); and (4) men have trouble walking upright (e.g., "Laios" might mean left-sided, and "Oedipus" might mean swollen-foot, both implying difficulty in walking). The significance of these admittedly hypothetical derivations is that they allow the fourth bundle or column to signify that humans were born from the earth: "In mythology it is a universal characteristic of men born from the Earth that at the moment they emerge they either cannot walk or they walk clumsily" (SSM, 215). Thus the fourth column contradicts the third, in which the slaying of monsters symbolizes the denial of the theory of autochthony (human birth from the earth). This permits Lévi-Strauss to assert that column 4 contradicts column 3 in the same way that column 2 (the underrating of blood relations) contradicts column 1 (the overrating of blood relations), a parallelism that gains significance from the structuralist maxim that "contradictory relationships [within myths] are identical inasmuch as they are both self-contradictory in a similar way" (SSM, 216).

Lévi-Strauss's next and culminating paragraph in this analysis is a prime illustration of the succinct and even elliptical style with which he often challenges the reader:

> Turning back to the Oedipus myth, we may now see what it means. The myth has to do with the inability, for a culture which holds the belief that mankind is autochthonous . . . , to find a satisfactory transition between this theory and the knowledge that human beings are actually born from the union of man and woman. Although the problem obviously cannot be solved, the Oedipus myth provides a kind of logical tool which relates the original problem—born from one or born from two?—to the derivative problem: born from different or born from same? By a correlation of this type, the overrating of blood relations is to the underrating of blood relations as the attempt to escape autochthony is to the impossibility to succeed in it. Although experience contradicts theory, social life validates cosmology by its similarity of structure. Hence cosmology is true. (SSM, 216)

According to Lévi-Strauss, then, myth employs a homology to validate the cosmological contradiction between a traditional belief in autochthony and the empirical discovery of human generation: it shows that the contradictions in our thinking are like (homologous with) the contradictions in our social reality. Thus the cosmological contradiction between primitive tradition and science is validated by the analogous and real social contradiction between the overrating and the underrating of blood relations. The social contradictions show that the structure of reality is itself contradictory. The function of myth is to make this entire situation—a reality riddled by social and intellectual contradictions—tolerable.

If we look again at the cryptic two sentences that conclude the passage quoted above—"Although experience contradicts theory, social life validates cosmology by its similarity of structure. Hence cosmology is true"—we can see that Lévi-Strauss is simply drawing out the consequences of what he has already argued: within cosmology, the scientific experience of human generation contradicts the traditional theory of autochthony; but social life demonstrates a similar structure of self-contradiction concerning the value of blood relations, and so the social contradiction validates the cosmological contradiction. Cosmology is "true" in the sense that it displays the same structure of contradiction found in social reality.

Lévi-Strauss's analysis of the Oedipus myth grants priority to social over intellectual contradictions: the problem is generated by a conflict between mythical and scientific intellectual convictions, while the "solution" is found in the homologous real contradictions within actual social experience. This may be why he treats Freud's psychological theory about Oedipal complexes as a modern version of the myth rather than as a preeminent interpretation of it (SSM, 217). Despite this emphasis upon social reality, Lévi-Strauss avoids explaining myths in terms of their particular social and historical elements. For him, the content of myths is as arbitrary as the individual signs that stand for concepts in a linguistic system (SSM, 209). What counts is the mental structure that gives binary form to the various contents provided by the social and natural environments. Social oppositions (paternal/maternal lineage or patrilocality/matrilocality) and polarities within nature (night/day, winter/summer, or east/west) are of less interest to him as objective contradictions than as symbolic vehicles by which the mythmaking mind shapes and is shaped by the reality in which it lives.[4]

In "The Effectiveness of Symbols,"[5] which deals primarily with a shamanistic intervention in a difficult child birth, Lévi-Strauss illustrates a different type of contradiction. Much of the article is devoted to a clever comparison between shamanism and psychoanalysis: both bring to consciousness previously unconscious conflicts; both provoke experiences in which those conflicts can be identified and resolved; and both require a knowledgeable guide, whether shaman or psychoanalyst (ES, 198). In both cases also the patient is manipulated mentally by means of symbols rather than physical intervention: "It is the effectiveness of symbols which guarantees the harmonious parallel development of myth and action" (ES, 201). Lévi-Strauss does not ignore the differences between the two practices, yet he presents them less as direct opposites than as inversions of one another. In psychoanalysis the patient constructs an individual myth from personal experiences stored in the unconscious, tells it to the psychoanalyst, and then, by transference, puts words into the mouth of the psychoanalyst. In shamanism, however, the patient receives a myth based upon social experiences and told by the shaman who presumes to speak for the patient (ES, 199). Here the binary opposition of elements takes the form of inversion, which

---

4. This is clear in Lévi-Strauss, "The Story of Asdiwal," in *The Structural Study of Myth and Totemism*, ed. Edmund Leach (London: Tavistock Publications, 1967), 1–47.

5. In *Structural Anthropology*, 186–205; hereafter cited as ES.

has the ironic effect of implying a greater correspondence between the two than most psychoanalysts would care to admit.

Beyond these interesting similarities and inversions, Lévi-Strauss sees a deeper structural identity between psychoanalysis and shamanism, for both are expressions of "atemporal" structural laws, laws that constitute "what we call the unconscious" (ES, 202). Indeed, it appears that Lévi-Strauss wants to correct psychoanalysis by an appeal to shamanism, for he declares them to be identical on the ground that the unconscious is now understood to be a universal symbolic function rather than "the repository of a unique history" (ES, 202–3). The unconscious is made up of impersonal and universal laws, and personal experiences are processed by those mental structures just as diverse foods are processed indifferently by the stomach. The individual and personal aspects that psychoanalysis still, to a great extent, preserves are displaced by a structuralist "crossroads" theory of the unconscious. Although its contents are "infinitely varied," the laws by which it operates are few, just as there are "very few structural laws which are valid for all languages" (ES, 203). Lévi-Strauss wants to employ this structuralist principle to guide our understanding of music as well as myth and language, indeed, of all intellectual activities except science.

In *Myth and Meaning,* Lévi-Strauss takes pains to stress his respect for modern science (*M&M,* 5–14). He describes himself as a faithful reader each month of *Scientific American,* and reveals that his first intellectual fascination as a child had been with geology. The sort of science that interests him, however, is the search for the invariant, for laws or structures that endure through all the changes that a phenomenon undergoes. In fact, it was the puzzling similarities that occur among myths originating in cultures that have had no contact with one another that initially attracted him to mythology. Lévi-Strauss contrasts a structuralist approach with scientific reductionism. Whereas structuralism identifies parallel formal structures, or homologies, in such different phenomena as culture and nature, reductionism tries to understand complex phenomena by translating them into simpler terms, as when individual behavior is explained by distinctive genetic codes. Lévi-Strauss insists that the richness of culture cannot adequately be understood by reducing it to just one aspect of nature (e.g., genetic causes);[6] therefore a structuralist method is necessary to reach a fuller understanding of human thought and behavior.

In fact, the structuralist method developed by Lévi-Strauss is what he

---

6. He does imply, however, that a common origin of mental and physical experience may one day be found in "the structure of the nervous system" (*M&M,* 8).

calls in an earlier work "a science of the concrete."[7] He states that the parting
of science from mythological thinking occurred when, in the seventeenth
and eighteenth centuries, "it was thought that science could exist only by
turning its back upon the world of the senses, the world we see, smell, taste,
and perceive" (M&M, 6). Science rejected everything concrete and particular for abstract truths and universal laws. Lévi-Strauss denies that science
is a superior method of thinking, for he believes that "the same logical
processes operate in myth as in science, and that man has always been
thinking equally well" (SSM, 230). Technology shows that the only real difference between primitives and moderns is in the materials on which the
mind works. A steel ax is better than a stone ax not because it is better made
but because steel is superior to stone (SSM, 230).

Due to its concrete and particular form of expression, myth is no longer
intelligible to scientifically trained readers. Lévi-Strauss sees his task as the
scientific explanation of myth, that is, the unraveling of the concrete partic-
ularities of myths in order to reveal the structural laws that govern them. He
cannot employ reductionist methods, because they all deny the essentially
intellectual character of the structures of binary opposition. They flatten
out the contradictions that characterize human thought, by reducing it to
a simple result of one or another material cause. In contrast, structuralist
analysis explains myths in terms of formal homologies that preserve their
intellectual character.

As a paradigm of theoretical interpretation, Lévi-Strauss's structuralism
is very instructive. In contrast to Skinner's behavioral reductionism, Lévi-
Strauss makes binary opposition the intellectual center of his attention.
But he also joins Skinner in assuming the objective stance of a scientific
observer. Rarely does Lévi-Strauss show any interest in what the "native"
interpretation of a myth might be. Likewise, he disavows any personal
involvement or freedom of choice where his scholarly works are concerned.
His claim of detachment and belief in determinism is certainly equal to
Skinner's. Both see themselves as scientists, and both understand science as
the objective explanation of all reality, including subjective meanings. They
presuppose a fundamental binary opposition between objectivity and subjectivity that is characteristic of theoretical interpretation.

Lévi-Strauss's denials of personal agency—his conviction that chance,
rather than choice, guides his actions—continually reminds the reader of
the ambiguous relation between the writer and his writings. In some respects

7. Claude Lévi-Strauss, The Savage Mind (Chicago: University of Chicago Press, 1966),
1–33.

he is like the sorcerer Quesalid, a Vancouver Indian who recognized that his art involved deception, but who came to believe in his own powers nonetheless. In a long discussion of Quesalid in "The Sorcerer and His Magic,"[8] Lévi-Strauss is adamant: "Quesalid did not become a great shaman because he cured his patients; he cured his patients because he had become a great shaman" (SM, 180). What made him into a great shaman was a social structure, "a system of oppositions and correlations" in which he found himself in polar relations with patients on the one hand and with society on the other (SM, 181–82). He too was just a crossroads. And yet he became a great shaman, a sorcerer who could heal people of (presumably real) illnesses. Is the structuralist method of analysis also a sort of deception by which our contradictory ills are overcome by homologies? Is Lévi-Strauss a scientist, as he claims to be, or a structuralist sorcerer, a scholarly shaman whose ingenious analyses have so impressed others that he ultimately, like Quesalid, falls victim to his own self-deception?

An Anthropological Negotiator

Not all social theorists are willing to sacrifice the freedom, significance, and identity of the thinking individual on the altar of structuralist determinism in the manner of Lévi-Strauss. One of the strongest proposals for balancing one half-truth (that thinking is governed by impersonal structures or forces) with another (that thinking is a volitional act of a free person) is that of Mary Douglas, a British anthropologist. Her crosshatch method of analysis shows that societies provide a limited range of possibilities to individuals, who are free to choose among those options.[9] Although Douglas does not address myth directly, her discussion of cosmology indicates how she would interpret myths with similar contents.

Douglas was led to develop her new method by anthropological debates over the nature of culture. One position views culture as autonomous or *sui generis*, and therefore amenable to explanation in terms of its own patterns and themes; the other treats culture as the product of child-rearing customs, and therefore determined by forces outside of itself. Douglas comments

8. In *Structural Anthropology*, 167–85; hereafter cited as SM.
9. Mary Douglas, *Cultural Bias*, Occasional Paper no. 34 of the Royal Anthropological Institute of Great Britain and Ireland, London, 1978. See also *Natural Symbols: Explorations in Cosmology*, rev. ed. (New York: Pantheon Books, 1982).

that the first position shields culture in "a glass case," whereas the second fails to account for the obvious fact that individuals "so manifestly do overcome and transform their cultural origins" (2). The task she sets for herself is the development of a model that will reflect the actual reciprocity of the two poles of this opposition. She applauds those few anthropologists who have attempted to match personality and culture without bifurcating them in an impossible autonomy or welding them into a rigid determinism. Her goal is to demonstrate how individuals transact or negotiate (two of her favorite words) among the cultural options available to them.

Douglas presents her new model as consisting of two primary axes that she labels grid and group: "grid" is defined as "a dimension of individuation" and "group" as "a dimension of social incorporation" (7). Although her labels are well chosen, it is important to realize that both terms are multivalent: the entire system might be called a grid, and every part of it represents a different type of group. Douglas does not reject the general uses of grid and group, but she employs the two terms only in her own technical sense.

Grid is primarily a matter of rules (8). In a high-grid culture, individuals have relatively little choice about their means of livelihood, whom they will marry, their religious affiliation, where they will live, or other aspects of their lives. Low grid indicates that the culture leaves a much greater range of options open to the individual. Even so, individuals may find that certain professions, marriage partners, religious groups, or particular neighborhoods will be viewed with disapproval by their families and friends. The designation here is a relative one: no culture can function without some rules, and every culture grants individuals at least a modicum of freedom. Yet the distinction is an important one: in high-grid cultures the individuals transact on a relatively restricted scale, whereas in low-grid cultures individual freedom is substantially greater.

In contrast to the explicit and implicit rules that characterize grid, "group" refers to the boundaries that include or exclude individuals (7). Strong groups have very clear boundaries distinguishing members from nonmembers, whereas weak groups do not. Members of strong groups are likely to avoid relating to those outside their group. They will attempt to transact as much of their lives as possible—religion, family, work, social life, recreation, and so forth—within the group. The group provides them with their identity. In contrast, individuals who participate in weak groups enjoy a multiplicity of affiliations, like to transact significantly with a variety of people who are not bound by membership in any one group, and think of their identity in individual terms. As with grid, the group classification is a relative one along an axis from weak to strong, with the understanding that group boundaries are rarely either totally determinative or totally absent.[10]

The variety of possible grid-group interactions demonstrates Douglas's commitment to mediating the contradiction between deterministic theories of culture and those that assert cultural autonomy. As she comments on the relation between individuals and their environments: "Grid-group analysis treats the experiencing subject as a subject choosing. It does not suppose that the choices are pre-determined, though costs may be high and some of the parameters may be fixed. The method allows for the cumulative effect of individual choices on the social situation itself: both can interact, the individual and the environment, and either can move, because *the environment is defined to consist of all the other interacting individuals and their choices*" (13; emphasis added).

This last clause is crucial to understanding the way in which Douglas is a transactional thinker. Because so much of her analysis involves the rhetoric of social structure, she is sometimes taken for a determinist in spite of herself. But such a reading ignores her understanding of the social environment as the matrix of individuals who are, to a significant extent, freely choosing their own locations on the social grid-group map. Environmental social structures are the sum total of the previous choices of the members (presumably those who have died as well as those still alive) of a society. All social interactions are to be understood as transactions between or among individuals who could have decided to transact differently. Their freedom is real, although never unrestricted. Douglas is not a psychologist, and there is little discussion in her works of why individuals choose this or that alternative. She is an anthropologist whose primary interest is social theory, and her stated goal is to show that social structures influence, but do not totally determine, individual identities, which in turn influence the cultures of which they are a part.

Every organization can be located in terms of how grid and group reciprocally interact within it, resulting in four general types: (A) low grid/weak group; (B) high grid/weak group; (C) high grid/strong group; and (D) low grid/strong group. Douglas arranges these four possibilities along two intersecting axes, a vertical axis moving up from low grid to high grid, and

10. Douglas does seem preoccupied with the question of individuals who try to opt out of cultural contexts altogether, in search of a no-grid/no-group utopia. She discusses both hippies and hermits in this regard, but never tries to make the case that such a state could be fully attained in social reality.

a horizontal axis moving from left for weak group to right for strong group. The four quadrants created by the axes are assigned letters, starting with A in the lower left and proceeding clockwise to B, C, and D (Fig. 1).[11]

Figure 1

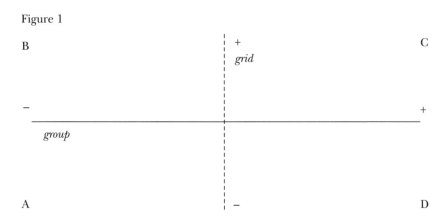

In quadrant A we find the weak groups promoted by modern secular society, where a high value is placed upon the social mobility that accompanies relatively low commitment to institutions and organizations (companies, families, churches, clubs). Douglas enjoys poking fun at the common belief that modern secular society is historically unique by pointing out that Melanesian and some African societies are also low-grid/weak-group (11). She sometimes refers to quadrant A simply as "Low Grid" (21), for it is characterized by a lack of formal rules governing individual behavior and relationships. Moreover, since group boundaries in A are always somewhat ambiguous and subject to change, it is also weak-group. Those who thrive in such a culture tend to be entrepreneurs and competitive individualists, for they neither want nor receive support from others. Curiously, Douglas suggests that the only way for these freewheeling individualists to gauge their success is by the size of their following.

Quadrant B illustrates how Douglas's categories presuppose the importance of individual choice. There the groups are weak, and yet they have very strong external boundaries, which should result in strong groups. The solution to this riddle lies in Douglas's explanation that most members of such organizations are "controlled from somewhere else, since they belong to no

11. In *Natural Symbols* Douglas uses the same pattern, but reverses the letters for the two left quadrants, so that A is upper left and B lower left. Their content, however, is identical to that in the same position in *Cultural Bias*.

group" (17). In other words, these people have been placed in rule-governed institutions: prisons, nursing homes, military units, and so forth. Although individuals in such situations can, as individuals, "embrace [the rules] willingly" (18), their participation in the group is involuntary, so the strength of the boundaries consists in the fact that they are walls and fences that have been imposed. Thus "the individual has no scope for personal transactions," and is restricted to a few options that are "fully defined and without ambiguity" (20). Although behavior is rigidly constrained and rule-governed by a power that remains aloof and impersonal, those without any power in the institution may well constitute the majority of participants (as in a prison).

Douglas uses the shorthand "strong group" for quadrant C, which actually refers only to those strong groups that also have high grid. Her descriptions sometimes suggest that the Roman Catholic Church might be a good example, but she rejects that suggestion on the grounds of size. International organizations, countries, and social classes are too large and internally too diverse to constitute groups in which members, although unable to know personally all other members, actually experience "pressure from face-to-face situations to draw the same boundaries" as all other members and (in relation to grid) "to explain to each other why they behave as they do" (15). Douglas prefers the example of old family firms that are a tradition in Europe, as portrayed in Thomas Mann's novel *Buddenbrooks* (37–38). Such institutions have an internal formal organization that is complex and hierarchical, and which results in more capacity for resolving internal conflicts without schism (20). They can grow both bigger and older, but the individuals within them have little mobility, for their roles and status are defined for them by the group's traditional rules.

As for quadrant D, Douglas emphasizes that the strong group boundaries define the social experience and, in extreme cases, the entire lives of members (19–20). Individuals are defined dualistically either as members of the group or as its opponents. Little interaction with nonmembers is encouraged. An obvious example of such a group is any sect or cult that adheres to the dualistic belief that only its members will be saved, and therefore considers meaningful relationships with people outside the group impossible. Because the strong group in quadrant D has a weak grid, there is great mobility within the group with regard to tasks and status. The rules of the group's culture rarely prevent an individual from moving into a new role. However, as in any weak grid situation (D or A), the means for resolving internal conflicts are not adequate, so conflicts are often repressed, or else they lead to "covert factions" within the group and ultimately to schism

(19–20). There is also a tendency for a charismatic leader to emerge who can dominate the other members of the group. Douglas refers to this as the "Big Man" phenomenon (11–12).

Although Douglas does not discuss mythology as such, she does give clear indications of how grid-group analysis would approach actual myths in their distinctive cultural contexts. In *Natural Symbols* she also provides a diagram of the grid-group quadrants and their typical cosmologies (Fig. 2).[12]

Figure 2

B		+ grid		C
	success-cosmology; syncretist, ritualism		complex regulative cosmos; combination of dangerous and benign elements; ritualist	
	potential millenialism, private magic			
–				+
	group			
	benign, unstructured cosmos; unmagical, weakly condensed symbols, personal religion		dual philosophy divided between warring forces of good and evil; irrational, dominated by witches using magical objects; ritualist for counter-witchcraft	
A		–		D

This diagram of the four types of cosmology can aid in the interpretation of the example of attitudes toward death, one of the examples discussed in *Cultural Bias* (32). Among groups in quadrant A, death is rarely discussed, for a person's life and death are validated individually rather than in relation to the group. The meaning of life and death is strictly a private matter, a function of personal religious or philosophical choice. Such practices as abortion, suicide, and euthanasia may also be treated as legitimate personal choices in the face of serious problems. They are equally accepted by people

12. *Natural Symbols*, 105, where the content of all four quadrants corresponds to that in *Cultural Bias*, but the designations A and B are reversed.

in quadrant B, but simply as a necessary escape, not as the exercise of a justifiable individual right. Douglas does not say how death is viewed by B, but the impression given is that it is constantly thought about and discussed as an ever-present possibility.

It is in strong groups that death has real status. Heroic suffering for the group is especially celebrated in quadrant C: "A favorite form of myth that feeds group consciousness tells of lives laid down for group survival" (32). Funerals are major events in the life of the group, and the families of those who have departed are treated with warmth and concern—in sharp contrast with A, where widows are forgotten soon after their husbands have died. Abortion, suicide, and euthanasia are treated as public rather than private matters, and normally disapproved. When the grid weakens in quadrant D, the importance of the deceased individual's life is seen less in terms of group survival (as in C) and more as a sign of the imminent arrival of the expected apocalyptic climax (29–30).

It may be helpful to draw out further the implications of Douglas's grid-group analysis of attitudes toward death for the myths that will be found among the four quadrants. In A there will be relatively few myths in which significant figures die, and they will not be elaborated. The vast majority of myths will portray young and healthy individuals overcoming obstacles on their way to success of one kind or another. Death or any other form of suffering that does not produce clear and positive results will be minimized as absurd intrusions on life as it ought to be. This is a culture that creates Horatio Alger and Superman myths.

In B there is a much greater awareness and acceptance of the ever-present possibility of death, but it is not in any way glorified or idealized. The mythical heroes are likely to be those who escape the system altogether. Whether the escape is accomplished by a daring adventure (a jailbreak), a supernatural intervention (a miraculous healing or pardon), or even blind luck (winning a lottery) is not important. What counts is deliverance by any means from the cultural system that has denied the individual all power and autonomy.

The high status conferred upon death in quadrant C means that myths portraying victory as accomplished through the death of a leader or a hero will be cherished in such groups. Members will often hope to die for the group in an equally sublime manner, and those who do so will be revered in the group's mythic memory. Christianity and Islam have produced abundant examples of this sort of culture. In contrast, the small dualistic sects in quadrant D will create myths that deal with the coming Armageddon, the eschatological battle between good and evil. Individual deaths will be meaningful only in relation to that concern. The myth of an imminent and possibly fatal clash with demonic secular authorities, such as the one that inspired the Branch Davidian community near Waco, Texas, illustrates this sort of mentality.

This discussion has shown that Douglas employs a transactional way of understanding myth. Just as Ellul looks for equilibrium between technique and individual choices, Douglas believes that social forces and individuals mutually influence each other, that different cultures must be understood in terms of the individuals who transact within and among them, and that interpreters must seek "a match between subjective and objective criteria" (18). All this points toward a dialectic of reciprocity. Starting from theoretical binary oppositions that are common in sociological theory, Douglas rejects the assumption that such polarities necessarily constitute firm contradictions, and sets out to show instead how the poles are points of reference for those who reciprocally transact between them.

This transactional, reciprocal framework places a high value on individual choices, interpersonal communication, the dynamic character of cultures and communities, and the historical diversity of individuals and groups. Douglas's approach clearly contrasts sharply with Lévi-Strauss's cavalier dismissal of individual intentions, interpersonal relations, the historical dynamism of cultures, and the real diversity of persons and communities. Douglas develops a method that can serve as a tool; Lévi-Strauss claims that he is nothing but a tool in the hands of the structuralist method. With this contrast before us, we are ready to move on to a transformational thinker who tries to unite the opposing poles that serve as grist for Claude Lévi-Strauss's binary manipulations and as opportunities for Mary Douglas's negotiating individuals.

A Modern Mythmaker

Joseph Campbell's readers sometimes seem to divide neatly into two camps: uncritical admirers and very hostile critics. Although that binary opposition itself might be suitable material for dialectical analysis, my interest here is not in Campbell's credentials as scholar, guru, or citizen, or in what motivates his fans and critics. It is his enthusiastically transformational approach to myths that makes Campbell a fitting third author for this chapter. His paradoxical vision of the meaning of life and the limitations of myth is sometimes lost in readings of his work that focus upon the narrative and psychological dimensions of his interpretations. For an understanding of both the psychological and the transformational aspects of Campbell's conception of myth, and their relation to one another, *The Hero with a Thousand Faces* is an excellent resource.[13]

According to Campbell, the message of myth is, in the first instance, psychological. Whereas Lévi-Strauss treats Freud's interpretation of the Oedipus story as one more version of the myth, Campbell finds in Freud and Jung two theorists to whom we can turn for help in finding our way through the intricate mysteries of myth. In decoding the patterns of dreams, they also provide tools for the understanding of myths, understood as collective expressions of the same psychological truths: "Dream is the personalized myth, myth the depersonalized dream; both myth and dream are symbolic in the same general way of the dynamics of the psyche. But in the dream the forms are quirked by the peculiar troubles of the dreamer, whereas in myth the problems and solutions shown are directly valid for all mankind" (19).

Here Campbell is drawing on Jung's theory of archetypal images, according to which the unconscious is a reservoir of symbols of meaning. In myths, dreams, fantasies, artistic activity, and play, these symbolic images enter into consciousness and convey to it deeper truths than those subject to the control of the rational mind. The father god, the cosmic mother, the female counterpart within all males (anima), the male counterpart within all females (animus), and the shadow archetype that represents the rejected aspects of one's self—these are but a few of the images that Jung identifies and Campbell appropriates from him. Campbell also leans heavily upon the thematic theories of Freud, including his interpretation of the Oedipal myth as a dramatic account of the repressed desire that every son supposedly has to kill his father and marry his mother. This effort to synthesize the conflicting views of Freud and Jung could in itself be construed as an example of paradoxical thinking.

Campbell's abilities as a storyteller shine as he develops this psychological interpretation of myth. His interest in individual rather than social dynamics leads him to select myths that center on a hero: "the man or woman who has been able to battle past his personal and local historical limitations to the generally valid, normally human forms" (19–20). The story of this adventure varies slightly from culture to culture, but all expressions conform to what Campbell calls the "monomyth." This is a threefold pattern of (1)

13. Joseph Campbell, *The Hero with a Thousand Faces*, 2d ed. (Princeton: Princeton University Press, 1968).

withdrawal from family and society to pursue one's heroic destiny; (2) initiation into the mystery that is the truth of human life; and (3) return with
that knowledge to family and society. Each of these movements embraces a
number of symbolic challenges, encounters with divine helpers and
demonic enemies, and opportunities for the hero to persevere or to turn
back in defeat.

Campbell's idealization of the hero figure is no doubt a primary reason
for the enormous popularity of his work. In retelling the myth of the Minotaur
he offers some insight into how he hopes to affect his readers (23–25). The
Minotaur is a dangerous beast that prowls the passages of a Cretan labyrinth
constructed by the artist-scientist Daedalus. Theseus is the hero who must
slay the Minotaur, and Ariadne, who is in love with him, asks Daedalus for
advice on how Theseus can find his way out of the labyrinth after killing the
beast. His solution is a skein of thread that the hero can unwind as he enters
the maze and that he will be able to use to retrace his steps. Campbell
praises Daedalus as a "hero of the way of thought" (24), whose discovery of
truth gives us freedom. Freud and Jung would seem to be his modern counterparts, for they have charted the dark passages of the unconscious. It is
clear that Campbell views every reader as a potential hero like Theseus, for
he writes that "we have only to follow the thread of the hero-path" (25).
Where does that leave Campbell himself as author of the book? Is he not
our Ariadne, a guide who will, having consulted our modern Daedalus figures (Freud and Jung), provide us with the thread by which we can find our
way through the labyrinth of the unconscious? Campbell is writing less to
explain myths than to inspire us to pursue our own hero-paths.

All of this involves a very strong affirmation, not of narcissistic individuality (386), but of individuals as creative heroes. Each of us has a purpose
to fulfill and a role to play. We find ourselves in meaningful relationships
with others who are likewise pursuing their own hero-paths. The psychological dimension of myth calls us to realize our own potential, to learn to
express the truth of who we are, to throw off anything that might inhibit
our growth. It is a resounding affirmation of the personal identity of every
human being.

Campbell also proposes, however, deeper interpretations of myth that
reveal "the inadequacy of any merely psychological reading" (178). One of
these might be called a "phenomenological" approach, with the qualification
that Campbell consistently uses the term "phenomenal" in an equivocal
way. In its primary meaning, "phenomenal" refers to anything that appears
to our five senses, which Campbell renders more abstract by referring to

the "phenomenal realm of names and forms" (89). For psychological interpretation, the phenomenal world of appearances is a major constituent of
reality, but for Campbell, it is symbolized by an ogre of Buddhist legend
named Sticky-hair: the five weapons of the senses are useless in battle with
him, for they all stick harmlessly to his hair (85–88). Only "the divine thun-
derbolt of knowledge" can overcome this "monster of phenomenality" (89).
Campbell finds this theme confirmed in Christian symbols also, "through
the sacramental operation of which, man, since the beginning of his day on
earth, has dispelled the terrors of phenomenality and won through to the
all-transfiguring vision of immortal being" (143).

This sacramental operation of Christian symbols is discussed as part of
the second movement of the monomyth—initiation. Specifically, Christian
symbols appear in the section on "Atonement with the Father." Campbell
employs Freudian categories (130) to represent God as a terrifying dragon
(the superego) intent upon punishing the opposing dragon of sin (repressed
id). He marshals a number of stories to illustrate the fearsome father theme,
and the resulting need for atonement (at-one-ment). Once again, it is the
phenomenal world that is the key to this terror, a terror that can be conquered by the hero only with the realization that "the sickening and insane
tragedies of this vast and ruthless cosmos are completely validated in the
majesty of Being" (147). Since God has created this cosmos, such a validation
also constitutes atonement with him. As in the biblical story of Job, who was
subjected to unbearable sufferings for no apparent reason, the challenge is
to glorify God in all circumstances, not to hold him accountable (147).

It is clear, however, that the word "God," like all other symbols, is seriously
implicated in the phenomenal realm. Since Campbell thinks that we are all
terrified by phenomenality, his attitude toward myths and symbols can be
characterized as a qualified enthusiasm. He affirms the power of myth and
symbol to inspire individuals to pursue the hero-path. But he also understands them as inextricably linked with the phenomenal realm, which provides their form and their content. Myths and symbols may point beyond
the world of sensation, names, and forms; but they depend upon the senses,
names, and forms to achieve that very act of pointing: "Myth is but the penultimate; the ultimate is openness—that void, or being, beyond the categories—
into which the mind must plunge alone and be dissolved. Therefore God
and the gods are only convenient means—themselves of the nature of the
world of names and forms, though eloquent of, and ultimately conducive
to, the ineffable. They are mere symbols to move and awaken the mind,
and to call it past themselves" (258).

This view of symbols helps to explain Campbell's ambivalence toward such monotheistic religions as Judaism, Christianity, and Islam. As religions that have historically placed a very high value upon assent to specific affirmations concerning God, they have all forcefully rejected the notion that it is possible or desirable to employ other symbols of our own choosing or to transcend the symbol "God" altogether. Campbell quotes Jung's ironical comment aimed at Christianity: "'The incomparably useful function of the dogmatic symbol [is that] it protects a person from a direct experience of God'" (202). The problem here lies not, it appears, in the symbols themselves, but in the way they are employed by religious thinkers and authorities. Campbell implies that symbols, when properly understood, can symbolize that which is ineffable and therefore is, strictly speaking, beyond all symbolization: "Symbols are only the *vehicles* of communication; they must not be mistaken for the final term, the *tenor,* of their reference. . . . The problem of the theologian is to keep his symbol translucent, so that it may not block out the very light it is supposed to convey" (236).

Because myths and symbols point beyond themselves to a truth that transcends all forms and contents, it is an easy matter for every individual or culture to read the forms and contents it cherishes into its myths and symbols. Campbell lists a half dozen of the most popular explanations of myth, from Frazer's theory that it attempts to explain nature to the Christian Church's doctrine of revelation, and concludes: "Mythology is all of these. The various judgments are determined by the viewpoints of the judges" (382).

What, then, is this direct experience that transcends all forms and contents and reveals the truth that myths and symbols can point to but can never capture? When the hero finally leaves behind the gods, goddesses, demons, and all the other mythical and symbolic projections of the unconscious mind, what is left?

Beyond atonement within the realm of myth and symbol lies apotheosis, which literally means deification, and which renders all the categories of the conscious mind "translucent" to a higher reality. The world of phenomenality is made up of binary oppositions, or contraries (93), and atonement does not go beyond balancing those poles by some sort of relative reconciliation. Apotheosis, however, reveals that the opposing poles are really identical, that the human hero seeking the divine Father is in fact also divine. This paradoxical identity of the human subject and the divine object shares the dialectically circular structure of Kuhn's paradigms, despite the great difference in content.

Campbell extends the identity of opposites to all the other archetypal oppositions that he has discussed: The Void and The World, Eternity and Time, Nirvana and Samsara, Truth and Illusoriness, The God and The Goddess, The Enemy and The Friend, Death and Birth, Subject and Object, Yang and Yin, and so on (171n). The supreme symbols embrace within them this ultimate and mystical coincidence of opposites. The Word Made Flesh unites the divine with the human. The Bodhisattva myth reveals the androgynous character of the Ultimate that is both God and Goddess and also "the annihilation of the distinction between life and release-from-life" (163). Nirvana, which is the state in which all desire has been extinguished, is not different from Samsara, the world of change, in which desire for stability or for any sort of change from the status quo normally dominates. In the Bodhisattva myth, the hero attains Nirvana only to give it up and return to this transitory and dangerous world in order to share the gift of knowledge with others who may be seeking it.

Thus the hero is transformed by a new consciousness of the nature of reality, but the world itself appears different only from this higher perspective: "The objective world remains what it was, but, because of a shift of emphasis within the subject, is beheld as though transformed" (28). To reach this understanding it is not enough to grasp Campbell's theory; we must ourselves be transformed and transfigured. Real readers are also participants, each carrying a skein of thread into the labyrinthine unconscious. Although psychological knowledge can be expressed in theories and the limits of the phenomenal realm can be illustrated by myths, mystical understanding must be the result of direct and personal experience.

This transformational interpretation of myth confronts us with paradoxes at every turn. Campbell's central theme is the individual hero, whom he analyzes using the tools of ego psychology. Yet his final goal is the esoteric knowledge that takes us beyond the illusion of ego altogether. Like all the other binary oppositions mentioned by Campbell, that between ego and non-ego is ultimately transcended. Myth is said to provide solutions to the problems we humans face. But myth is also only penultimate: the ultimate is a mystical realization that cannot be expressed in words, symbols, or myths. So myth does not provide the ultimate solution, and yet we cannot hope to attain that solution without the help of myths and dreams.

It might be possible to explain these paradoxes as nothing more than the inevitable tensions between different stages of development: Campbell never claims that the psychological ego and the mystical non-ego coexist in consciousness simultaneously, or that mythical symbols and direct experience are really the same. The problem is, Campbell never really explains much at all about what the hero does upon returning, or how a man or woman who has brought back that mystical ultimate boon then negotiates living once again in the world as one ego among many, a person in society who cannot always escape from words and myths into an ineffable void.

As if to anticipate this question, Campbell closes *The Hero with a Thousand Faces* with a chapter entitled "Myth and Society." There he allows that "the individual can only be an organ" of society (383). He even implies, in direct contradiction to the hero-path presented earlier in the book, that it is not necessary to leave society in order to realize the Truth: "[J]ust as the way of social participation may lead in the end to a realization of the All in the individual, so that of exile brings the hero to the Self in all" (386). Yet Campbell does not see this as a viable solution in the modern world, where societies no longer provide the myths and symbols that can guide their members toward the truth: "[T]oday no meaning is in the group—none in the world: all is in the individual. But there the meaning is absolutely unconscious" (388). This is why the modern hero must begin with the psychological interpretation of dreams, struggle with the phenomenal meanings of myths and symbols, and ultimately push through to the center of the mystery alone. Societies and even traditional religions are no longer any help, Campbell believes. Our need is for a new Theseus, or our need is for each of us to become Theseus, to enter the labyrinth of our unconscious in faith that the thread of mythical meaning provided by Campbell will prove to be a reliable lifeline. "It is not society that is to guide and save the creative hero, but precisely the reverse" (391).

It appears, then, that Campbell has offered an affirmation of society only to take it back almost immediately. Perhaps there was a time when institutional religions and the culture of entire societies could guide people to a conscious apprehension of the truth. Today, he seems to be saying, only the individual journey into the unconscious will suffice. Perhaps there is a social theory that incorporates the mythical and mystical values Campbell promotes throughout the book. But his only concrete suggestion is that the hero return to call other individuals to pursue the same path. There are no longer any shortcuts or group programs available. Everyone must make the journey alone, for modern society has severed its own spiritual roots. Only through myths and dreams will any individual establish a strong contact with those roots. Campbell believes in the power of myth to produce, even now, heroes who are psychologically transformed, aware of the dangers of the phenomenal world, and ripe for spiritual transfiguration. This is the greatest function of the hero: to set an example by pursuing the mystic path, for the hero's "passing and returning demonstrate that through all the contraries of phenomenality the Uncreate-Imperishable remains, and there is nothing to fear" (93).

. . .

No doubt Campbell would happily include Lévi-Strauss and Douglas in his list of interpreters of myth whose theories simply express their own viewpoints. But he could also point out the ways in which he is overcoming the opposition between the structuralism of Lévi-Strauss and the grid-group analysis of Mary Douglas. Transformational interpretation attempts to unite the binary oppositions of theoretical interpretation with the thrust toward harmony of transactional interpretation. Although Campbell understands the dialectical goal as an identity that dissolves differences rather than a unity that paradoxically highlights them, his appeal to the coincidence of opposites certainly reveals him to be a fundamentally paradoxical thinker. Moreover, his insistence upon the need for every individual to experience directly the truth communicated through myths and symbols further demonstrates that his understanding of myth is ultimately in terms of its transformational power.

Campbell shares much with our other interpreters. Like Lévi-Strauss, he surveys a wide variety of myths from all over the world, virtually ignoring cultural differences among them. If anything, Campbell is even more hostile than Lévi-Strauss to the demand of historians that we study each myth in its unique sociohistorical setting (249, 256). But his alternative to historical contextualization is not homologies among formal structures of contradiction; it is the mystical identity of opposites. Lévi-Strauss is capable of relating myths in a wonderfully interesting manner, but he considers the stories significant only insofar as they confirm the formal abstract logic of contradiction to which he is philosophically committed. Campbell is an even better storyteller, yet the truth he seeks lies neither in the narrative nor in the structures embedded in it but in the transformational experience to which it points. Campbell is not engaging in a scientific analysis of myth at all. He is promulgating old myths and proposing a new one of his own: the myth of the hero who struggles with the psychological ego and the phenomenal world of duality until realizing that it is all illusory. For Lévi-Strauss, the oppositions are real, and the alleged overcoming of them is an illusion. Campbell sees it just the other way around.

With Mary Douglas, Campbell affirms the centrality of the individual who is trying to steer a course through stormy waters. In fact, he goes far beyond her, in that he believes that individuals really can and must leave their social moorings altogether for a time. This possibility fascinates and troubles Douglas, but she never embraces it. Yet Campbell's individualism does not involve the corollary affirmation of radical freedom. He admits that important choices are made by the hero during the journey, but he also affirms very strong notions of chance and destiny. Once again, he seems to want have it both ways at once, to claim that freedom and destiny are paradoxically the same, just as individuals best serve their society by realizing their particular identities as individuals. In terms of Douglas's categories, Campbell appears to be proclaiming a low-grid/weak-group gospel using materials produced by societies that are generally high-grid and always strong-group. His hero abandons society for a time rather than negotiate with it.

These are three overlapping yet ultimately very different interpretations of myth. Individually each can be read as an example of its type: theoretical, transactional, or transformational. Together, the three illustrate how the types talk both with and past each other. The dialectics of contradiction, reciprocity, and paradox all begin with binary oppositions, but they treat those oppositions in very different ways. The formal stance of Lévi-Strauss collides with the social particularity emphasized by Douglas, and neither seems to envision a leap like Campbell's over the entire phenomenal realm to a transphenomenal mystical vision. From the individual as crossroads we move to the individual as negotiating agent to the individual as a hero who is identical with everything that had previously been perceived as other. And they all can find numerous illustrations to support their interpretations in the abundance of mythical narratives.

We have, then, three incompatible strategies for reading myths. Lévi-Strauss may claim that all views are equally valid (*M&M*, 4), but his notorious attack upon Jean-Paul Sartre shows that he does not really mean it.[14] His formal method of analysis has a brilliance that cannot be found in Douglas or Campbell, and makes his theoretical reading of myths intellectually the most challenging and often the most interesting of the three. Although they would certainly reply that it is much too abstract and formalistic to do justice to the rich and complex content of mythology, it is a more comprehensive and satisfying program precisely because it goes beyond myth to present a theory of mind. The binary character of myth, according to

14. *The Savage Mind,* chap. 9.

Lévi-Strauss's structuralist approach, is to be understood as but one of the many creative products of the bifurcating human mind.

Douglas's commitment to balance and common sense makes her grid-group analysis the most plausible of the three, for she alone tries to do equal justice to the social forces that shape myths and the freedom of individuals to accept or reject them. While individuals simply disappear from the picture painted by Lévi-Strauss and are torn from their social and historical contexts by Campbell, Douglas is able to situate them as living persons interacting with, and choosing among, real alternatives. The resulting interpretation of myth is nuanced according to the particular social context in question. Varieties are shown to be significant differences in social structure, not merely deviations from the formal binary pattern. The result is philosophically less ambitious than the one attempted by Lévi-Strauss, but it is better able to provide an account of how the varieties of myth arise.

Campbell's vision of a transcendental mystical truth makes his interpretation the most poetic and inspiring of the three, even while his paradoxes sacrifice Lévi-Strauss's formal rationality and Douglas's ability to present a picture that rings true to life. Like many other transformational thinkers, Campbell claims that he is able to include alternative types within his own, just as he tries to build his mystical interpretation of the meaning of myth upon the psychological foundations laid by Freud and Jung. The difficulty is that Campbell's primary explanation of that mystical coincidence of opposites is, like so many phenomenological claims, based in a circular fashion upon his own interpretation of myths that he has selected for that very purpose. Campbell does not offer a comprehensive survey of all myths, including those that have no hero figure. Nor does he deal with the problem that confronts every philosophical monism, namely, how to affirm the identity of all particular opposing poles without collapsing them into each other so completely that there is no longer anything particular to be united. Campbell's embrace of an undifferentiated identity rather than an internalized tension within a paradoxical unity is reminiscent of some Romantic thinkers as well as monistic mystics of many religious traditions. This identity comes perilously close to a coincidence of opposites without any real opposites to coincide, one that could even undermine the paradoxical character of transformational interpretation.

3

Frontiers in History

One of the salient characteristics of modern thought is its preoccupation with history. We routinely expect to understand ourselves and our societies in terms of our historical contexts, on the assumption that we are, to a significant extent, products of our social environments. We believe in historical progress as an ideal if not always a reality, and the conviction that world history somehow moves forward, even if in a somewhat zigzag manner, undergirds much historical analysis.

Implicit in this notion of historical progress is the concept of a frontier. Every time we speak of a scientist, a scholar, or an artist as working at the "cutting edge" of a discipline, we assume that the discipline in question is moving in a discernible direction toward a new and better future. Each discipline has such frontiers, although not every practitioner within each discipline will agree about what the true frontier is. That disagreement forms the focus of this chapter, in which I discuss several ways of understanding the frontier that faces us as interpreters of history.

Lee Benson wants to approach history and historiography theoretically as an objective scholar. The matter of method is all the more urgent for him due to the great number of historians committed to some sort of historical relativism. Benson writes as though the most significant frontier is the establishment of history as a rigorous social science. For a transactional approach to history I turn to E. H. Carr, who analyzes almost every question by dividing it into a polar opposition that he then shows to be a reciprocal relation rather than a contradiction. Carr views history itself as a dialectic in which the past and future reciprocally interact to produce the present, which is the real frontier in all historical development. Reinhold Niebuhr is less interested in the methodological frontier of academic historians or the actual frontier of historical progress than he is in the spiritual frontier that emerges when historians inquire about the ultimate meaning of events. The meaning he finds is a paradoxical attempt to embrace both theoretical and transactional interpretations in an understanding that transforms both the historical reality and the historian simultaneously.

Frontiers in History and Historiography

The "frontier thesis" of Frederick Jackson Turner, which is the target of a vigorous attack by Lee Benson in *Toward the Scientific Study of History*,[1] provides a convenient point of departure for consideration of a theoretical approach to history. Benson is distressed about the influence of Turner's 1893 essay, "The Significance of the Frontier in American History," upon the public and historians alike. Turner's frontier thesis, which dominated historical studies through World War II and popular imagination even to the present, certainly has the virtue of simplicity. It states that, prior to the late nineteenth century, the West had been open territory that rewarded the heroic efforts of those rugged individuals who braved dangerous obstacles to settle it, but that in 1890 the last free land was claimed and that with it the open frontier disappeared. For Turner, the existence and subsequent closing of the frontier define the spirit of Americans and their history.

The extent to which Turner became a model for the next generation of historians is demonstrated by Carl Becker, a historian who both extols Turner and defends a relativistic position that Benson considers incompatible with history as a discipline capable of providing reliable knowledge.

1. Lee Benson, *Toward the Scientific Study of History: Selected Essays of Lee Benson* (Philadelphia: J. B. Lippincott, 1972).

This direct clash between Becker's celebration of relativism and Benson's opposition to it is especially evident in their conflicting evaluations of Turner's frontier thesis. A brief account of Becker's assessment will set the stage for a look at Benson's critique of Turner.

Carl Becker first encountered Turner as an undergraduate at the University of Wisconsin. His reminiscences, related in a long 1927 essay on his mentor,[2] are nothing less than reverent: "Serious indeed the man was, you never doubted that, but not solemn, above all not old, not professionally finished; just beginning rather, zestfully and buoyantly beginning, out for adventure, up to something, in the most casual friendly way inviting you to join in" (193). The impression given is that Turner was like the pioneers he so admired: brave, energetic, good-humored, committed. A rugged individual out of place in the world of academic conformists. He had the marks of a charismatic leader, a person who charmed others by the sheer force of his personality: "The answer [given by Turner to a question] was nothing, the words were nothing, but the voice—the voice was everything: a voice not deep but full, rich, vibrant, and musically cadenced; such a voice as you would never grow weary of, so warm and intimate and human it was. I cannot describe the voice. I know only that it laid on me a kind of magic spell which I could never break, and have never wanted to" (194; cf. 232).

For Becker, Turner is the very image of objectivity, but he makes that claim only after redefining the concept. The familiar academic ideal of objectivity as detachment bred of rigorous scholarly training seems to him to be only "a set of artificially induced and cultivated repressions . . . the best substitute for ideas yet invented." In contrast, Turner's objectivity "seemed rather to spring from that intense and sustained interest which an abundance of ideas can alone generate" (208–9). Turner did not care about scholarly conventions and accepted methods. He was an independent thinker whose interpretations of historical events were always fresh and "personal" rather than burdened with "scholastic dust" (212). Becker's praise for Turner leans heavily upon this reconception of scholarship as what might be called personal objectivity.

Certainly the suggestion that all American history is related to the closing of the frontier—that the four previous centuries were only the "first phase" of our history (222–24)—was a strikingly original contribution. Becker stresses that Turner's explanations of historical developments never appeal to a "universal answer," still less to "the Transcendent Idea, or any of

2. Carl L. Becker, "Frederick Jackson Turner," in *Everyman His Own Historian: Essays on History and Politics* (Chicago: Quadrangle Books, 1966), 191–232.

its many poor relations" (213, 214). History illustrates a process of social evolution that is determined not by some historical "Reason" or by class struggles but by the actions of ordinary people trying to carve out lives for themselves in ordinary ways.

For Lee Benson, Frederick Jackson Turner was less a great historian than a prolific mythmaker. He rejects the entire frontier thesis on the grounds that free land had not disappeared by 1890, or even by 1900, and not many people at that time thought that it had (85). Benson proudly identifies with the tradition of scientific history so reviled by Becker. The quotations from Francis Bacon and René Descartes with which he opens his book both call for more progress in science. Benson even points to Ranke's dictum—that historians should "tell it like it was"—as a worthy ideal (175).

As Benson sees it, Turner's frontier thesis was indeed the product of a universal idea, namely, the theory of free land promulgated by Marxist historian Achille Loria as the key to economic evolution and therefore to all historical development in the American colonies: "Clearly, the Loria-Turner thesis was economic determinist in character, despite the romantic metaphors and symbols used to state and support its propositions" (179). The attraction of the free-land concept was that it assumed a virgin beginning in America, which in turn implied that the historian could see in America a recapitulation of the stages of economic growth that were long past in Europe. Because free land continued into the twentieth century, long after changes attributed to its disappearance by Turner (e.g., Populism) were under way, an entirely new historical analysis is needed.

Benson also attacks the effort of Ray Billington in *Westward Expansion* to salvage Turner's thesis by arguing that the frontier was a psychological one, a perception of the loss of open expanse and unspoiled opportunity (181–83). The basis for this claim is the *Census Bulletin* of 1891, which Billington erroneously represents as implying that the frontier had closed, and which, in any case, very few Americans (not even Turner himself) had read by 1893 (183). For these reasons, Benson concludes that the widespread belief in the closing of the frontier and its impact on American society was a myth unwittingly created by Turner himself, not by the *Census Bulletin* and certainly not by general knowledge of the historical facts. In contrast to Becker's picture of Turner as an objective scholar who was personally engaged with his work, Benson dismisses the frontier essay as "a series of remarkably sweeping assertions supported by a hodgepodge of selective and sporadic quotations from scattered primary sources, travel accounts, and secondary works. Given the sketchiness of his research, the self-assured tone adopted by Turner in his early essays cannot be justified (188 n. 34). Lamenting that the myth of the closed frontier has been "the most influential set of ideas yet presented in American historiography" (189), Benson implores historians not to forget their responsibility to strive for professional standards of accuracy.

Like many defenders of a rigorously objective method, Benson is very concerned about the question of data selection. Every researcher must decide which data are relevant to the inquiry at hand, and that is one of the points where scientific objectivity is most vulnerable to attack. For example, Benson is particularly interested in the assertions made by historians about public opinion. He suggests that Turner in fact created the public opinion (that the frontier had closed) that he then set out to analyze. We can see more clearly what Benson understands as a social scientific approach to history if we look closely at his methodological program for the analysis of public opinion.

Benson's long essay "An Approach to the Scientific Study of Past Public Opinion" (105–59) opens with a dilemma: since "relevant opinion surveys or polls" do not exist for most of American history, and since scientific study of past public opinion has not yet occurred, how can such study be accomplished now? In a careful discussion of the concept of public opinion, Benson borrows from the field of social psychology a distinction between opinions and attitudes: "As defined here, an opinion always connotes a *position* on some specific government action or general course of action; an attitude represents a persistent, general *orientation* toward some individuals, groups, institutions, or processes, but it does not necessarily result in a specific position on specified public issues" (108). The example Benson offers is drawn from another area on which he has worked and written a great deal—the causes of the American Civil War. In the 1840s, many Americans held negative attitudes toward slavery, but that does not prove that the same number held the opinion that the government should intervene to abolish it.

Benson outlines a rigorous method for the study of past public opinion. Historians should, "*in sequence,* try to (1) reconstruct the distribution of opinion on specified issues over time, (2) reconstruct and explain the formation of opinion, (3) reconstruct and explain the impact of opinion upon policy" (138). He stresses that the three directives should be followed in order, since it is crucial to understand the distribution of a public opinion over time in order to be able to assess who was instrumental in forming that opinion and what impact it had on government policy. Specific guidelines for examining each of the three themes are developed. Significantly, voting records are valued most highly for establishing the opinions actually held on issues of importance (151–58).

To revisit the example of the causes of the Civil War, Benson complains that Harriet Beecher Stowe's *Uncle Tom's Cabin* has not been shown to have influenced public opinion sufficiently to justify Abraham Lincoln's quip that the conflict was "'Mrs. Stowe's War'" (96). He chides intellectual historians for agreeing so uncritically with Lincoln's analysis. The issue, in his view, is the verification of causal claims: historians should "demonstrate the state of public opinion on specified issues before they assert that public opinion produced specified effects ultimately resulting in war and assign it relative weight as a causal factor" (94–95). True, Benson does not review the very impressive facts that point toward the great influence exerted by Stowe's novel. *Uncle Tom's Cabin* sold 350,000 copies its first year in print; it became the basis for a hit play; and it spawned countless toys, games, and other trinkets. Given that it was first published in 1852, almost a decade before the outbreak of the Civil War, Benson's skepticism about the influence of *Uncle Tom's Cabin* could be questioned. He would no doubt reply that this is evidence only about the state of public attitudes toward slavery, not about public opinion on government policies and official decisions, evidence that is objectively verifiable only on the basis of voting records.

As it is for all theoretical thinkers, methodology is a matter of great importance for Benson. Following Aristotle, he distinguishes among scholarly disciplines according to their aims, their subject matter, and their methodology (196). Benson is perfectly willing to concede that different aims can be legitimate with regard to the same historical subject matter, and that therefore those conflicting aims will employ diverse methodologies. He denies that this concession opens the door to a "subjective" relativism about historical truth, since all he has endorsed is a functional distinction among scholarly aims (197). Indeed, he even admits that "there is not and cannot be any such thing as 'the discipline of history.' Instead, there are a congeries of related scholarly disciplines, all equally entitled to be described as historical in character" (198).

Benson describes four distinct activities that can be considered historical work. Some treat history as entertainment, in the deep sense of a kind of literature that portrays "the human comedy"; others engage in history as a search for identity through the study of a specific group that includes but also transcends the historian; a third group practices history as a philosophical broadening beyond the parochial customs and values of one's own group; and the fourth type of historian strives to function as a social scientist: "[T]his historical discipline focuses on past human behavior in order to contribute to the overall scientific study of human behavior, past and present. Its primary goal is not to provide specific advice for decision-makers in specific situations; instead, it is to help develop general laws of human behavior that can aid human beings to identify the alternative courses of action available to them in specified types of situations, as well as make rational choices among alternatives in order to best achieve desired outcomes" (199).

It is this fourth type that claims Benson's professional allegiance. He is committed to explanation rather than inspiration. Benson admits that all historians have social contexts and individual experiences that shape their work, but he denies that this personal dimension validates their contributions. The personal stake of the historian is ultimately irrelevant to the scholarly value of historical endeavors. What is needed is greater attention to those methods that will insure objectivity and reliability in historical analysis.

Benson acknowledges that historians of earlier generations have attempted to function as social scientists. He mentions Turner and others as examples of an experiment that failed. But he refuses to take their failure as decisive for the project itself. For one thing, they did not have the benefit of the elementary fourfold distinction among types of history that he has provided. For another, there has been no concerted effort to produce a new generation of historians trained in the social scientific methods that will yield tangible results. In his words:

> [W]e cannot determine whether a genuinely scientific history is possible until we radically revise the undergraduate and graduate history curricula and train a "critical mass" of historians in the scientific style of analysis, i.e. explicit conceptualization, theory construction, model building, systematic comparison, standard criteria of measurement. Because such training is nowhere available (although winds of change can be detected in a few institutions), because the four roles have not been separated out effectively, the concept of *scientific history* has essentially been an honorific term devoid of real content. (200)

Benson's program for making historical research a rigorous social science shows us a more moderate version of objective theoretical understanding than Skinner's or Lévi-Strauss's. He concedes that historians are persons with differing goals and therefore legitimate methodological differences, but this does not imply for him that history is in any way inaccessible to objective study. He also maintains clear and distinct oppositions in his treatment of binary concepts. Parallel to his preference for objective over subjective methods, he insists that conclusions about public opinion be based upon voting records, which are behaviors subject to observation, rather than expressed attitudes, which are little more than feelings.

The means that Benson advocates for the development of history as a social science are thoroughly methodological. He believes that proper techniques in research will result in more reliable explanation of causal relations. The historian is an observer whose first responsibility is to manipulate the historical data and the tools of the trade according to the methodological rules established for social science. The presumed goal throughout is for the scholar to remain in total control of the material and the procedures of historical interpretation. This commitment to objectivity and detachment in causal explanation distinguishes objective theoretical analysis from other approaches to causality. All interpretations must deal at least implicitly with causal questions, but only objective theoretical understandings make them the center of methodologically rigorous disciplines.

Benson realizes that historical studies cannot yet boast a "critical mass" of young scholars trained in the methods of social science. This is the most significant contemporary frontier facing historians. I now turn to a transactional writer who rejects this theoretical understanding in favor of a paradigm based upon reciprocity rather than contradiction, and a vision of the frontier as a dynamic relation within history rather than a methodological challenge for academic historians.

The Present as Frontier

One of the most widely read works in recent philosophy of history is Edward Hallett Carr's *What Is History?*[3] The primary reason for this popularity is no doubt Carr's humorous and accessible style. But his book's popularity is also due to the way in which he presents himself as a moderate who can ferret out and reconcile the partial truths buried in the more extreme positions of others. Whereas Ellul's commitment to reciprocity is

3. Edward Hallett Carr, *What Is History?* (New York: Vintage Books, 1961).

embedded in his occasional references to equilibrium and Douglas's is explicitly stated only as her point of departure, Carr structures several of his lectures around an explicit and complex dialectic of reciprocity, an effort to balance the polar oppositions that have dominated previous debates.

Carr opens his lectures with the provocative observation that two editions of the *Cambridge Modern History* contradict each other: in 1896 Lord Acton called for "ultimate" history, which Sir George Clark dismissed in his 1957 condemnation of any notion of "objective" historical truth (3–4). Carr delights in poking fun at—and a lot of holes in—the simplistic faith in facts that he attributes to such objectivistic historians as Lord Acton. He deftly shows how even allegedly pure primary sources are inevitably biased by the perspectives of the original historical participants. He calls upon the great British philosopher, R. G. Collingwood, for support in establishing three principles of interpretation: that historical facts are never pure, that historical interpretation requires not objectivity but imaginative understanding, and that the past can be viewed only through the eyes of the present (23–28).

However much Carr may appear to be agreeing with Sir George Clark and the subjectivist position that he attributes to Collingwood, he then turns the tables and criticizes Collingwood for abolishing objectivity in history and for subordinating rigorous analysis of facts to the tyranny of contemporary, pragmatic concerns (29–31). It turns out that Carr is unwilling to privilege either the facts over interpretation (objectivity) or interpretation over the facts (subjectivity):

> The historian starts with a provisional selection of facts and a provisional interpretation in the light of which that selection has been made—by others as well as by himself. As he works, both the interpretation and the selection and ordering of facts undergo subtle and perhaps partly unconscious changes through the reciprocal action of one or the other. And this reciprocal action also involves reciprocity between present and past, since the historian is part of the present and the facts belong to the past. . . . [History] is a continuous process of interaction between the historian and his facts, an unending dialogue between the present and the past. (35)

Reciprocity, interaction, dialogue: these dialectical terms—so characteristic of transactional interpretation—are taken up again by Carr when he addresses the issue of society in relation to the individual. He asserts that the much-discussed "antithesis" between them is "imaginary," really "no more than a red herring drawn across our path to confuse our thinking" (69). But Carr is not content simply to reject the opposition between society and the individual. His analysis develops further the reciprocal relations between the historian, who is "part of the present," and the facts, which "belong to the past." As for the historians, they always look at the past through the lens of their own present: "Great history is written precisely when the historian's vision of the past is illuminated by insights into the problems of the present" (44). Although he illustrates this point by showing how several conservative historians altered their viewpoints with the changing times, Carr admits that similar variations are evident in his own work and that of all historians. (Indeed, although Carr has been criticized by Benson and others for writing a book that deals more with what history should be than with what it is,[4] his interest in the complexity of what historians actually do is clear in this and in many other parts of the book.) Every historian is an individual whose work can be understood only in relation to the "historical and social environment" that shaped that unique individuality (54). The person who creates historical facts is also a product of history.

When he returns to the question of the facts, Carr casts it also as a putative dichotomy: significant historical facts are to be understood either as the actions of free individuals or as the products of impersonal social forces (54). He derides historians who focus upon such powerful individuals as "Bad King John and Good Queen Bess," while ignoring the social forces that produced them (57). But he has equal disdain for any claim that historical actions are guided by a big idea or higher power, something that renders all individuals mere pawns in a game that remains unintelligible to them: "I have no belief in divine providence, world spirit, manifest destiny, history with a capital H, or any other of the abstractions which have sometimes been supposed to guide the course of events; and I should endorse without qualification the comment of Marx: *History* does nothing, it possesses no immense wealth, fights no battles. It is rather *man*, real living *man* who does everything, who possesses and fights" (60–61).

---

4. See Benson's "On 'The Logic of Historical Narration,'" in *Philosophy and History: A Symposium*, ed. Sidney Hook (New York: New York University Press, 1963), 36. Since Benson considers more significant the question of what history should be, his criticism is really an unintentional compliment. For my part, I find Carr's analysis to be a typically reciprocal interplay between comments on what historians actually do and jibes at them for failing properly to understand that they are in fact doing it.

The question is, how does Carr understand "man"? Not as a pawn of some higher power, and equally not as a consciously independent historical agent. He even invokes the aid of the just-rejected notion of "divine providence" and Hegel's famous "cunning of reason" (one form of "history with a capital H") to argue that the consciously intended results of individuals' actions are often utterly different from the actual effects they have (62–65). For Carr, history is thoroughly human, and humans are individuals who are products of their societies. A great individual might influence the future shape of social forces, but only as one in a myriad of influences. The antithesis between society and the individual is a red herring because complex social and individual elements are reciprocally related within every person.

All this should make the dialectical structure of Carr's thought quite clear. The mutual interaction between the historian of the present and the facts from the past leads to a deeper probing of them both for their identical internal reciprocal dialectics between individual concerns and social forces. Carr employs this dialectic of reciprocity as a basis for interpreting two other major issues, progress in history and the status of history as a science. He defends his belief in the former by stating again his fundamental premise: "Progress in history is achieved through the interdependence and interaction of facts and values. The objective historian is the historian who penetrates most deeply into this reciprocal process" (174–75). Since history is the changing relationship between the present and the past, progress can result whenever the present conquers the future on the basis of the past. Indeed, the openness of history to progress turns the present into a frontier, an intersection of past and future where possibilities abound. Only in hindsight will historians be able to discern how the road that was taken followed rationally from the previous conditions.

On the question of history as a scientific discipline, Carr observes that most of the common objections are based upon misunderstandings of history. Some assert that history deals exclusively with unique events, while science explains general laws and patterns. Carr replies that this misses the extent to which history is "concerned with the relation between the unique and the general" (83). The power of prediction characterizes science, but is often denied to history. Carr's answer is that scientific method involves prediction in controlled experiments, but only statistical probabilities, not predictions about individual cases. Moreover, historians also aim to provide "general guides for future action which, though not specific predictions, are both valid and useful" (87).

Carr also objects to the misconception of history as necessarily involving religious and moral issues. This long and interesting discussion gives him an opportunity to castigate religion for appealing to a *"deus ex machina,"* or a "joker in the pack," to explain historical suffering (96). Carr's own justification for the suffering caused by violent change is that it is "indigenous in history," a natural part of every struggle in which "[t]he losers pay" (102). His final appeal, however, is to history as a movement that cannot be evaluated according to transcendental standards of right and wrong, but only by such immanent and linear historical criteria as progressive or reactionary. Historical phenomena are to be judged by how much they help history to progress, how much they advance the frontier where past and future reciprocally interact to produce the present, not by absolute religious or moral standards (108).

Those who charge that history is too subjective to qualify as science show that they misunderstand not only history but also science itself. This objection poses an interesting challenge for Carr, since it appears to employ a dialectic of reciprocity to characterize history and thus to prove its unscientific character. The argument is that historians, like all social scientists, study humans, whereas natural scientists study nonhuman phenomena. Thus the subjects and the objects of social scientific investigations are both human: "[S]ubject and object belong to the same category, and interact reciprocally on each other" (89). Carr's rejoinder challenges the theoretical approach to knowledge that is presupposed in the objector's view of science, according to which subject and object must be opposed to one another. He argues that this binary structure is inadequate as a characterization of historical knowledge and equally as a description of contemporary scientific theories, especially those in physics. He offers no examples, but does affirm the "interrelation and interdependence" of subject and object in all knowledge, including science (93). Thus the difference between the social sciences and natural science is one of degree rather than kind. Carr boldly implies that science no less than history requires a dialectic of reciprocity.

A more general appeal to reciprocity is employed to answer the objection that history, unlike science, teaches no lessons: "Learning from history is never simply a one-way process. To learn from the present in the light of the past means also to learn from the past in the light of the present. The function of history is to promote a profounder understanding of both past and present through the interrelation between them" (86). In other words, if the historian can understand the past only in relation to questions shaped by the present, it is equally true that the present can be grasped only as that which has been shaped by the past. But then we do learn from the past, and it is history that teaches us those lessons.

Only in his lecture on causation in history does Carr depart significantly from a dialectic of reciprocity. He again sets out from what he takes to be a binary opposition: each historical event can be understood either as determined by historical causes or as the result of chance. Here Carr's dialectic is perspectival rather than reciprocal, for there is no interaction between the two poles: "All human actions are both free and determined, according to the point of view from which one considers them" (124). Carr never suggests, as Douglas would, that events must be understood as mutual interactions between causal determinations and chance occurrences. Nor does he admit, with Kuhn, that causes and chance are united in the midst of their opposition, rendering interpretation of events inevitably circular. Carr believes that the historian's task is to distinguish rational causes from those that are merely accidental, which he expresses by quoting Hegel's famous maxim, "'[W]hat is rational is real, and what is real is rational'" (139). Most important, the responsible historian will avoid the contemporary tendency to exaggerate the role of chance in history (133). This shows that Carr is less balanced on this issue than on the others he discusses. Where causation is concerned, he opts for objective rationality and avoids the subjectivity implied in every appeal to accident. His defense of an objective theoretical, rather than a transactional, type here shows that the boldness he demonstrated in arguing for reciprocity in science does not hold up when he turns to causal analysis as such, where theoretical rationalism clearly dominates his thinking.

·Except for his treatment of causation, Carr is a paradigmatic example of a transactional interpreter of history. Whereas Benson is concerned only with establishing objective methods by which historical facts can be validated, Carr considers the quest for such objectivity misguided. Rather than assume a binary opposition in which one of the two poles is embraced and the other rejected, Carr prefers (except for the question of causal freedom and determinism) to view the two poles as interacting with each other, as working together toward a harmony that is rational and stable. Carr readily affirms that all historical events are relative to their contexts, but he also wants to reject relativism (161), to base history upon a firm scientific footing, and to avoid attributing too great a role to either individual historical agents or to individual historians. As he sees it, the relativity of historical knowledge and the status of history as a (social) science mutually interact with and support one another.

Not surprisingly, Benson has real difficulty grasping the reciprocal context in which Carr understands the relativity of historical judgments.[5] Although he admits that he and Carr share a commitment to "the aims of a socio- logical historian," Benson misconstrues Carr's position as a belief that "arbi- trary value judgments determine what historians do."[6] What this illustrates is the tendency of a theoretical thinker to assume that everyone must ulti- mately take a position for or against a given issue, such as the relativity of historical knowledge. Benson fails to grasp the transactional paradigm by which Carr views the historian's individual relativity in interaction with the collective objectivity of society.

Carr's transactional commitment to history as a dialogue between past and present raises the question of mastery over the subject matter. Dialogue makes manipulation difficult. Likewise, the emphasis upon interrelation- ship between the individual and society, or the present and the past, leads to a sense of common humanity shared with those being studied, and this in turn inspires caution in a historian and makes theoretical closure more difficult.

A related question asks about the historian as both the agent behind these approaches to history and as a product of history. Benson minimizes the extent to which all historians are shaped by their communities. His sci- entific and methodological detachment restricts any interest he might have in the historian as a product of history. But Carr brings this sense of the socially conditioned self to the foreground. His interpersonal image of the historian contrasts sharply with Benson's ideal of the historian as a method- ologically impassive social scientist.

However, it must be admitted that Carr's reciprocity is more a way of thinking than an actual relation among individuals. His concept of self is certainly a social one, but the dialogue between the historian and the facts is not a dialogue between two persons. If the facts can speak at all, it is only by virtue of the historian's ability to impute speech to them. While the his- torian must choose to submit to the facts as not only objects of knowledge but also shapers of self, the facts make no comparable choice. Thus impor- tant aspects of Carr's dialectic of reciprocity are strangely impersonal, lack- ing the mutual intentionality that characterizes most reciprocal relations.

Finally, the frontier metaphor succinctly expresses these conflicts. For Turner, the frontier was a place of power and rebirth, a site where battles

5. See ibid., 32–42.
6. Ibid., 40, 35.

were won and lost, where old ways of life were either validated or overcome by new ones. Becker does not so much affirm that geographical frontier as he praises the imaginative power and influence of Turner's contribution to our understanding of American history. In so doing, he subtly recasts the frontier image as a method rather than a place. This sets the stage for Benson, who rejects Turner's frontier as a myth and argues for a rigorous new discipline of history as a social science. This methodological frontier represents a power struggle just as much as Turner's frontier did, but it is a power struggle that takes place in universities rather than on the prairie. Carr's understanding of history requires that the metaphor be shifted even farther away from its geographical origin. For him, history is always a complex interrelationship of past and future that the historian must participate in and explain at the same time. The frontier is the present, that moving place where the past and future meet. Since Carr believes that historians are, like everyone else, created by and part of the ongoing process of history, he does not seek a fixed theoretical point on which to base a method. Rather, he remains committed to probing the contradictions of life and historical knowledge in order to find a deeper reciprocity.

The Frontier Within

It is no coincidence that the search for a transformational interpreter takes us, with history as it did with myth, to a religious thinker who not only writes about religious ideas but is inspired by a spiritual vision. The connection, although not logically necessary, is a natural one. Especially in the modern world, where religious faith has been marginalized and often trivialized by a secular rationalism long dominant among intellectuals,[7] paradoxical thinkers have often found their home in religion and the arts, two areas that preserve a more open attitude toward the nonrational aspects of life.

Among paradoxical religious writers, only a few have found large numbers of readers among their fellow believers and also among those who share neither their faith nor their capacity for paradox. Such a writer was Reinhold Niebuhr. One of the great theological minds of twentieth-century America, he seems to have had as much influence upon secular social

7. See Stephen Carter, *The Culture of Disbelief: How American Law and Politics Trivialize Religious Devotion* (New York: Basic Books, 1993).

scientists as upon theological colleagues. Niebuhr was given what is perhaps the highest honor accorded to a religious philosopher, an invitation to deliver the Gifford Lectures at Edinburgh University in 1939. Volume 2 of the resulting publication, *The Nature and Destiny of Man*,[8] is a systematic analysis of his Christian understanding of history. Many of its central ideas are expounded less technically in a book published two years earlier, *Beyond Tragedy*.[9]

The theme of *Beyond Tragedy* is announced as "Christianity's dialectical conception of the relation of time and eternity, of God and the world, of nature and grace. It is the thesis of these pages that the biblical view of life is dialectical because it affirms the meaning of history and of man's natural existence on the one hand, and on the other insists that the centre, source and fulfilment of history lie beyond history" (*BT,* ix). As Niebuhr explains, a dialectical relation is one that negates or qualifies its own affirmation: "The eternal is revealed and expressed in the temporal but not exhausted in it" (*BT,* 4). This dialectical doubleness pervades Niebuhr's thinking, as the use of such phrases as "double affirmation," "twofold character," and "synthesis" throughout the Gifford Lectures attests.[10] As it happens, the term that best captures what Niebuhr is doing—one that he employs more sparingly than we might expect—is "paradox."

In addition to the substantive theological paradoxes that absorb most of his attention, there is also a hermeneutical paradox to which Niebuhr constantly appeals. He expresses it using Saint Paul's words in 2 Cor. 6:4–10: "We do teach the truth by deception. We are deceivers, yet true" (*BT,* 3). The very act of employing symbols to express Christian faith involves an element of deception. Niebuhr admits that this renders Christianity less rational than other faiths and philosophies. Buddhism, he thinks, is more rational than Christianity, for it simply declares the world to be evil. Spinoza is also more rational, for he thinks the world is so good that it is identical with God. Niebuhr takes the consistency of these opposing views as marks of their rationality. In contrast, Christianity teaches that God created a good world, but that the world cannot be identified with God, for it is imperfect. Given the ambiguities of a world that is both good and imperfect, the creation myth resists full rationalization. It is a story that deceives, yet is true

---

8. Reinhold Niebuhr, *The Nature and Destiny of Man,* vol. 1, *Human Nature;* vol. 2, *Human Destiny* (New York: Charles Scribner's Sons, 1943); hereafter cited as *NDM.*

9. Reinhold Niebuhr, *Beyond Tragedy: Essays on the Christian Interpretation of History* (New York: Charles Scribner's Sons, 1937); hereafter cited as *BT.*

10. E.g., *NDM,* 2:46, 47, 53.

(*BT,* 7). Niebuhr makes the same case for the story of the Fall, which is deceptively portrayed as an objective, historical event, even though it conveys a truth that, he believes, "can only be known in [subjective] introspection" (*BT,* 12).

As for the central substantive paradox of time and eternity as expressed in the Christian belief that the eternal God became incarnate in Jesus of Nazareth during the reign of Herod the Great, Niebuhr concedes that "[t]he idea of eternity entering time is intellectually absurd" (*BT,* 13). However, it is also a truth, an affirmation about a historical event that reveals the character of both Christian faith and human history. Because this central truth cannot be rationalized, it employs the deceptive language of myth (e.g., the Virgin Birth) and is simultaneously true, and by its truth it subverts all metaphysical systems. Niebuhr thinks the doctrine of the two natures (divine and human) in one person (Christ), affirmed at the Chalcedonian Council in 451, is an example of theology's futile attempts to rationalize the truths expressed in stories (*BT,* 16). If so, it is indeed a failure, for the paradoxical claim that Christ is one person fully uniting two mutually exclusive natures without mixture or confusion is hardly rational in any ordinary sense of the term.

Niebuhr handles the theory of atonement differently. Although the story of the vicarious death of Christ has, in his view, deceptively led to such morally outrageous theories as atonement by means of substitution, this fact is not responsible for its rejection by rational thinkers. Rather, it is rejected because the conception of human nature that has conquered the modern world entirely ignores the role that evil and tragedy play in life, especially "the simple but profound truth that man's life remains self-contradictory in its sin." The result is a "false optimism" that leads to despair (*BT,* 18, 20).

In the Gifford Lectures Niebuhr develops his thinking on the Atonement as "the paradox of the divine mercy in relation to the divine wrath" (*NDM,* 2:56). Appealing to the Incarnation as a model, he insists that justice and forgiveness are one, as the Father and the Incarnate Son are one, yet also that justice and forgiveness are two, just as the Father and Son remain two distinct persons. Niebuhr's criticisms of atonement theories that try to rationalize this paradox are aimed primarily at the classical dramatic view that Christ's death was a ransom paid by God to the Devil (which portrays a God of mercy but not of justice) and Anselm's juridical view that Christ suffered for others in order to satisfy God's wrath (which implies a God of justice but not of mercy). The latter is sometimes called the theory of substitution, but both views provoke in Niebuhr the moral outrage referred to above; worse yet, he believes that both dissolve "the paradox of grace" (one of his favorite phrases) in their efforts to render the Atonement rational.

Another theme that is mentioned in *Beyond Tragedy* and developed in the Gifford Lectures is the paradox of foolishness and wisdom. Niebuhr repeatedly alludes to Paul's statement in 1 Cor. 1:23–24 that the crucified Christ is foolishness to the Greeks and a scandal to the Jews, but nonetheless the wisdom of God and the power of God.[11] Thus a foolish proclamation (one man's death means eternal life for all) in fact reveals the wisdom of God; and a religious scandal (God had a Son who died ignominiously) is the revelation of God's power. This fundamental paradox serves as a justification for all the other paradoxes that Niebuhr finds in Christian faith. If human reason cannot reliably distinguish between foolishness and wisdom, then any effort to refute all paradoxes simply because they are paradoxical is preempted.

One of the most troublesome Christian declarations that deceives while being true concerns the Last Judgment and Second Coming of Christ. The return of Christ, says Niebuhr, has been the occasion for more deceptions and illusions than any other Christian doctrine. Yet it is also the belief that "distinguishes Christianity from both naturalistic utopianism and from Hellenistic otherworldliness" (*BT*, 21–22). It alone makes the point that the meaning of history will never be found within history, for it will be revealed only at the end of history. Yet that meaning is not above history, in some spiritual realm that is unrelated to this world. To divide meaning from temporal existence, Niebuhr suggests, is the way of rationalism: "It is therefore impossible to express the Christian idea of salvation in purely rational terms, for they suggest that temporal existence is, by its very temporality, a corruption of ultimate reality. The pattern of life is not corrupted by historic existence but in historic existence. Thus the Kingdom of God must come in history" (*BT*, 192).

To apply to Niebuhr's thought the central metaphor of this chapter: the frontier that gives meaning to history is the Kingdom of God, the entry of the eternal and infinite mercy and justice of God into the temporal and finite world of corruption. That entry has already occurred throughout history; it is decisively expressed by the Incarnation, Crucifixion, and Resurrection of Christ;[12] and it gives ultimate meaning to the historical realm of diachronic temporality by pointing toward the Last Judgment and Second Coming of Christ, which will be "the end of history" (*BT*, 190).

The frontier of historical meaning, then, is in, but not of, history, just

11. To cite just one example, *NDM*, 2:54.
12. Niebuhr discusses the meaning of the Resurrection claim in *NDM*, 2:294–98.

as Christians are said to be in, but not of, the world (John 17:15–16). Thanks to the gift of freedom, all human beings encounter contradictions in history, contradictions that cannot be avoided, although they will be overcome by God. The paradox lies in the fact that they will never be overcome within history. As the end (goal and termination) of history, this overcoming repudiates all false optimism based upon a utopian denial of contradictions within history. Indeed, implicit in Niebuhr's vision is the idea that the contradictions of history are highlighted and even intensified by the promise of their overcoming. Whereas Campbell welcomes paradox as an escape from the contradictions of this world into the bliss of identity, for Niebuhr redemption is won by the suffering symbolized by the Cross: the ultimate paradoxical unity is available only inwardly, in faith. As long as history endures, the Kingdom of God cannot be identified with any external institution or historical actuality. Just as "the Kingdom of God is within" (Luke 17:21), the true frontier in history is not, as for Carr, the temporal present; it is the presence of the revealed yet hidden God within history, a presence discernible only by faith.

The attack that Niebuhr mounts on various forms of modern thought provides a helpful look at how a transformational thinker both affirms and rejects interpretations based upon a theoretical dialectic of contradiction. In one example, he also demonstrates how transformational interpretation can engage secular political and social movements. Niebuhr's position is that such movements fail to appreciate the paradoxical complexity of historical reality. Fascism resorts to a romantic "tribal simplicity" that, when combined with modern technology, results in "the sadism of a concentration camp."[13] Communists also promise to overcome the tensions of modern life, totally missing the fact that "the creative forces of history" are the very forces that "destroy the harmonies of nature. That is a paradox which has not dawned upon the consciousness of any simple-minded modern, whether liberal or radical" (*BT*, 145). No matter how harsh his criticisms, Niebuhr does not simply reject these theoretical perspectives on social and political questions. Rather, in each case he shows how they try to build an entire position based upon a limited truth that, by itself, is inadequate to the full reality of history, a reality that cannot be rightly understood apart from the frontier of God's presence in history.

Likewise, while many modern thinkers try to cope with conflicts between religious and scientific truth by subordinating one to the other, Niebuhr assumes that they must function simultaneously, even if on different levels.

13. *BT,* 143–44. This judgment was published in 1937.

Those who reject the resulting tension will inevitably trade the full truth for a comfortable but inadequate simplicity. Thus, on the one hand, religious literalism "corrupts ultimate religious insights into a bad science," while, on the other hand, "[t]he adolescent sophistication of modernity expresses itself in finding scientific answers for religious questions" (*BT*, 148). Neither form of theoretical literalism—the religious or the rationalistic—can attain to the "childlikeness of a wisdom which has learned the limits of human knowledge" and "therefore approaches life with awe, hope and fear" (*BT*, 149). This is also the wisdom that is necessary to embrace paradoxes in those situations where they alone are adequate to the truth.

In his reflections on a theme from Jeremiah, chapter 17—that to trust in man brings a curse, whereas to trust in God brings blessings—Niebuhr cites examples that represent a variety of theoretical types of interpretation. All of them are guilty of optimism, which Niebuhr judges a "more dangerous" threat to faith than despair, because "[o]ptimism and human self-sufficiency are almost identical" (*BT*, 115). This occurs especially when citizens idealize their nation and praise the collective man who lives for the nation, forgetting that "[n]ations are also mortal" (*BT*, 118). Niebuhr praises Augustine for teaching the Christian Church that it should not despair over the fall of Rome and the failure of the Roman ideal, for every earthly city trusts in itself rather than in God, and is therefore doomed to self-destruction. In the twentieth century, some have been more likely to trust in youth, while others extol the wisdom of the poor and oppressed. These are all theories that identify human being with what is at best just one aspect of a full humanity. They are useful abstractions, but not worthy objects of ultimate trust. The same must be said for intelligence, which is an especially tempting ideal for modern scientists and rationalists. Niebuhr in no way condones "ignorance and obscurantism," but he emphatically insists that no man can be trusted, "particularly if he be intelligent man" (*BT*, 125).

Significantly, Niebuhr includes among those who are not to be trusted several versions of Christians. Even "the redeemed man in the church" is still a sinner in need of God's grace, and therefore not a proper object of trust. This is where Augustine went wrong, for his identification of the heavenly city of God with the church "was responsible for the great heresy of Roman Catholicism, the heresy of identifying the church with the Kingdom of God and of making unqualified claims of divinity for this human, historical and relative institution" (*BT*, 121). Yet Protestantism does not come off much better, for it makes the mistake of trusting in human piety. It rightly rejects the church and the priesthood as mediators that can be trusted, and then falls into the same error in a different form by trusting in the individual believer as one who knows and does God's will (*BT,* 123). The permutation of this Protestantism that draws Niebuhr's greatest ire is the liberal Protestant effort to join piety with rationalism, an effort that yields the conclusion that "[t]he man to be trusted is the man who is both pious and intelligent" (*BT,* 126). Rather than a healthy unity of vigorous faith with sharp intelligence, Niebuhr continues, this marriage often produces only an "enervated sentimentality."

Niebuhr's three examples—Catholic, Pietist, and liberal Protestant—demonstrate that not every religious identity has a transformational character. All three interpret faith according to a simplistic binary paradigm that does not do justice to the transforming paradox of grace. Niebuhr's preoccupation with pride and with the arrogance of self-confidence leads him to cast all such inadequate positions in the abstract form of theoretical interpretation. But all three of these historical Christian identities have also found expression as both transactional and transformational perspectives.

If one image expresses the paradoxical power of Christianity as Niebuhr understands it, it is the belief that God's Messiah comes into this world as a suffering servant. This is a power that reveals itself in weakness (2 Cor. 12:9), for it shows that "pure goodness, without power, cannot maintain itself in the world. It ends on the cross. Yet that is not where it finally ends. The Messiah will ultimately transmute the whole world order" (*BT,* 177–78). Just as true power reveals itself paradoxically in powerlessness, those who seek to destroy pure goodness are themselves "the best people" of their time (*BT,* 182). No one strove any harder to observe the Law than the Pharisees, yet it was they who led the attack on Jesus. Rather than condemn them, Niebuhr urges his readers to acknowledge their good intentions and understand what had to happen, then as now: "The Kingdom of God must still enter the world by way of crucifixion" (*BT,* 185). It confirms, rather than abolishes, "the contradictions in which human nature is involved," and its expression in the idea of the Second Coming of the Messiah "contains some of the basic paradoxes of the Christian religion" (*BT,* 187–188). In particular, it shows that God can and will redeem both creation and humanity from sin. Creation does not have to be destroyed, and humans have not succumbed to total and irredeemable depravity. Although this idea of salvation cannot be expressed in rational terms, it illustrates that God, by the crucifixion of the suffering servant, has "absorbed the contradictions of historic existence into Himself," and that "the foolishness of God is wiser than the wisdom of men" (193).

•   •   •

For history, then, there are also different dialectics and various types of interpretation. It can be analyzed theoretically as a discipline that must strive to be more objective and correspondingly less subjective; it can be treated transactionally as a dialectic of reciprocity between subjects and objects; or it can be viewed as a realm of paradox, in which truth lies neither in the historian's vision nor in the historical world as such. Rather, truth is found in the transformations that occur within history but cannot be understood simply as products of it.

For the interpreters I have discussed, history is the exploration of a frontier, but the various frontiers could not be more dissimilar. Benson is unwilling to validate Turner's frontier thesis as an important imaginative construct. He acknowledges its influence, but only as a very misleading myth. A genuine frontier does exist for historians in the challenge to subject their work to the standards of rigorous social science. We might call this a methodological frontier. Benson never compromises his theoretical commitment to maintaining a sharp opposition between objective and subjective methods. Carr prefers to mediate that opposition by a dialectic of reciprocity typical of transactional interpretation, according to which the historian's subjectivity is the product of objective social forces and the objective social forces are in part shaped by the actions of subjective individuals. He argues that history is the interrelationship between past and future, with the present serving as a movable and progressive frontier. Niebuhr's transformational interpretation takes this dialectic one step further. Although he never discusses subjectivity and objectivity as such, his constant appeal to paradox makes clear that he would see this as yet another debate over one of the contradictions of history, contradictions that are real and yet are also overcome in a paradoxical unity that transcends a merely reciprocal reconciliation. For Niebuhr, the truth that defines the frontier of historical meaning is God's presence in history, an objective presence that, like the subjective faith that discerns it, is in, but not of, history.

For working historians, Benson's practical advice on how to do the job better will no doubt have an immediate appeal. His ability to expose the sloppy thinking behind so many historical analyses, especially those that appear to sacrifice the very possibility of historical knowledge on the altar of relativism, is a welcome relief to many who are laboring in libraries to discover what really happened and why. On very clearly defined questions of fact, a theoretical type of understanding will almost always have the greatest heuristic value, for it defines a discipline and rigorous methods that show a historian how to perform their task. But Benson's objective theoretical understanding accomplishes this at a price that is too high to pay in the eyes of some historians and many philosophers of history. His methodological sophistication excels on technical matters, but ignores the question of the role of the historian in the shaping of history. Little wonder that he finds himself at loggerheads with Becker, whose notion of personal objectivity remains utterly opaque to him.

Carr's transactional response to this dilemma is to point out that all historians are both objective and subjective in all their historical work, and that their objectivity and subjectivity mutually influence one another. His dialectic of reciprocity helps to lead us out of Benson's philosophical cul-de-sac. It also clarifies many important questions: the nature of historical facts, the role of social forces in history, the place of individual historical agents, the problem of progress, and some aspects of the scientific status of history as a discipline. Carr suspends that dialectic when dealing directly with the issue of historical causation, but there are ways in which he could have employed reciprocity there also. That is not the only limitation of Carr's program, however. He does not, as Benson would be quick to point out, offer us any help on how to do history. The common criticism of his book—that it is more about what history ought to be than what it is—seems oddly inverted: basing his proposals upon what he observes real historians to be actually doing, Carr tells us a lot about how we ought to understand that process, but almost nothing about how to do it better. If Benson is all practice and little theory, Carr offers, despite his Marxist leanings, almost all theory and precious little practice.

When we turn to Niebuhr, it seems for a moment as though we have left the realm of history altogether. There is no discussion of historical methods here, and nothing about the relation between the historian as subject and the historical objects to be understood. Benson's historiographical concerns and Carr's epistemological preoccupations are equally ignored in favor of another question: What is the meaning of history? Why should we bother to study it at all? To a devout secular historicist, this may be a nonquestion, for the belief that we are products of our natural and historical environments alone entails a presumption of the value of history. For Niebuhr, as for most transformational interpreters, this is not enough. If the only meaningful "frontier" for history is to be found in the squabbles of historians or in the historical present, which is little more than our "progress" from a questionable past into a dubious future, then it hardly seems worth the effort. For transformational thinkers, the choice is not between a spiritual significance within history and a merely secular significance; it is between meaning in history and meaning that lies utterly beyond history, that is neither in nor of historical existence. The major competition for orthodox incarnational faith over the two millennia of Christian history has come, I suspect, from such ahistorical and otherworldly alternatives as Gnosticism. So, if Benson teaches us how to do history better and Carr sharpens our self-understanding as we do it, it is Niebuhr who helps us to deal with the paradox of history as the locus of transcendent meaning.

4

Variations on the Theme of Love

Does any word cause more confusion than "love"? What other concept leads to such frequent and serious misunderstandings? No doubt the intimacy and intensity of love result in more conflicts in understanding than is the case with any other topic treated in this book. It provides a striking example of how differing views of the same phenomenon can result from the three types of interpretation, of how sometimes three authors appear to be using the same word for utterly different realities.

The three texts I have chosen for this chapter on interpretations of love are Roland Barthes's *Lover's Discourse,* Erich Fromm's *Art of Loving,* and Søren Kierkegaard's *Works of Love.* Each has been selected because it is both a powerful statement in its own right and a good illustration of, respectively, theoretical, transactional, and transformational interpretation. Although Kierkegaard wrote in the 1840s, Fromm in the 1950s, and Barthes in the 1970s, there is no indication that the later authors had read the books on love by the earlier ones. Kierkegaard is usually regarded as one of the first existentialist philosophers; his thought is dominated by a religious motive and Christian categories. Fromm presents himself as a secular psychologist with a strong commitment to Marxist humanism. Barthes's works are prominent among those of postmodern literary theorists. He wrote extensively on semiology and literature, with frequent allusions to Buddhist concepts. *A Lover's Discourse* was published in French in 1980, just three years before Barthes was fatally struck while crossing a Paris street. It was an immediate best-seller in France. In it we see that theoretical interpretation need not always pursue objectivity, so long as it assumes or reflects a binary opposition between objectivity and subjectivity.

Love as Discourse

It is tempting to employ the postmodern stylistic device of crossing out the words in the title of this section. Barthes denies that *A Lover's Discourse* is a "discourse on love" or even on the lover—"the amorous subject and what he is."[1] Rather, it deals only with what the lover says. To treat Barthes's book as an essay about "love as discourse" falsely implies that he argues that love can be defined as discourse. Nevertheless, he does attempt to peer into a corner of the mystery of love through an examination of "fragments d'un discours amoureux" (the wording of the French title of the work). Whatever we can learn about love in this essay is accessible to us only insofar as a lover's discourse is also a discourse on (or by) love, an image of love as it is inscribed (or inscribes itself) in a lover's discourse. So the title of this section may stand, though qualified, for it may be that the essay does not, after all, teach us anything about love.

Second qualification: Barthes (or the narrator of his book) announces that he will not describe the lover's discourse; he will simulate it, speaking it in the first person singular (3). He also observes how others speak it, especially literary lovers. Werther is mentioned so constantly that *A Lover's Discourse* could be read as a gloss on Goethe's classic *Sorrows of Young Werther,* which is praised as "pure discourse of the amorous subject" (205). But even this commentary does not constitute analysis: "[D]iscourse on love though I may for years at a time, I cannot hope to seize the concept of it except 'by the tail': by flashes, formulas, surprises of expression, scattered through the

---

1. Roland Barthes, *A Lover's Discourse: Fragments,* trans. Richard Howard (New York: Hill & Wang, 1978), 5; originally published as *Fragments d'un discours amoureux* (Paris: Éditions du Seuil, 1977).

great stream of the Image-repertoire" (59). And that is as it should be, for any abstract discourse on love in general is nothing more than a covert way of addressing someone amorously (74).

The "Image-repertoire" (storehouse or theatrical stock of images) is a leading figure in *A Lover's Discourse*. It appears as a great stream of monologue, like the pure discourse of *Werther*. Third qualification: Barthes's focus is on a lover's discourse, not the discourse of a pair of lovers. There is no dialogue here. This lover's discourse is not with an other, the beloved, for the other also resides within the Image-repertoire. The flow of the lover's discourse is generated "by means of the Image-repertoire's capital" (70), not by shared experiences. Reality is imaginary, for the image is *"the thing itself"* that "always has the last word" against any so-called knowledge (132–33). *A Lover's Discourse* is organized into eighty short fragments, or entries, alphabetically arranged; each traces the speaking of an image. Each also begins with a synopsis, as, for example, this fragment on reverberation: "Fundamental mode of amorous subjectivity, an image reverberates painfully in the subject's affective consciousness" (200).

The lover does not examine, explore, analyze, evaluate, or express the Image-repertoire. The lover, as lover, is the monologue that issues from the Image-repertoire: "The power of the Image-repertoire is immediate: I do not look for the image, it comes to me, all of a sudden" (214). If there is a question of control, it is the Image-repertoire that controls the lover: "[E]verything around me changes value in relation to a function, which is the Image-repertoire; the lover then cuts himself off from the world, he unrealizes it because he hallucinates from another aspect the peripeteias of the utopias of his love; he surrenders himself to the Image, in relation to which all 'reality' disturbs him" (90).

Language equivocates. It creates artificial abstractions such as the infinitive "to love." In the lover's discourse, *"I-love-you* must be understood . . . [as] a single word, . . . beyond syntax and . . . structural transformation" (147). *I-love-you* "belongs" neither to linguistics nor to semiology, but to music (149). Like the Image-repertoire from which it comes, it is too immediate for the hierarchies of sentences, nuances, and differing usages. It is "always true" (148), but of course it is true from a perspective that considers "reality" a disturbance.

The contemporary lover speaks a lover's discourse despite the fact that this discourse is "completely forsaken by the surrounding languages" (1). Marxist discourse is silent on love; psychoanalytical discourse affirms it as a lost memory; and "Christian discourse, if it still exists, exhorts him [the contemporary lover] to repress and to sublimate" love (211). Even so, Barthes often exploits mystical discourse. Ruysbroeck appears in many fragments, uttering praise, to cite just one example, of "the joy of which one cannot speak" (55)—an encomium on the love of God that Barthes transposes into an image of erotic love. As the many references to Buddhist concepts testify, the mystical joy that is in view here is more an impersonal ecstasy than an interpersonal love relation: "[B]y a movement one might well call mystical, I love, not what he is, but *that he is*" (222).

This fact—that the beloved simply *is*—releases the flow of the Image-repertoire. The characteristics of the loved one are secondary because the true object of erotic love is less the other person than the lover's mother, the most powerful image in the entire repertoire. The image of the Mother evokes feelings of abandonment, waiting, reunion. Like mystics experiencing the darkness of not feeling loved by God, the lover links the beloved's coldness with "the Wicked Mother" (113). The "infantile" response to being abandoned is a shifting "brutally to the genital" (48), such that in intercourse "the Image-repertoire goes to the devil" (104). Abandonment is followed by waiting, a small boy waiting each evening for a bus to bring the Mother home from work: "[T]he buses would pass one after the other, she wasn't in any of them" (15). Interminably waiting for a telephone call from the beloved, and overcome with anxiety, the lover feels a desperate need for "the healing call, the return of the Mother" (38–39). The "return to the mother"[2] abolishes and fulfills all desires with its "motionless cradling," an incestuous enchantment (104). The image of the Mother is, then, a contradictory one: "[T]he gratifying Mother shows me the Mirror, the Image, and says to me: 'That's you.' But the silent Mother does not tell me what I am: I am no longer established, I drift painfully, without existence" (168).

The contradiction between the image of the loving Mother and the image of the wicked Mother is echoed in every dimension of experience. Sensations are contradictory (50); feelings of happiness and wretchedness occur simultaneously (22); the beloved is experienced "contradictorily" as both "a capricious divinity . . . *and* as a heavy, *inveterate* thing" (220). The beloved can also seem responsible for this constant state of contradiction: "[T]he other alternates actions of seduction with actions of frustration" (125). The lover responds to all these contradictions by becoming intentionally contradictory himself. He utters the *I-love-you* as a force opposing other, hostile

2. Barthes uses here "the Mother" (*la Mère*) and there "the mother" (*la mère*), with no apparent systematic distinction.

forces (153). He affirms a modern reversal, by which the ravisher becomes the passive party and "loved *object*," while "the ravished object . . . is the real *subject* of love" (188). Lover becomes beloved, and subject becomes object. And vice versa. The "amorous system" is a web of contradictions to which the lover yields: "I order myself to be still in love and to be no longer in love." There is no escape within the system: "If it were not in the 'nature' of amorous madness" to pass, to cease of itself, no one could ever put an end to it (143).

The connection between contradiction and system is a primary tenet of structuralist and poststructuralist thinking. The reality experienced by the lover is "a system of power" (89) that opposes him, much like the attacks that must be repelled by the *I-love-you*. The lover survives in this hostile system more as a site than as an individual: "The lover's solitude is not a solitude of person (love confides, speaks, tells itself), it is a solitude of system: I am alone in making a system out of it (perhaps because I am ceaselessly flung back on the solipsism of my discourse)" (212). To embrace a structure does not assure happiness, but it does offer a place to live, a location that the lover can reject and explore and perversely enjoy all at the same time, like the ancient monk who lived on top of his column (46). The discourse of a lover is this sort of structured system, the same for all lovers, the basis upon which lovers can identify with each other: "Identification is not a psychological process; it is a pure structural operation: I am the one who has the same place I have" (129). "The structure has nothing to do with persons; hence (like a bureaucracy) it is terrible" (130). There is a frightening pain here, but also a release from ethical responsibility for behavior: "I suffer, but at least I have nothing to decide; the amorous (imaginary) machinery here operates all by itself, within me" (64).

And yet the lover does decide, for even morality does not escape the dialectic of contradiction in *A Lover's Discourse*. The notion that love occurs "at first sight" is a myth, admittedly a very powerful myth in our sentimental age, but the lover's structural site entails the admission that "I never fall in love unless I have wanted to." It is a decision that must be made before the lover will respond to "a release switch" that serves as "bait" (190). Once that bait has been taken, the lover is entrapped in a system in which all decisions seem to be made by the loved one, or even by other forces that control "*his* dependency," a double subjection that seems to the lover "altogether unfair" (83). There is, then, a sort of decision to lose the power of decision, a submission to a structure and system that preempts any further or alternative submission or rebellion. Ecstasy displaces responsibility (12). Ethics is seen as conformist and morality as philistine (84). Marriage is defined as a system for those who wish to be "pigeonholed" rather than as a relation-ship (45–46), a system that promotes argument (204). The lover derides "[t]he moral tax levied by society on all transgressions" (178) even while he admits "the moralism of anti-morality" (176).

The self-contradictory dimension of a lover's discourse arises from the Image-repertoire itself. When an image "comes to" the lover, it is not sub-ject to his control or decision: "It is afterwards that I return to it and begin making the good sign alternate, interminably, with the bad one" (214). This oscillation is not an ethical logic of either/or (62), by which a choice is made that can then become the plumb line for subsequent behavior. The either/or of contradiction maintains both poles of the opposition in a rad-ical tension, refusing to choose one over the other, since it is controlled by the theoretical system of structural oppositions. In contrast, transactional thinking would affirm the obligation to choose between alternatives in ethical matters, in order to be able to go beyond mere contradiction to the reciprocal dialectic of interpersonal relationships. A transactional thinker could not fathom the lover's fascination with two simultaneous yet contra-dictory embraces, the maternal and the genital, and his affirmation of the desire "to rediscover, to renew the contradiction—the contraction—of the two embraces" (105). In particular, the association of contradiction with contraction is incomprehensible from a reciprocal perspective. There is an alleged reciprocity in "what is euphemistically called *dialogue*," but it is really only the give-and-take of argument (204) and the determination of each partner to have the last word (207). There are also occasional moments where the lover admits to reciprocity with the beloved, as when "we mother each other reciprocally" (224), yet the tone of the relation throughout is much more one of opposition; the only enduring "reciprocity" is the lovers' mutual manipulation.

Paradox is also mentioned in *A Lover's Discourse,* and paradoxical self-contradictions abound, but these also turn out to be, upon closer exami-nation, varieties of oscillation or manipulation rather than a genuine unity within opposition. The centrality of manipulation as a theme in *A Lover's Discourse* is evident. It appears both in the images of the relation of the lover with the beloved and in later reflections upon that relation. The lover finds himself in an "amorous duel" in which each is trying to subject the other (121). He is torn by the *will-to-possess* (conquest) and the *non-will-to-possess* (submission), but he cannot unequivocally affirm either (232). He con-strues "total union" as "the fulfillment of ownership" in which each enjoys an "absolute appropriation" of the other (226), and he complains that he alone is kept waiting: the loved one never waits, significantly, since the capacity to make someone wait is "the constant prerogative of all power" (39–40). Every aspect of the lovers' relation, even their comments to each other about a rival for the beloved's affection, is part of a strategy of manipulation (65–66).

Although some of these manipulations are characterized as paradoxical, it would be erroneous to conclude from them that *A Lover's Discourse* employs a dialectic of paradox in the transformational sense. For example, the lover sees a paradox in the fact that the image of love as ever new is itself "the most worn-down of stereotypes" (151), but this is little more than an ironic observation. He calls it a paradox that he continues to believe that he is loved, but that is clearly a self-deception: "I hallucinate what I desire" (187). His frequent use of Ruysbroeck's mystical paradoxes is suggestive, but those references play a largely metaphorical role, for they never affirm the existence of the reality that generates the paradox for the mystic (234).

Using "dialectic" in the sense of the unfolding of an objective reality, the lover denies that amorous discourse is dialectical, for "it turns like a perpetual calendar" (7), a self-enclosed system. He also denies that he is a dialectical person, for he demands a love that is total or nothing, being unable to conceive of a love that develops (163). Yet the lover is very aware that the beloved is beyond his control. Embedded in *A Lover's Discourse* is a theory of the other. When the lover writes that he loves his beloved not for his personal qualities but for the fact that he is, he is repeating the idea that being in love is a structural relation within a system of amorous sites and signs. Lover and beloved are both sites. *I-love-you* and keeping the other person waiting are signs. In this structuralist sense, the other is virtually a cipher, a nonperson who stands for the desired one, who is always leaving (13) and always absent (15). Within this structure of opposition, the lover and his other establish each other in truth (229), simply because neither could occupy his site without the other over against him. Being opposed, the other remains impenetrable, despite the fact that the lover knows him better than anyone else does (134). That is also why ecstatic "engulfment" by love results in a loss of the other as other (11), for it abolishes the entire oppositional structure of self and other.

In denying the "dialectical" nature of love and of himself, the lover is not repudiating this structural opposition of impersonal signs. He is rejecting dialectic in the more conventional sense of a binary relation in which both poles contribute to the whole: reciprocity or paradox. He is also affirming the silence he has imposed upon the loved one (3), the totally unilateral character of this entire relation, and the solipsism of his lover's discourse. Indeed, it is never clear in *A Lover's Discourse* whether we are reading reflections on an actual relationship or simply the solitary imaginings of a poetic spirit whose primary knowledge of love has come from reading books like *The Sorrows of Young Werther.*

This poeticizing of the other amounts to a self-projection into the other (49).[3] Barthes often indicates that the lover's feelings for the beloved involve a great deal of transference from the mother. There are also a number of references to dependence upon one's analyst. In both cases the implication is that love is a way of characterizing a particular kind of self-involvement, either the infant's need for the mother or the patient's employment of the analyst in order to achieve greater self-understanding. Neither infant nor patient relates to mother or analyst as an*other* person, an individual who has needs and desires also and who is free to engage in the relation or not. From the perspective of infant or patient, love is the lover's impersonal dependency upon an other who is assumed to be entirely oriented toward the lover.

The text expresses this poeticized other quite bluntly. The lover loves not the other person, but love itself (31). The lover's discourse stifles the other, for it is little more than soliloquy (165–66). The lover's other "would be born" only if he could unite "all the others in a single person" (228). The lover resents any suffering experienced by the loved one that he (the lover) has not caused, for he thinks it shows that the loved one does not really love him (57). "Adorable" is a "rather stupid word," but it does convey the fact that the other "produces in him [the lover] an aesthetic vision" (18–19). In so many ways the point is made: a lover's discourse is a product of the lover's Image-repertoire, not of an actual relationship with a real *other* person.

To be sure, there are moments when the lover's solipsism yields to an acknowledgment of an other who cannot be manipulated or poeticized. To "discover in the other another myself" (199) can mean that the other expands my world and identity. An entire fragment is devoted to the theme of exile from the Image-repertoire, an exile that includes a conscious sacrifice of the Image-repertoire necessary for the lover's survival. This sacrifice is touted as a "proof of love," a "mourning for my beloved" in which

---

3. This may help to account for the ambiguity of the gender of the beloved, who is usually referred to in masculine terms but also sometimes with feminine pronouns. No explicit indication of gender is ever stated, so the pronouns result in an ambiguously (but not paradoxically) bisexual discourse.

"I liquidate my transference . . . *for I love the other still*" (108). There are also others who are third parties to the love affair, such as those who gossip about the beloved, leading the lover to condemn any use of the third-person pronoun: "[Y]ou are never anything but you, I do not want the Other to speak of you" (185).

But these moments of apparently real otherness are also best understood as part of the poeticizing process. When others speak of the beloved, the lover protests, not out of a deep appreciation for the beloved but because he cannot tolerate any relation, beyond his control, between the beloved and others. When the lover does not reply to a love letter, his "image changes, becomes *other*" (158). This otherness is negative, signifying the lover's inability to manipulate the beloved. In other words, the lover cannot appreciate any positive otherness in the beloved: "Everything about the other which doesn't concern me seems alien, hostile" (220). And: "[I]n the realm of amorous sentiment . . . , I refuse to recognize the division of our image, the other's alterity" (221).

Whereas the theoretical thinkers in earlier chapters have championed objectivity over subjectivity, here there is no effort to present the lover's discourse as a discipline governed by an objective method. In that sense, *A Lover's Discourse* is an example of a subjective theoretical type of understanding. Objectivity is disdained, but the structure of binary opposition between objectivity and subjectivity is maintained. The beloved stands in a strangely hostile relation to the lover: the alien object of love over against the subject who loves. The conflict between them remains constant. Since neither object nor subject is sharply defined, they sometimes seem to be little more than poles in that conflict, abstract signs pouring out of the lover's subjective Image-repertoire. Indeed, *A Lover's Discourse* could be said to be doubly subjective: first, in its refusal to submit to any criteria of objectivity; and second, in its preoccupation with the lover's subjective discourse.

A Lover's Discourse asserts that the loved person is a site, a polar other, a replaceable function within the system of amorous discourse. The insights that it offers into the psychology of this romantic solipsism are marvelous, but it can be called love only in a very restricted sense. Love is subsumed in a semiotic theory on the one hand and in erotic desire for a possibly imaginary loved one on the other. The beloved is frequently mentioned, but almost always in strangely impersonal or reifying language. In ordinary usage, love between persons cannot occur unless both parties will it. It is a relation that they believe to be based upon a mutual attraction of each toward the other as an individual, rather than the internal repertory of images of either of them alone. Perhaps a theoretical understanding of love is an oxymoron, for love as a relation between persons may require transactional categories. There is no interpersonal relation of mutual affirmation in *A Lover's Discourse*, only desire for the silent, impenetrable other, who may be nothing more than a projection of the lover's own self. The lover and beloved are both sites within the Image-repertoire that is the system and structure of love. The contrast between this subjective theoretical interpretation of love and the more conventional transactional understanding that we are about to visit could not be sharper.

Love as an Art

Erich Fromm's *Art of Loving* is a complex and provocative book,[4] far more difficult to grasp than it at first appears. Although Fromm intentionally devotes most of the essay to his theory of love, that theory does not represent a "theoretical" type of interpretation; despite the fact that his theory of love culminates with a long section on the paradoxical character of the love of God (by far the longest of the several sections on the various objects of love), the theory is neither paradoxical nor even religious; and even though he specifically designates love as an "art," no aesthetic aspects of love are explicit or implicit in his discussion. Indeed, it sometimes seems as though Fromm intends to disguise the character of his own argument. In any case, he thereby inadvertently provides me with a welcome opportunity to demonstrate how my dialectical analysis suggests questions that can lead to more nuanced readings of complex texts.

Fromm is adamant that love is an art. The general resistance to viewing love as an art that must be learned is due to a number of confused beliefs: that love occurs because one is lovable, that the challenge of love is to find a lovable object and to acquire it, and that love is simply a matter of falling in love. Fromm protests that all of these views are mistaken: love is an art that requires mastery of both theory and practice in a blend that he calls "intuition, the essence of the mastery of any art" (5). This argument forms the basis for a point that is repeated throughout the book: "Love is an activity, not a passive effect; it is a 'standing in,' not a 'falling for'. . . . primarily

---

4. Erich Fromm, *The Art of Loving: An Enquiry into the Nature of Love* (New York: Harper & Row, 1956).

giving, not receiving" (22). In short, love is not an experience that happens to us; it is an activity that we must learn and practice.

According to Fromm's theory, there are four basic elements that can be found in all forms of love as an activity: care for the loved one; a sense of responsibility for the other; respect, which means "concern that the other person should grow and unfold as he is" (28); and knowledge of the beloved, knowledge that can be gained only "in the *act* of love" (31). What is striking is his clear emphasis upon love as something that one person does "by one-self" (107). Although there obviously must be another person for the lover to love, Fromm argues that the objects of love are secondary to the lover's own character: "Love is not primarily a relationship to a specific person; it is an *attitude*, an *orientation* of *character* which determines the relatedness of a person to the world as a whole, not toward one 'object' of love" (46).

It is not surprising, then, that Fromm stresses the role of the will in love, even in romantic love: "To love somebody is not just a strong feeling—it is a decision, it is a judgment, it is a promise" (56). For this commitment to stand, "the mastery of the art must be a matter of ultimate concern; there must be nothing else in the world more important than the art" (5; cf. 110). This is strong language, and Fromm reinforces it by stating that it applies equally to music, medicine, and carpentry: all are arts that require a total commitment. If this is not simply hyperbole or a call for multiple ultimate concerns, then Fromm must believe that the ability to love is one expression of a psychological gestalt that governs a person's entire being. Again, the emphasis is upon love as an art and practice in which an individual must be fully engaged.

This assumption is also implicit in Fromm's discussion of the practice of love. He declares that "love is a personal experience which everyone can only have by and for himself" (107). Although this makes any thought of a rigid program impractical, there are three standard requirements: discipline, concentration, and patience (108–9). Here also the accent is on how a person can grow into a mature lover, not on the dialectics of love relationships. Learning to love is an art, and prerequisite to that art one must become a person who is capable of being an artist: "With regard to the art of loving, this means that anyone who aspires to become a master in this art must begin by *practicing* discipline, concentration and patience throughout every phase of his life" (110). This is the sense in which the concern to love, like other concerns, must be ultimate: together they all follow from a person's commitment to living "every phase of his life" as an artist.

The intensity or totalism of this activist understanding of love as an art is matched by the universalism of its scope. As we saw above, love is an attitude toward the entire world, not just a preference for a particular person. That is why Fromm considers brotherly love to be the "most fundamental kind of love, which underlies all types of love" (47). Brotherly love is love for all human beings, a love utterly free of any exclusivity. Although it presupposes the equality of all human beings, brotherly love does not deny that some people are needier than others. This acknowledgment does not threaten its universality, however, for brotherly love never seeks a reward: "Only in the love of those who do not serve a purpose, love begins to unfold" (48).

A theory that advocates such a totalistic and universalistic understanding of love might appear to demand profound self-denial. But Fromm strongly endorses self-love in his discussion of the objects of love, and he condemns the identification of self-love with selfishness that he finds in thinkers as diverse as Calvin and Freud (57). Against them, he cites the biblical teaching that one must love one's neighbor *as oneself*. Love of self is not the opposite of love for others; rather, they both follow equally from the "love of man as such" (59). Without love of self, there can be no love of others; and without love of others, no love of self is valid. The true opposition is not between love of others and self-love but between self-love and selfishness (60). Selfishness often masquerades as love by engaging in "oversolicitous" behavior, thereby showing that it is really "neurotic 'unselfishness'" (61). One of Fromm's many quotes from the medieval mystic Meister Eckhart speaks to this issue: "'Thus he is a great and righteous person who, loving himself, loves all others equally'" (63).

It is true that what we call self-love is often narcissism, and Fromm has a great deal to say about that psychological aberration. In his view, the narcissist is a case of arrested development, a stage of seeking to be loved that should have yielded to the stage of learning to give love, which normally occurs about the age of eight (40). Narcissists may appear to love other persons, but they are really only loving a person whom they think of as a part of themselves (50). This is not a genuine form of love: "[T]he main condition for the achievement of love is the *overcoming* of one's *narcissism*" (118). To do this, it is necessary to learn to see others objectively, as they are, and not simply as they might meet one's own emotional needs.

The opposite of narcissism, and the crown of a person's development in learning the art of loving, is reason. This is why Fromm's fourth element in love is knowledge, for it is impossible to know others in the intimacy of love without first knowing them in an objective, "psychological" way (31).

Reason is self-awareness in an attitude of humility that makes objective or detached knowledge possible (120). Reason is not, for Fromm, the opposite of faith. Faith is necessary for anyone who would practice the art of loving, but it is a "rational faith . . . rooted in one's own experience of thought or feeling" (121). This faith is not a matter of assent to particular doctrines. It is the courage and vision that are necessary to perform any art—or any science—well.

These aspects of Fromm's discussion of love appear to point toward a concept of love that manifests, like Barthes's discourse, a lack of interest in the other as other, the loved one without whom love cannot be a relationship. However different the two theories might otherwise be, Fromm's essay has a structural and impersonal dimension that seems very theoretical. He calls love an art, and he describes that art in terms of self-discipline. But Fromm assumes throughout that love is a relational reality. He never suggests that his art of loving might be an activity of the imagination.

The acme of the art of loving, human reason, is also present at the beginning of the need for love relationships. Reason is self-awareness, and the first inkling that we have of our own need for love is our reason's awareness of the fact that we are alone, confined by the inevitability of death to a separateness that "is the source of intense anxiety" (8). Fromm also locates shame and guilt in this sense of separateness, on the curious assumption that the taboo on nakedness was an invention of the Victorians (9).[5] Be that as it may, anxiety over separateness is what motivates human beings both to seek love and to love, whether the object of that love is a child, a sexual partner, or God. Moreover, "above the universal, existential need for union rises a more specific, biological one: the desire for union between the masculine and feminine poles," a polarity that exists "*within* each man and each woman" (33). This opposition within each person combines with the sense of separation from other persons to produce a psychology oriented toward the achievement of both intrapersonal and interpersonal union. Although many seek to escape from their separateness in ecstatic consciousness (whether induced by drugs or some other means), through social conformity, and by activities that are creative and productive, Fromm clearly believes that none of these can substitute for the union of human love: "The unity achieved in productive work is not interpersonal; the unity achieved in orgiastic fusion is only transitory; the unity achieved by conformity is only

---

5. See Exod. 32:25 for one of numerous indications that nakedness was equally offensive to the ancient Israelites.

pseudo-unity. Hence, they are only partial answers to the problem of existence. The full answer lies in the achievement of interpersonal union, of fusion with another person, in *love*" (18).

Although all forms of love involve fusion for Fromm, he singles out erotic love as "the craving for complete fusion, for union with one other person" (52–53). He insists that mature erotic love is both exclusive and heterosexual. He defends marriage as an enduring (although not absolutely indissoluble) commitment (53, 57), and he opines that same-sex relations lack the polarized differences necessary to achieve the "polarized union" of love, just as many heterosexual relations have the polarized differences without the union (34). Fromm is generally wary of "the deceptive character of sexual desire," which can arise from so many sources other than love (54). But, when combined with the decision and commitment of brotherly love (56), sexual love remains for him a profound and valid expression of the art of loving.

In addition to inner and outer polarities, Fromm also affirms the conflicts that will arise in any love relationship. Love is not validated by the absence of conflict, but by constructive "working together" in the midst of conflict: it is "a constant challenge" (103). This working together precludes any manipulation of one by the other, for manipulation occurs only when one party does not have faith in the potentialities of the other (124). A mature love preserves the integrity of and respect for each unique person, in contrast to both masochism and sadism (20).

Mutual integrity and reciprocal respect point to the centrality of freedom in a love relationship. "'Love is the child of freedom,'" Fromm quotes from a French song (28). The need to respect the freedom of the loved one is particularly evident in motherly love, a subject to which Fromm frequently returns. A loving mother offers the unconditional acceptance that is so vital to an infant and young child. But the mother must also be able "to wish and support the child's separation" and to go on loving despite it (51–52). Genuine love overcomes the anxiety of separation even as it respects and promotes necessary separation within the relationship.

That mother's love overcomes separateness by respecting the need for separation sounds almost paradoxical. Likewise, Fromm's emphasis upon love as an art performed by an individual appears to contradict his insistence upon love as an interpersonal relationship based upon mutual respect for the other's integrity, a contradiction that could be overcome only by a paradoxical concept of their unity. However, a closer look at what Fromm says about paradoxical thinking demonstrates that he remains a reciprocal thinker and that his view of love presupposes a transactional paradigm of interpretation.

Although mother's love is only implicitly paradoxical, Fromm appeals to paradox frequently in his discussion of the love of God. The concept of God plays an interesting and highly equivocal role in *The Art of Loving*. On the one hand, Fromm is fascinated with the development and variety of concepts of God, and he devotes more space to God than to any other object of love (63–82). On the other hand, Fromm makes it clear that he is not a theist, that he thinks of God as a projection "in which man has expressed his experience of his [own] higher powers" (72). A mature religious individual is one who has outgrown spiritual narcissism and spiritual authoritarianism alike and "has incorporated the principles of love and justice into himself, where he has become one with God . . . to a point where he speaks of God only in a poetic, symbolic sense" (81). Thus Fromm considers the efforts of mystics to experience the union of self with God a distinct improvement over the efforts of traditional monotheists to acquire knowledge about an external and alien God.

The teachings of mystics provide Fromm with strong evidence for the importance of paradox. He cites Brahmanical thinkers who taught that oppositions are simply created by the perceiving mind, for reality itself is not dualistic (76). In one particularly striking passage, Fromm declares: "The world of thought remains caught in the paradox. The only way in which the world can be grasped ultimately lies, not in thought, but in the act, in the experience of oneness. Thus paradoxical logic leads to the conclusion that the love of God is neither the knowledge of God in thought, nor the thought of one's love of God, but the act of experiencing the oneness with God" (78).

The fact is, however, that Fromm is really very far from becoming a paradoxical thinker. Although he values experience more than doctrine, he applauds mystics, not because of their transcendental and transformative experiences, but because the knowledge they attain through those experiences confirms his humanistic belief in the identity of the divine with the human. Fromm believes that the benefit of mystical experience is simply a greater emphasis upon moral behavior, an increased tolerance for others, and a deeper commitment to the ongoing task of self-improvement (78–79). He seems to forget about love of God when he discusses what he takes to be the primary mark of true love: productivity.

Fromm frequently states that "[g]enuine love is an expression of productiveness" (59), both when discussing love of others and also when describing self-love. He takes from Marx the principle that "love is a power which produces love" (25), that mature love grows beyond the need to be loved into the ability to give love before receiving it (40–41). This love is not an instrumental, calculated maneuver to manipulate the other into loving in return. It is an expression of the lover's character, of the fact that the lover is a loving person toward all others. But this love is reciprocal, for, in Marx's own words, "'[i]f you love without calling forth love, that is, if your love as such does not produce love, if by means of an *expression of life* as a loving person you do not make of yourself a *loved person,* then your love is impotent, a misfortune'" (25). Although reciprocal love refuses to manipulate the other, it does not conceive of love as a unilateral giving without regard to the loved one's response. It is mutual love, in which the lovers exchange respect for each other's integrity and freedom. It is, as it were, a labor theory of love, for it values love according to the effort it requires and the productivity it creates, not as a commodity to be brokered on the market or as a gift to be given indiscriminately, even to those who ignore or reject it.

Fromm's use of Marxist language throughout the book is more than just a rhetorical flourish. It provides the key to his theory of love. It also explains why he insists that love is a capacity rather than a relation: "It is an illusion to believe that one can separate life in such a way that one is productive in the sphere of love and unproductive in other spheres. Productiveness does not permit of such a division of labor" (128–29). Capitalism has given us the universal principle of fairness, which construes love as an exchange in which each party expects to get something having a value equal to that which is given. Against this, the universal brotherly love of neighbor is a caring for all others that enables them to love and care in turn. Only in this way does love achieve mutual integrity, reciprocal respect, and the interpersonal unity of productive work. Fromm's emphasis upon the difference between fairness and genuine love is perhaps an indication that they are easy to confuse, for capitalist and Marxist understandings of love both, at least in their humanistic forms, offer competing versions of a transactional approach to love.

Fromm's transactional interpretation differs from the approaches of Ellul, Douglas, and Carr. They all oppose theoretical thinking, but only Fromm is also interested in such transformational paradoxes as the love of God. In the final analysis, however, he is as far from the transformational view of love that I find in Kierkegaard as he is from Barthes's subjective theoretical position.

Paradoxes of Love

The book by Kierkegaard that contributes directly to this discussion is *Works of Love*,[6] a long discussion of the Christian understanding of the duty to love and the nature of love. Kierkegaard is a natural choice to conclude this chapter, for he is also the writer from whom I have learned most about the dialectics of paradox.

I begin with an aspect of Kierkegaard's thought that has brought him a great deal of criticism over the years: his emphasis upon the single individual.[7] This is a constant refrain throughout his writings, one that is expressed in *Works of Love* in a number of ways, among them this remark about faith: "[T]he essence of faith is to be a secret, to be for the single individual; if it is not kept as a secret by every single individual, even when he confesses it, then he does not believe" (28). Since faith is critical to human identity for Kierkegaard, it follows that individuals are basically "single" in his view. Relationship is secondary.

But Kierkegaard does not stop with setting the single individual above the world of reciprocal relationships; he also restricts access to a person's individuality. While such transactional thinkers as Fromm extol mutual respect for the integrity and individuality of the other, which presupposes reciprocal self-revelations, Kierkegaard insists that any distinctive elements that we can reveal to others are of no interest to Christianity, which considers such matters "nothing but worldliness" (71). Identity for Kierkegaard is not the visible or socially accessible individuality, but a much more elusive uniqueness: "Just look at the world that lies before you in all its variegated multifariousness; it is like looking at a play, except that the multifariousness is much, much greater. Because of his dissimilarity, every single one of these innumerable individuals is something particular, represents something particular, but essentially he is something else. Yet this you do not get to see here in life; here you see only what the individual represents and how he does it. It is just as in the play" (86–87).

In other words, Kierkegaard believes that there is a limit to human efforts at self-revelation. They do not penetrate to the core of who we really are in relation to God, and they never will "here in life." He disagrees with those who claim that human relations constitute our entire identity, especially

6. Søren Kierkegaard, *Works of Love*, trans. Howard V. Hong and Edna H. Hong (Princeton: Princeton University Press, 1995).
7. See, for example, Martin Buber, "The Question to the Single One," in *Between Man and Man*, trans. Ronald Gregor Smith (New York: Macmillan, 1965), 40–82.

when they call "the person who wants to hold to God . . . self-loving" (128). Whether they take this stand for the sake of some personal advantage in the world or for a social identity within the context of community is a negligible difference: "What the world honors and loves under the name of love is an alliance in self-love" (119). Only individual uniqueness makes it possible for each person to have a genuine relationship with God (230), quite apart from the world or even the individual's community.

The individual's identity in relation to God also takes priority over social relations in marriage. Because love is a matter of conscience for Christianity, Kierkegaard writes, a pastor who marries two people does not address them with the familiar "Thou." By speaking to the bride and the groom individually with the formal "You," the pastor addresses their individual consciences, expressing the Christian conviction that every person must be regarded "first and foremost . . . individually as the single individual" (138). Certainly they both should have genuine love for the unique personality of the other, and not merely a narcissistic love for one's own distinctiveness as reflected in the other (269). But the real basis for their love is not their interpersonal relationship at all; it is the prior relationship that each of them has with God. True love is a relationship among three rather than just two persons (303), a paradox Kierkegaard frequently mentions in *Works of Love* and to which I return below.

In Kierkegaard's view, erotic love is merely a form of self-love, and self-love does not deserve to be called love (7). Christianity, he insists, does not condone self-love; it simply presupposes its existence, and then sets out to break it. He writes about the biblical command to love your neighbor as yourself: "When the Law's *as yourself* has wrested from you the self-love that Christianity sadly enough must presuppose to be in every human being, then you have actually learned to love yourself" (22–23). Whereas Fromm enthusiastically endorses self-love, Kierkegaard believes it must be "wrested" from the individual by Christianity. This also is a paradox, for the result is not simply the annihilation of self-love but its transformation into authentic self-love, which Kierkegaard later defines as love toward God (107).

Self-love takes many forms. It can avoid becoming dependent upon the beloved due to fear of commitment (38), or it can be a commitment based upon a spontaneous preference for the other that seeks stability in vows of friendship and sexual fidelity (52). Both friendship and erotic love suffer from this preferential character. In themselves, they are simply versions of self-love, love that is bestowed upon an other who is judged lovable, the other as one's own *"other I"* (57) rather than the other simply as other, with no thought of results or reward. Self-love is also evident in parental love, for an expectation of future reward often drives parental care (349–50).

The mere fact that a particular love displays self-sacrifice does not demonstrate that it is genuine rather than self-love, for the sacrificial lover can easily desire that the sacrifice be fully understood and appreciated by the loved one. In contrast, authentic love expects no reward or recognition, not even Fromm's productiveness of generating love in the beloved: "[T]he inwardness of Christian love is to be willing, as reward for its love, to be hated by the beloved (the object)" (131). Any desire for reciprocal love is "a lower view of love, therefore a lower love that has no view of love in itself" (237). Indeed, it is impossible for there to be any deception in true love, for nothing has been expected of the beloved. Whoever complains about being deceived in love "thereby denounces himself as a self-lover" (238).

In all of this Kierkegaard rejects self-love and equally love that is merely reciprocal, at the same time that he affirms a higher conception of self-love and the authenticity of mutually loving the individuality of the other as other. The tendency we have seen of transformational interpretation simultaneously and paradoxically to reject and affirm critical aspects of theoretical and transactional thinking is already apparent. That Christian love, at least according to Kierkegaard, is thoroughly paradoxical is also clear from his discussion of one sort of love that is not susceptible to the charge of being covert self-love: love of neighbor.

The New Testament version of the command to love your neighbor is pronounced by Jesus just before relating the parable of the Good Samaritan (Luke 10:27–37). Although Kierkegaard does not refer to this parable directly, his understanding of neighbor-love is clearly influenced by it. In the parable, Jesus tells of a man attacked by robbers and left for dead. After a priest and a Levite pass him by, a member of the despised Samaritan nation goes out of his way to help the suffering man. Jesus affirms the Samaritan as the true neighbor, a provocative judgment in several ways: it criticizes the priest and the Levite who did not help the man (as temple officials, they no doubt needed to avoid the ritual defilement that would come from touching a bleeding or dead man); it accords higher honor to a Samaritan than to Jews; and, most startling, it inverts the question of how to identify one's neighbor. By praising the Samaritan and telling his interlocutor to go and do likewise, Jesus demonstrates that the real question concerns not who deserves to be treated as a neighbor but who is willing to act like a neighbor by virtue of actively loving and helping anyone in need.

Kierkegaard assumes that the neighbor is not someone who qualifies for love by virtue of national identity or geographical proximity or any other common bond. Indeed, we should never even raise the question of who might be our neighbor: "There is not a single person in the whole world who is as surely and as easily recognised as the neighbor. You can never confuse him with anyone else, since the neighbor, to be sure, is all people. If you confuse another person with the neighbor, then the mistake is not due to the latter, since the other person is also the neighbor; the mistake is due to you, that you will not understand who the neighbor is" (51–52).

Kierkegaard comments that pagan cultures offer remarkable examples of erotic love and friendship, but none of love of neighbor, since pagan love is always based upon a "passionate preference" and admiration for the friend or the beloved: "The neighbor, however, has never been presented as an object of admiration" (54). The neighbor is loved not because of his or her beauty, intelligence, skill, creativity, personality, or moral character. The neighbor is to be loved simply as a neighbor, another human being.

For erotic love and friendship to become genuine love, they must also be neighbor-love. It is not enough for a husband and wife to add to their erotic love an obligation to love their neighbor. Nor are conjugal love and friendship based upon mutual attraction, while neighbor-love is strictly nonpreferential and therefore requires a special gift from God. No, the full paradoxical force of the command to love one's neighbor is revealed in Kierkegaard's application of that command directly to marriage and friendship. A special love for a spouse or friend can be genuine love only if it is based upon a prior neighbor-love for that person. To love anyone in any way at all we must first love that person as our neighbor, nonjudgmentally, exactly as we love every other neighbor (140–41). The paradox of preferential love is that, to be authentic love, it cannot be based upon preference. To be in a special relationship such as marriage or friendship is to love a person as one's neighbor—that is, without distinguishing among persons—while simultaneously loving that same person on the basis of a preferential passion.

This is why Christians are also enjoined to love their enemies: "[T]he one who truly loves the neighbor loves also his enemy. The distinction *friend or enemy* is a distinction in the object of love, but love for the neighbor has the object that is without difference" (67–68). To love one's neighbor is thus to be a neighbor to every other human being, whether friend, foe, or stranger. This recalls the surprising inversion suggested by Jesus, that the question is not who qualifies as my neighbor but whether I am loving as a true neighbor ought.

If love of neighbor includes love of enemies, it will often have to take the form of forgiveness. According to Kierkegaard, love does not forgive the sin of another, contingent upon that person's changed behavior, repentance, or even desire for forgiveness. To love is to seek "a mitigating explanation" (289), to know "nothing about the past" (314), and "to need to forgive already when the other person has not had the slightest thought of seeking forgiveness" (336).

Although Kierkegaard is rightly understood as a philosopher who extols passion, and although he explicitly defines love as "a passion of the emotions" (112), it is also the case that he thinks love is better understood as an action than as an emotion. The title of his book *Works of Love* indicates his plan to consider "love in its outward direction" (282). The idea of love as an act is developed in the maxim that it is *"our duty to remain in love's debt to one another,"* which in turn is based upon Rom. 13:8: "'Owe no one anything, except to love one another'" (177). The distinction between duty and debt is both subtle and significant. To love one's neighbor is a duty. Therefore the duty to love one another would merely be redundant, for everyone is our neighbor. But Kierkegaard insists that we have a duty to be in debt to the one we love. Loving another goes beyond the mere fulfillment of a duty to a profound sense of "infinite debt" (176). This debt is incurred not by the person who receives the love but by the lover. To focus on the duty to love is to dwell upon oneself, but to feel oneself in love's debt to the other is to make love a matter of total attention to the other rather than a relation in which one uses the other to fulfill the duty to love.

This debt of love is action. It is not fanatical or fanciful action, for a debt of love that fulfills the duty to love "removes from love everything that is inflamed, everything that is momentary, everything that is giddy" (188). Kierkegaard's point is that the debt of love is neither just ideal nor merely a strong emotion. It is the demand for certain behavior, an action that must be constant. Love is a work, a work from which the lover never takes a rest (190). And the secret of human love, the power which makes it possible and to which it testifies, is God.

Despite the overwhelming emphasis throughout *Works of Love* upon love as human action, there is no doubt about the divine source of love for Kierkegaard: "Just as the quiet lake originates darkly in the deep spring, so a human being's love originates mysteriously in God's love. Just as the quiet lake invites you to contemplate it but by the reflected image of darkness prevents you from seeing through it, so also the mysterious origin of love in God's love prevents you from seeing its ground" (9–10). As the source of all human love, God is invisibly present in every love relationship. Normally love is construed as a relation between two persons, but God is the third, the *"the middle term"* (107) that unites two people in love. Therefore love is initially from God and for God, and only secondarily from and for another human being. To love God is to love everyone (including oneself), and to love anyone rightly is to love God. No one should ever seek to be the object of another person's love, since "the only true object of a human being's love is *love,* which is God" (264–65).

The theological characterization of the ability to love is that it is a gift of God's grace: "It is God, the Creator, who must implant love in each human being, he who himself is Love" (216). True forgiveness, as we saw above, is an expression of the debt of love that is offered long before it is requested. According to Kierkegaard, God loved us first as Creator and then loved us again as Redeemer by offering us a reconciliation that we had not requested (336). Thus the Atonement provides a model of love.

The transformational dialectic of paradox that permeates Kierkegaard's discussion of love merits further emphasis. We have already seen it at a number of points: preferential love is based upon admiration and attraction, but to be genuine love it must first be neighbor-love for the loved one, resulting in a paradoxical Christian love for friend or spouse that is really an expression of love for God as the source and object of all real love. Thus friendship and marriage are triadic relations in which the direct relation between the two human beings is paradoxically affirmed and sustained by the love relation that each individual has with God. The strength of the friendship or marriage resides in the fact that the two people love each other in the same way that they love every other neighbor. As Kierkegaard sums up: "The merely human view of love can never go beyond mutuality: the lover is the beloved and the beloved is the lover. Christianity teaches that such a love has not yet found its true object—God. The love-relationship requires threeness: the lover, the beloved, the love—but the love is God. Therefore, to love another person is to help that person to love God, and to be loved is to be helped" (121). Neither calculation nor possessiveness in relation to the loved one finds a place in this kind of love (178, 266). Both entail manipulation of the other, and that is incompatible with the paradoxical unity-in-difference that Kierkegaard's sees as the core of Christian love.

It is hard to imagine a more transformational understanding of love than this one. Friendship, erotic love, love of enemies, even neighbor-love are all radically changed by being understood as love from and toward God.

Whereas self-love is always worrying about its right to this and its right to that, real love transforms the lover by what Kierkegaard calls redoubling: "[T]he one who loves is or becomes what he does" (281). To love is to be transformed into a vessel of love. To give love to anyone is paradoxically to receive it from God and to be changed by it.

The idea of redoubling brings us to the most radical aspect of Kierkegaard's view of love: that God too is part of its paradoxical and transforming dialectic. In love, the eternal enters a person, and then "this eternal redoubles in him in such a way that every moment it is in him, it is in him in a double mode: in an outward direction and in an inward direction back into itself" (280). The implication is clear: God exists as love and in love. Without people to love and be loved by, the love that is God could not exist in the world. Love is not simply a gift from God, who remains on high; it is the presence of God as the source of unity in every love relation. The "transformation of the eternal" takes self-love and changes it into duty (34). At the same time, in Christ the eternal is itself transformed into thc reality and presence of God in our midst: "[H]e was love and yet he did everything out of love and wanted to bring salvation to humanity, and by what means? By the relationship with God—because he was love" (111).

•   •   •

We have viewed love as discourse, art, and work. As a discourse emanating from the Image-repertoire, love exemplifies the way in which theoretical interpretation sets the subject/lover over against the object/beloved and assumes that any interaction is fundamentally manipulation. As an art, love transacts an ethical commitment to an interpersonal relationship by a lover who hopes productively to nurture a reciprocal love in the beloved. And as work, love is obedience to God's command to love the neighbor, an obedience that is paradoxically possible only by the transforming grace of God's own love, which is the middle term in every love relationship.

These portrayals of love have also shown us a new aspect of each of the three types of interpretation. Whereas Skinner, Lévi-Strauss, and Benson all typify objective theoretical approaches and disavow any kind of subjective interest, Barthes's lover's discourse assumes, as it were, the opposite position. Objectivity in argument is disdained, and the objectivity of the other is seen as a challenge to the lover in his attempts subjectively to control and exploit the loved one. Barthes is the first subjective theoretical thinker we have encountered. The new aspect in Fromm's reciprocal understanding of love is his very real interest in matters that appear to be paradoxical.

Ellul, Douglas, and Carr are all busy arguing against theoretical positions, and never (in the works examined here) consider the possibility of paradox. In Chapter 5 we shall encounter another transactional interpreter, Martin Buber, who takes that possibility seriously. Finally, Kierkegaard is really the first example presented here of a transformational thinker who is primarily concerned with showing how a paradoxical dialectic goes beyond one that is merely reciprocal. Campbell and Niebuhr offer only passing criticisms of transactional understanding, and the alternatives to circular hermeneutics considered by Kuhn all seem thoroughly theoretical. Paul Ricoeur, however, whom I discuss in Chapter 6, is another transformational interpreter who takes transactional understanding seriously.

One way to evaluate what is really at stake in each of these three understandings of love is to revisit one of the most revealing questions that we can ask ourselves about our own view of love: where do we stand on the question of possessiveness? If we assume that love is fundamentally erotic—and by eroticism I mean not primarily sexual desire but the deeper desire to possess the other, to have the beloved for one's own—then a theoretical interpretation will suit us best. That will also be true for the inverse form of love, when the desire is primarily to be held, to be possessed by the other. In either case, the lover presupposes a fundamental dichotomy, an opposition in which one person is active and the other remains passive. Theoretical love marginalizes mutuality and the integrity of the other as other. However common it may be in actual relationships, it hardly seems worthy of the name of love.

Fromm's call for reciprocity in love is certainly a much more plausible and attractive challenge. With his emphasis upon mutual regard for the other and the other's freedom, Fromm expresses the essence of a transactional understanding of love. He grounds this understanding in a strong claim for the priority of brotherly love, a love that both undercuts all exclusivity and inequality and also undergirds all genuine love. Thus the possessiveness of what many take to be normal or natural love is tempered by the ethical demand for brotherly love. For Fromm, brotherly love rules out any question of manipulation, mutual or otherwise. Although he treats love as an art and activity that must be learned, focusing more upon the individual who loves than the actual relation between lovers, Fromm presupposes and points toward the sort of dialogical relationship that is articulated more fully by Martin Buber (Chapter 5).

At first glance, Kierkegaard's emphasis upon love of neighbor seems to echo Fromm's call for brotherly love. Both are universal. Both demand a nonpreferential love for the beloved as the necessary foundation for any and all genuine preferential love, even that in marriage. Fromm, however, understands brotherly love within a context of mutual respect, while Kierkegaard portrays love of neighbor as higher than any reciprocal relationship. For him, all love must be grounded in and derived from love of (from and for) God. We are to love the neighbor simply because God is love and God commands neighbor-love. There is to be absolutely no thought of what our love might accomplish in—or, even less, elicit from—the other. Love of enemy is simply one more version of this neighbor-love. The truth of preferential love lies, therefore, not in its mutuality but in its paradoxical expression of love of God and neighbor. Kierkegaard may actually undermine his own statement about the validity of preferential love within God's love by his harsh comments on reciprocal relationships. If transformational understanding is to be fully paradoxical, then it must embrace what is true in both theoretical and transactional views even as it rejects their shortcomings. Just as Fromm writes much about the love of God but seems to understand only human love, Kierkegaard extols the love of God so exclusively that he risks having it annihilate love among human beings.

5

Dialectics of Identity

This chapter deals with three thinkers for whom dialectic is itself a central theme in at least some of their writings. This allows me to explore that dimension of the typology in greater depth, and to clarify what it means to say that a text is governed by a dialectic of contradiction, reciprocity, or paradox. As in earlier chapters, I have attempted to choose representative texts for each of the writers discussed, but the extent to which the dialectical pattern discernible in a selected text also governs other books by the same writer goes beyond the parameters of this discussion.

The three writers I have chosen for this inquiry are often classified as existentialist philosophers. Although none of them employs that label as a comprehensive self-description, all three are intent upon grounding all abstract statements in the concrete realities of human existence. At times their views on truth and religion seem more psychological than philosophical or theological. This is because they believe that no system of thought is valid unless it addresses the question of what it means to be a person. In terms of my typology, this question becomes an inquiry into three existential dialectics of identity.

I begin with Friedrich Nietzsche, whose rich and varied writings can only be partially represented here. His bold attack on Christian morality and religion as promoting unhealthy, rather than "manly," instincts in *Twilight of the Idols* and *The Anti-Christ,* both written in 1888, is based upon an explicit theoretical embrace of contradiction. Thirty-five years later Martin Buber published *I and Thou,* a work of poetic philosophy that grounds human identity in the reciprocity of relational transactions. It was certainly written in part as a direct and critical response to Nietzsche. Finally, in 1952 Paul Tillich published one of his major works, *The Courage to Be,* in which the fundamental dialectic of identity is portrayed neither as conflicting instincts nor as relationships, but as a transforming and paradoxical unity of despair and faith. All of these writers have exerted incalculable influence on twentieth-century thought, influence extending far beyond the ranks of existentialist philosophers. Together they will help us to probe more deeply the dialectical character of the three types of interpretation.

The Fruitfulness of Contradictions

Numerous themes in the two works by Nietzsche before us could provide a point of departure for this discussion: will, power, instinct, joy, and the "overman" are just a few. I am going to begin with a passage on freedom, a passionate statement that touches on many aspects of Nietzsche's vision:

> For what is freedom? That one has the will to self-responsibility. That one preserves the distance which divides us. That one has become more indifferent to hardship, toil, privation, even to life. That one is ready to sacrifice men to one's cause, oneself not excepted. Freedom means that the manly instincts that delight in war and victory have gained mastery over the other instincts—for example, the instinct for "happiness." The man *who has become free*—and how much more the *mind* that has become free—spurns the contemptible sort of well-being dreamed of by shopkeepers, Christians, cows, women, Englishmen and other democrats. The free man is a *warrior.*—How

freedom is measured, in individuals as in nations? By the resistance which has to be overcome, by the effort it costs to stay *aloft*.[1]

Three aspects of this passage can serve to guide the discussion of Nietzsche's values: responsibility, determination, and vitality. Freedom is, first of all, "the will to self-responsibility." Although Nietzsche has—and certainly cultivated—the image of an antimoralist, a philosopher exposing good and evil as illusions (55), in truth his opposition to morality is firmly grounded in his deep commitment to a different moral vision. In his view, Christian morality and religion have made the mistake of promoting various lists of dos and don'ts (47). Since everyone will at some point fail to satisfy those demands, the result will inevitably be a sense of remorse and humility (21, 26). Nietzsche opposes those attitudes: "conscience" should lead us to step out ahead of others, to assert our own cause boldly, to know what we want, and to work tirelessly for it (26–27). A major mistake of Christian morality is that it makes us accountable to one another and to God. Nietzsche rejects all such accountability (55) in favor of self-responsibility: the self is accountable only to itself, but (and this is critical to understanding him) the self is radically accountable to itself.

Self-responsibility will, according to Nietzsche, "preserve the distance which divides us." Nietzsche boasts (43) that he has succeeded, against Christianity, in spiritualizing both sensuality (by showing that it really is love) and enmity (by showing that it is healthy). The spiritualizing of enmity is neither a Nietzschean version of the Christian injunction to love one's enemies nor an endorsement of the Church's tradition of trying to destroy its enemies. Rather, it asserts "the value of having enemies." For example, "we immoralists and anti-Christians see that it is to our advantage that the Church exist" (43). It is important in life to have enemies to oppose.

What Nietzsche's morality requires above all is determination. Only determination can make us indifferent to the hardships we encounter, hardships that may deprive us of leisure, abundance, or even life itself. Only determination can withstand the pressures exerted by conventional morality and religion to conform to their dictates. Determination is a matter of will: the willpower to resist the need to follow every stimulus (65), and the

1. Friedrich Nietzsche, *Twilight of the Idols* and *The Anti-Christ*, trans. R. J. Hollingdale (London: Penguin Books, 1968), 92. The 1990 edition, with a new introduction by Michael Tanner, is now widely available, but the pagination is inconsistent from printing to printing. Therefore I will give the page numbers from the older edition. In general, add 11 or 12 pages to find a cited passage in the 1990 edition.

will to affirm (non-Christian) tradition and authority, in contrast to the democratic egalitarianism of modern liberalism (93). Determination as the will to power that refuses to submit to the demand for humility is always "ready to sacrifice men to one's cause, oneself not excepted." It is such a total dedication to a cause that no price is too high to pay for its realization.

Yet this determination is the opposite of striving for a purpose. Nietzsche repudiates purposes as abstract ideals that have been invented precisely to keep people from attaining true freedom. Human beings are not created by God or even by themselves in order to become some ideal other than what they are: each of us is simply "a piece of fate" within the matrix of existence (54). It is foolish to demand change in people whose past and future have been determined by fate (46). Nietzsche admires Goethe for his ability to create himself, to embrace the totality of reason, sensuality, feeling, and will, for the skill of his cultural and physical accomplishments, for being a man in whom there was no weakness, "whether that weakness be called vice or virtue" (102–3). Goethe was also a child of fate, but one with healthy instincts who fully embraced his fate: "A spirit thus *emancipated* stands in the midst of the universe with a joyful and trusting fatalism, in the *faith* that only what is separate and individual may be rejected, that in the totality everything is redeemed and affirmed" (103). This, Nietzsche adds, is what he calls Dionysian faith.[2]

This combination of physical prowess and uninhibited joy brings us to the third aspect of freedom: vitality. Nietzsche proclaims the virtues of the warrior: courage, strength, and trust in one's own "manly instincts." The appeal to instinct is central in his thought, and deserves examination. It is not a denial of the importance of mind. In the passage quoted at the beginning of this discussion, Nietzsche emphasizes that freedom of the mind concerns him most of all. But the Nietzschean mind is quite different from that of most philosophers, for it is a mind attuned to instincts rather than to ideals.

Nietzsche indicates just how critical instinct is for him in a passage in which he opposes fate to moral free will: "[A] 'happy one' *must* perform certain actions and instinctively shrinks from other actions, he transports the order of which he is the physiological representative into his relations with other human beings and with things" (48). At another point he remarks that morality can be either healthy or antinatural, depending upon whether

2. In the glossary of names, Hollingdale comments that this description of Goethe "defines the *Übermensch* [overman or superman] more succinctly than any other single passage in Nietzsche's works" (203–4).

it is "dominated by" or turns "*against* the instincts of life" (45). The good instincts come naturally, and "[e]verything *good* is instinct—and consequently easy, necessary, free. Effort is an objection" (48). Likewise, every error reveals that the instincts have already lost their vitality. The maxim that one should not seek one's own advantage is "merely a moral figleaf for a quite different, namely physiological fact: 'I no longer know how to *find* my advantage.'. . . Disintegration of the instincts!" (87).

The references to physiology are a reminder that Nietzsche believes that the instincts are determined by a person's metabolism, and that he advocates the physiological study of animals—including humans—as machines: "[O]ur knowledge of man today is real knowledge precisely to the extent that it is knowledge of him as a machine" (124). But it is also true that there are just as many various instincts as there are diverse states of consciousness. Physical vitality is manifest in the instincts of energy, courage, and the will to power—those "manly instincts that delight in war and victory [and] have gained mastery over the other instincts." Those other instincts are instincts that would lead toward Christian morality and religion. Whereas the instinct toward joyous affirmation of the natural world is healthy, a contrary and decadent instinct for revenge results in rejection of the world, an unhealthy mental state that is shared by Christians and socialists (87).

We must return, however, to the instincts of the warrior. Only the warrior is truly free, and the only way to measure the extent of freedom in individuals or in nations is by "the resistance that has to be overcome, by the effort it costs to stay *aloft*." The fundamental instinct of the warrior is to dominate, and the drive to dominate is affirmed by Nietzsche in an all-encompassing way. One striking example is his portrayal of marriage as an institution that should be based upon three instincts: "the sexual drive, the drive to own property (wife and child considered as property), [and] the *drive to dominate* which continually organizes . . . the family . . . in a physiological sense . . . for a solidarity of instinct between the centuries" (94). He concludes that modern marriage is no longer secure in its indissolubility, as all strong institutions must be, because it is now based upon the idiosyncrasy of romantic feelings and the momentary passions that follow from them.

The fault for this state of affairs, according to Nietzsche, lies not with marriage but with modernity. In contrast to Goethe's embrace of the totality of his life, physical as well as cultural, the "modern" person is decadent by virtue of a "physiological self-contradiction" in which "instincts contradict, disturb, and destroy one another" (95). Nietzsche is a prophet of opposition, but he does not endorse indiscriminately any and every self-contradiction. He even likes to think of himself as having an affirmative nature, one that engages in "contradiction and criticism only indirectly and when compelled" (64–65). What compels him is the way in which modern instincts undermine the ability of manly instincts to overcome resistance—to achieve freedom by dominating one's unhealthy instincts and unhealthy pressures from others, rather than submit to domination by them.

Nietzsche's dialectic of opposition—his call to overcome resistance—is of a piece with his assertion of the value of having enemies to resist. His attack upon morality and religion is based upon the contradiction between his demand that individuals be self-responsible and the Christian or democratic/socialist demand that individuals subordinate their wills to God or to the majority of the people. Nietzsche approves of tradition and authority insofar as they establish a hierarchy in society within which individuals can find their natural and rightful place according to their own will to power over against the will to power of others. The reason that extraordinary determination is necessary is that the resistances to be overcome are so strong. Each individual must be a warrior because life itself is warfare. Opposition permeates every aspect of Nietzsche's thought. He is implacably suspicious of anything resembling peace: "One is *fruitful* only at the cost of being rich in contradictions; one remains *young* only on condition the soul does not relax, does not long for peace" (44). Peace of soul is desired by Christians, who want nothing more than "the moral cow and the fat contentment of the good conscience. . . . One has renounced *grand* life when one renounces war" (44).

This praise for war and contradiction does not lead Nietzsche to affirm dialectical reasoning. His contempt for dialectic echoes his dismissal of modernity as a morass of self-contradictions. The self-contradictions of both are born not of the freedom of a strong will to power but out of the instinct for revenge, the desire of the weaker to overcome the nobler: "[W]ith dialectics the rabble gets on top" (31). One example of this rabble was Socrates (30); another was Plato (106). In both philosophers, Nietzsche complains, the healthy Hellenic instincts had atrophied. He even calls Plato "an antecedent Christian" (106), for he opposed the "*noble* morality" in favor of a "*ressentiment* [resentment] morality" (135) that is characteristic of the Judeo-Christian spirit.

Nietzsche diagnoses the illness of Socrates and Plato—and of all dialectical thinkers—as a loss of trust in the senses. The senses "do not lie at all. It is what we *make* of their evidence that first introduces a lie into it, for example the lie of unity, the lie of materiality, of substance, of duration. . . . 'Reason' is the cause of our falsification of the evidence of the senses" (36). This condemnation is aimed at Heraclitus, although it was Socrates who elevated rationality to the status of a tyrant and savior, and with it moralism and dialectics (33). From Socrates to Hegel, the philosophical tradition has accepted reason's preference for abstract concepts over the concrete evidence of the senses.

Nietzsche's attack upon dialectical reason is not a call for abandonment of one's mind, as his own extraordinarily energetic thinking shows. What he opposes is the hegemony of reason over the senses, in contrast to the nobler path of subordinating reason to the senses and the healthy instincts. In fact, Nietzsche calls for educators who can teach the young to see, think, speak, and write, for these will produce "a noble culture" (65), not one based upon sentiment or arbitrary power. This praise for the immediacy of healthy instincts and sense experience over the abstractions of reason and language also entails a call for clarity of thought.

According to Nietzsche, Jesus was a teacher who denied the senses and demonstrated a physiological condition of "instinctive hatred of *every* reality" in favor of "a merely 'inner' world, a 'real' world, an 'eternal' world. . . . 'The kingdom of God *is within you*'" (141). This hatred of reality combines with a repudiation of enmity to produce the doctrine of redemption (142), a redemption in which "there are no more opposites" (144), no struggle, merely childlike faith. For Nietzsche, such faith is mere childishness, a symptom of "retarded puberty" (144) in which all the noble and warrior instincts are denied. Jesus, unlike Socrates and Plato, was no rationalist and no dialectician; yet his reduction of the realities of the world to the status of mere signs and symbols of an inner world equally undermines the manly instincts: "*Christian* values—[vs.] *noble* values: it is only we, we *emancipated* spirits, who have restored this greatest of all value-antitheses!" (149). Nietzsche concedes that Jesus (but only Jesus) actually lived according to his gospel of self-denial. Others who call themselves Christians suffer from "a psychological misunderstanding" (151). They are simply hiding their unhealthy instincts toward revenge beneath a shield of self-deceiving faith.

The rationality of Socrates and Plato, the inwardness of Jesus' teaching, and the hypocrisy of Christian faith all lead Nietzsche to what Paul Ricoeur has aptly called his "hermeneutics of suspicion."[3] As these two passages

---

3. Paul Ricoeur, *Hermeneutics and the Human Sciences,* ed. and trans. John B. Thompson (Cambridge: Cambridge University Press, 1981), 34.

show, he is equally suspicious of moral judgments and of claims to interpret the meaning of texts:

> To this extent moral judgment is never to be taken literally: as such it never contains anything but nonsense. But as *semeiotics* it remains of incalculable value; it reveals, to the informed man at least, the most precious realities of cultures and inner worlds which did not *know* enough to "understand" themselves. Morality is merely sign-language, merely symptomatology: one must already know *what* it is about to derive profit from it. (55)

> He who does not know how to put his will into things at least puts a *meaning* into them: that is, he believes there is a will in them already (principle of "belief"). (24)

Moral judgment is a symptom that can be diagnosed or decoded, but interpretation is triply false in its effort to discern a meaning. First, the interpreter engages in a self-betrayal by not knowing "how to put his own will into things." Second, the attribution of meaning to a text is a self-deception, for it denies that the interpreter is actually the one who has put a meaning into the text. Third, the affirmation of such meanings constitutes belief, namely, the belief that there is already another will at work in the text. But belief is always the opposite of truth (132). The hermeneutical truth that Nietzsche would endorse is presumably the demand that we approach every text as warriors, confident in our own ability to overcome all resistance and to know what the text is about quite apart from the author's understanding or any other obstacles or distractions.

However affirmative Nietzsche may consider his message, it is clear that these texts are resolutely oppositional as statements of truth. Nietzsche's own fruitfulness is that he is superlatively rich in contradictions, that he courageously opposes virtually all Western philosophy, morality, and religion, and that he does so not with the resentment of a defender of a lost cause but with all the conviction and exuberance of a victorious warrior. Perhaps the appearance of a contradiction between his claim to be affirmative and his unrelenting opposition is based upon a misunderstanding. Nietzsche is often condemned as a nihilist, who denies all meaning and truth. But surely that does not do justice to his joy in noble instincts and his affirmation of truth over against belief. His opposition to rationalistic philosophy and Christian faith comes not from a despairing nihilism but from the strength of his embrace of values that are best described as proudly pagan. Nietzsche certainly prefers to be affirmative rather than contradictory where the values of self-responsibility, determination, and vitality are concerned. Together they result in a freedom that he joyously celebrates.

This freedom of self is based upon a dialectic of opposition. Nietzsche's theoretical vision of human identity is structured by a series of contradictions: self-responsibility vs. accountability to others, determination vs. submission, vitality vs. atrophy of the manly instincts, understanding vs. interpretation, truth vs. belief—the list is almost endless. He sees every problem in terms of resistance, a challenge to be overcome, an opportunity to assert one's own will. Nietzsche never seeks compromise or even recognizes the need for, or fact of, reciprocal interdependence, let alone the inexorable reality of personal vulnerability. He utterly repudiates the moral or ethical concerns that drive transactional interpretation.

Although Nietzsche does not explicitly extend his love of contradiction to the relation between objectivity and subjectivity, his attack upon reason for its tendency to abstract from the senses, coupled with an aphoristic style that rarely develops an argument in the ordinary rational manner, shows that a subjective theoretical orientation guides *Twilight of the Idols* and *The Anti-Christ.* Nietzsche's physiological determinism is, to be sure, an objective element in his thinking, as is, for Barthes, the semiotic system according to whose rules the lover encounters the beloved. But the constant embrace of contradiction coupled with the refusal to acknowledge any objective rational methods by which his own pronouncements might be validated confirm the subjective theoretical character of Nietzsche's dialectic of identity.

It might appear that Nietzsche's use of contradiction is more transformational than theoretical. Certainly he refers often to the need for transformation. But note what he has in mind: "The man in this condition transforms things until they mirror his power—until they are reflections of his perfection" (72). This transformation is really a manipulation of "things"—ideas, texts, other people—so that they will become mere reflections of one's own will, power, and perfection. The conquering self is not transformed, nor is the conquest of the other likely to promote a transformation welcome to the other, who experiences only defeat, perhaps even annihilation. To speak of this as a dialectic of transformation is like claiming that war is a nurturing relationship. Of course, that is exactly Nietzsche's point. Enmity is good. War is the natural and proper state of human relations. The dialectic here is one of unrelenting opposition, not paradoxical unity.

Nietzsche repudiates dialectic because to him it always means an internal division or contradiction that allows the weaker to triumph over the stronger. To him, fruitful contradictions are those between the noble warrior and the forces that oppose him, not those within his own soul. Nietzsche does not seek a higher unity within these contradictions, even when he extols the Dionysian faith in fate as the redemption of everything within the totality. Fate is an impersonal force that makes no effort to take the transactional dialectic of identity up into itself. Dionysian faith follows inevitably from healthy instincts, not from choices made by a person on the basis of moral reflection. The transformation sought by Nietzsche will not reveal meaning, purpose, and a transcendent spirit. It will bring displacements and discontinuities. Nietzsche is a theoretical thinker who delights in contradictions and believes that they are fruitful as they stand. He remains deeply suspicious of all reciprocal or paradoxical efforts to overcome them.

Relationship as Reciprocity

A transition from theoretical to transactional dialectics of existence appears in a statement by Nietzsche that Martin Buber quotes twice: "'One accepts, one does not ask who gives.'"[4] For Nietzsche, this characterization of the process of inspiration or even "revelation" is one "that merely describes the facts," and the key facts are "necessity" and a total absence of choice.[5] Inspiration is an experience that simply happens to creative people. For Buber, it is a relationship: he agrees that one does not question the identity of the giver, but nevertheless one emphatically gives thanks (K:176, S:129).

What is received in such a transaction? It is, Buber continues, "a Presence

4. *I and Thou*, trans. Walter Kaufmann (New York: Charles Scribner's Sons, 1970), 158, 176. See also the 1958 translation by Ronald Gregor Smith (same publisher), 110, 129. I shall use both translations, referring to them parenthetically in the text as, for example, K:158 and S:110, citing first the translation that I have quoted (where appropriate). Not surprisingly, Smith emphasizes the theistic dimension of *I and Thou* that Kaufmann sometimes suppresses (for example, Smith will capitalize nouns such as "Center" or "Face," whereas Kaufmann does not). But Kaufmann is much more sensitive than Smith to Buber's use of traditional Jewish concepts (e.g., *teshuva*, K:107 and S:58; see note 8 below). References to the German text of *Ich und Du* are to Buber's *Werke*, vol. 1, *Schriften zur Philosophie* (Munich: Kösel-Verlag, 1962).

5. The statement is from part 3 of the section on *Thus Spoke Zarathustra* in *Ecce Homo*, in *Basic Writings of Nietzsche*, ed. and trans. Walter Kaufmann (New York: Modern Library, 1968), 756.

as power" that includes three things: first, "the whole fullness of real mutual action, of the being raised and bound up in relation"; second, "the inexpressible confirmation of meaning"; and third, the realization that this meaning can be received for this life but not experienced as something abstract that is not part of one's own concrete existence (S:110, K:158–59). It seems that Buber has quoted Nietzsche in order to turn his statement against him: the reason we do not ask who gives, he says, is because the fullness of relation, of meaning, and of concrete existence in the transaction are so profound. Receiving inspiration is not a matter of fate. It is the fruit of a relationship that is much deeper than any asking or any answer could express.

Buber's greatest contribution to contemporary thought is his development of the distinction between I-It experience and I-Thou relationships,[6] a distinction that corresponds to that between theoretical and transactional interpretation. An I-It experience is one in which the subject treats the other as an object, not as another subject. The I uses the It to achieve a goal, often a good and even important goal such as "the sustaining, relieving, and equipping of human life" (S:38, K:88). Without such I-It events, science and technology would be impossible, for they are based upon the concept of causal connections, and causality has "an unlimited reign in the world of *It*" (S:51, K:100). Furthermore, the histories of individuals and of cultures "both signify a progressive increase of the It-world" (K:87, S:37), and this increase is indeed a form of progress in terms of our ability to control and manipulate our environment.

Buber normally refers to the I-It dynamic as an experience rather than a relation. Experience is what happens when we acquire knowledge of something: "Man goes over the surfaces of things and experiences them. . . . He experiences what there is to things" (K:55, S:5), indifferent to whether those things are referred to as he, she, or it. It also does not matter whether the things experienced are inner or outer, mysterious or mundane: "The world as experience belongs to the basic I-It" (K:56, S:6); "any experience, no matter how spiritual, could only yield us an It" (K:125, S:77).

This experience of an objective It also shows why every interpretation of meaning that is determined by the subject alone is theoretical in character. According to Buber, such experience is located in the subject who has it, not in the object experienced or even in the space between the subject and

6. In 1841, Ludwig Feuerbach referred in passing to the religious consciousness as "the pregnant, complete unity of *I* and *thou*." See *The Essence of Christianity,* trans. George Eliot (New York: Harper & Row, 1957), 66. In contrast, Buber made the I-Thou relation the center of his philosophy.

the object (K:56, S:5). Only the subject really participates in an experience, for experience presupposes a consciousness of the experience that only the subject can have: "[W]hen the *I* of the relation has stepped forth and taken on separate existence. . . . Only now can the conscious act of the *I* take place. This act is the first form of the primary word *I-it*, of the experience in its relation to *I*" (S:23, K:74). The key to all theoretical interpretation—whether the result it seeks foregrounds the interpreted object (objective) or the interpreting subject (subjective)—is the control that the subject exercises over the entire hermeneutical operation.

An I-Thou relation is the opposite of this I-It experience. We experience nothing, but know everything, of the Thou that encounters us, for whatever we know of it we know not as a particular piece of information but as part of a relation that binds us together, a relation that is immediate and comes by grace, not by seeking (K:61–62, S:11). In other words, the I in no way controls the relation with the Thou. It is a communication in which the integrity of the other as other is never questioned.

As communication, the I-Thou relation would seem to be a language event. For Buber, however, speech is thoroughly ambiguous: "[M]any a spoken You really means an It to which one merely says You from habit, thoughtlessly. And many a spoken It really means a You whose presence one may remember with one's whole being, although one is far away" (K:111, S:62).[7] There is no language as such that can be trusted to preserve the freedom of the Thou and the pure immediacy of the I-Thou relation. To respond in speech to the Thou will bind the Thou over to the It-world. Silence alone can do justice to the power of the relation in its present being (K:89, S:39).

Nevertheless, speech is fundamental to human relations. While relations with nature are prelinguistic and those with spiritual beings have to create speech, relations among human beings enter fully into language (K:150, S:101). Buber sees in the scientific progress of the modern world a regress for language, since objectivizing speech has now replaced the more interpersonal expressions of so-called primitive peoples (S:17–18, K:69–70). The example he offers is the contrast between the modern "I am away" and the Zulu "someone crying out 'Mother, I am lost.'" Buber is not calling for a romantic return to premodern immediacy; he is attempting to show how

7. Kaufmann translates *Du* as "You" rather than "Thou," since "Thou" in English has now generally lost the intimacy that *Du* still carries in German. But "You" also lacks that intimacy, and so I will, with Smith, employ "Thou" except when quoting Kaufmann's translation.

inadequate modern theoretical language is to the full reality of human relationships. Indeed, it would be inaccurate to characterize the I-It as evil except in situations where it claims to be the truth of I-Thou relations (S:46, K:95). Buber admits that, just as all I-Thou relations inevitably slip into I-It experiences, an I-It experience can also be "transfigured to the point where it confronts and represents the You" (K:99, S:50). In history, however, the general direction seems to be away from I-Thou relations and toward I-It experience, which is due to the "decrease of man's power to enter into relation" (S:43, K:92).

I-Thou is the first "primary word," and it precedes the consciousness of the I. The I-It primary word comes after and out of the consciousness of the I, and is therefore always secondary to I-Thou (S:22, K:74). For Buber, this sequence is also manifest in the priority of person over individuality (Kaufmann: ego). Individuality is the self-consciousness of the using, experiencing subject within the I-It primary word. A person becomes self-conscious as a subjective person in relationship with other persons within the I-Thou primary word (S:62, K:112). Persons certainly have unique characteristics every bit as much as individuals do, but it is individuals that identify with those characteristics, whereas persons identify themselves simply as persons who exist in relation, without focusing upon unique traits (S:64, K:114). Although Buber concedes that no actual man or woman will ever be merely an individual or completely a person, the universal duality within each self will always reveal that self's character by emphasizing one pole or the other.

Whereas individuality may attain the control over objects that comes with particularizing analysis, it will also find itself enmeshed in the same deterministic web of causality that makes such (theoretical) analysis possible. This oppression can be escaped only by the person who "is not limited to the world of *It*, but can continually leave it for the world of relation," a world where freedom preempts causality by virtue of the power of decision (S:51, K:100–101). Buber opposes the notion of fate just as ardently as Nietzsche advocates it. The concept of return is no doubt the most succinct expression of this difference:[8] whereas Nietzsche's subscribes to a theory of causal determinism, Buber's return is a decision that can be made only in freedom

---

8. Return (*teshuva*) is as central to Jewish spirituality as turning or conversion is to Christianity, which makes Smith's choice of "turning" quite unfortunate, to say nothing of the fact that "return" is the usual translation of *Umkehr* (for this passage, see *Werke*, 1:160). For an analysis of the Jewish elements in *I and Thou*, see S. Daniel Breslauer's *Chrysalis of Religion: A Guide to the Jewishness of Buber's* I and Thou (Nashville: Abingdon, 1980).

and faith: "But the God-side of the event whose world-side is called return is called redemption" (K:168, S:119–20).

This reference to God recalls the second aspect of the Presence as power mentioned above, the "inexpressible confirmation of meaning" that results from inspiration: "Meaning is assured. Nothing can any longer be meaningless" (S:110, K:158). This meaning, Buber explains, is not a kind of knowledge that can be articulated and defended; yet it is more certain for the person who receives it than sense perceptions can ever be. Meaning is always a gift, always bestowed upon a person by the Giver. The connection between all meaning and the grace of God is illustrated by Buber's remark about the I-Thou in marriage, which "will never be given new life except by that out of which true marriage always arises, the revealing by two people of the *Thou* to one another. Out of this a marriage is built up by the *Thou* that is neither of the *I's*" (S:45–46, K:95). Every genuine I-Thou encounter is a meeting with the eternal Thou (S:6, K:57), which is the source of all meaning.

Another example is Buber's understanding of decision. We have already seen that the It-world is bound by causality, while the world of relation offers freedom through decision. This, too, is a matter of the relation to God: "Only he who knows relation and knows about the presence of the Thou is capable of decision. He who decides is free, for he has approached the Face [of God]" (S:51, K:100–101). This freedom extends beyond the merely personal aspects of life to such objective endeavors as politics and economics, which should remain in touch with the Thou in a "living relationship to the center" (K:98, S:49). Every genuine engagement with the world is an encounter with God, who embraces the world and all the persons in it. To separate God from the world is to relegate them both to the I-It realm of experience (S:95, K:95).

It is not immediately clear, however, how Buber understands the dynamics of this relation with God. On the one hand, he insists that it is not adequate to think of God theoretically as a mere principle (e.g., Being), idea, or mental construct: God "enters into direct relationship to us human beings through creative, revelatory, and redemptive acts, and thus makes it possible for us to enter into a direct relationship to him" (K:181, S:135). Likewise, the Thou that is realized in every relation is "consummated only in the direct relation with the *Thou* that by its nature cannot become *It*" (S:75, K:123). On the other hand, this direct relation is strictly qualified: "Although we on earth never behold God without world but only the world in God, by beholding we eternally form God's form" (K:166–67, S:118). The reason for this qualification involves the difference between the eternal

Thou and ordinary Thous. Whereas an individual Thou will always become
an It after "the event of relation has run its course" (K:84, S:84), the eternal Thou can never become an It; God can never be an object of experience (S:112, K:160). The tension for Buber is between an immediate
relation with God as Thou, which he emphatically affirms, and a direct
experience of God as a divine It, which he just as firmly rejects.

Buber's concern about the danger of all such claims for direct experiences of God echoes the condemnations of idolatry by the biblical prophets.
It also accounts for the long critique of mystical absorption, or immersion,[9]
in *I and Thou* (S:83–95, K:131–43), a section that is difficult to follow primarily
due to its use of mystical terms with relatively little clarification. Buber
begins with a series of nine contrasts between two types of absorption. One
is absorption through unification, which takes the self beyond the duality
of I and Thou; the other is absorption as identification, in which the duality
is not even acknowledged as a real starting point. In both, the fundamental
I-Thou relation is abolished. In his further development of these contrasting versions of absorption, Buber associates the first with the Gospel of John
and the second with the Upanishads and Buddhist doctrine. This leads him
back to a more general question: the status of mysticism as an experience
of unity without duality.

Here we arrive at the heart of Buber's concern. He is predictably critical
of the two theories of absorption, since they both seem to him to devalue
the primary word of I-Thou. But Buber refuses to identify all mysticism with
absorption. He confesses that he had once done so, but has now come to see
the difference between absorption through unification, which transcends
the I-Thou relation by asserting that two have become one; and a mysticism
of the soul by itself, in which the soul gathers all its energies into itself in
order to be able to "go out to the meeting" (S:86, K:134). This mystical exercise is preliminary to the I-Thou encounter, and is a unification only within
the soul as it prepares to meet the other. For Buber, this also reveals the
error of the claim made for absorption as unification with the other: "What
the ecstatic calls unification is the rapturous dynamics of the relationship;

---

9. Kaufmann considers "immersion" a great improvement over Smith's "absorption"
for Buber's *Versenkung* (K:125–26 n. 4). This is one of many interesting differences
between the translations. Certainly "immersion" is linguistically a better fit and is an
important term in Neoplatonic mysticism. Yet *Versenkung* can mean "absorbed in thought"
and, perhaps by extension from this usage, seems to be a more common term in mystical literature in general for the experience of loss of consciousness of self by virtue of
being solely conscious of Being or God. Curiously, Kaufmann also translates *versinken*
as "drown," as in "I and You drown" (K:134; *Werke,* 1:136).

not a unity that has come into being at this moment in world time, fusing[10] I and You, but the dynamics of the relationship itself" (K:135, S:87).

Buber's reluctance to see in the immediate relation with the eternal Thou an equally immediate experience of, or absorption in, that Thou is due both to his commitment to the priority of the I-Thou over the I-It and to his conviction that the eternal Thou meets us in every I-Thou relation. An opposition is often asserted between exclusivity and inclusivity in concepts of God. For Buber, however, "[i]n the relation with God unconditional exclusiveness and unconditional inclusiveness are one" (S:78, K:127). God is the eternal Thou who is the basis for all I-Thou relations. To speak of God as either beyond the world or in the world is to employ language that is appropriate only to the realm of It: "[B]ut to eliminate or leave behind nothing at all, to include the whole world in the *Thou*, to give the world its due and its truth, to include nothing beside God but everything in him— this is full and complete relation" (S:79, K:127). This brings us back to the first of the three elements of the Presence as power: "the whole fullness of real mutual action, of the being raised and bound up in relation."

The union of exclusiveness and inclusiveness in God is an example of the way in which Buber's language of relation sometimes implies a paradoxical understanding. Prima facie, relationships would seem to be based so squarely on "real mutual action" that they would inevitably be reciprocal in nature. But there are numerous points in *I and Thou* where a dialectic of paradox appears to be present. Is Buber better understood as a transactional or as a transformational thinker, or perhaps as a mixed type in which neither side clearly predominates?

Buber unequivocally embraces a paradox when he asserts that the tension between freedom and necessity is not to be resolved by abstract thought: it is an indissoluble antinomy or contradiction for the person who, standing before God, fully grasps the extent to which choosing God is simultaneously a matter of being chosen by God (K:143–44, S:95–96): "The You confronts me. But I enter into a direct relationship to it. Thus the relationship is at once being chosen and choosing, passive and active" (K:124–25, S:76). This paradox of the will in relation to God is restated in terms of feelings: the feeling of absolute dependence coexists with the feeling of utter freedom, and the feeling of being created, with that of being creative. As Buber succinctly puts it: "If one starts out from the soul, the perfect relationship

10. The German is *verschmilzt* (*Werke*, 1:137), which Smith renders as "dissolving." The word implies a fusion in which the distinct identities are lost through assimilation.

can only be seen as bipolar, as *coincidentia oppositorum,* as the fusion of oppo-site feelings" (K:130, S:81–82). The paradoxical character of a person before God appears also whenever we think about God as a person. By definition, a person's freedom is relative to the freedom of other persons, a relativity that cannot be true of God: "This contradiction is countered by the paradoxical description of God as the absolute Person, i.e. the Person who cannot be limited. It is as the absolute Person that God enters into direct relationship with us. The contradiction yields to deeper insight" (S:136, K:182).

If Buber were fundamentally a personalist, holding person and person-ality to be ultimate ontological categories, then he would indeed be a para-doxical and transformational thinker. But he is not. In fact, *I and Thou* stands as a far-reaching and profound attack upon any notion of the priority of individual persons.

We have seen that Buber writes of two primary words, the I-Thou and the I-It. From the perspective of classical personalism, the I in these two rela-tions remains constant, even as it moves from the world of the Thou to the world of the It and back again. For Buber, that is a serious misunderstand-ing. A central assertion in *I and Thou* is cast as an allusion to the openings of two biblical books, Genesis and John: "In the beginning is relation" (S: 18, K:69). Although it is true that we become aware of relation only through actual I-Thou encounters and I-It experiences, what they show us is that relation is the foundation and dynamic reality of every encounter and every experience. We are, to be sure, persons. But each of us is a person only by virtue of our concrete life in relation: "There is no I as such but only the I of the basic word I-You and the I of the basic word I-It" (K:54, S:4). This is Buber's constant theme: "Man becomes an I through a You" (K:80, S:28).

Since every I-Thou relation is one in which each I is a Thou and each Thou is equally an I, it is also true that "relation is reciprocity" (K:58, 67; S:8, 15).[11] As we saw in the example of marriage, when a relationship is true it is because both persons are revealing their Thou to the other. There are also negative examples, such as Napoleon, who recognized no reciprocal relation with other Thous and thereby became a "demonic *Thou*" for mil-lions (S:67, K:117). Whenever an I begins to use and to experience a Thou as an It rather than simply to encounter that Thou in relation, then they no longer meet one another in "the current of reciprocity" (K:80, S:29).

Just as reciprocal relations are the context within which persons come to

---

11. Kaufmann uses "reciprocity" for *Gegenseitigkeit* (*Werke,* 1:82), whereas Smith trans-lates it as "mutuality."

be, they are also the prerequisite for human communities. In a discussion of the role of emotions, Buber maintains that feelings alone cannot suffice to create true community among persons. There must be "a living, reciprocal relationship to one another," and this relationship must in turn have its source in "a living, reciprocal relationship to a single living center" (K:94, S:45). In other words, the reciprocity that governs all genuine relationships among persons constitutes the foundation for communities. More radically still, it is the character of the relation between humans and God. In one of his most striking claims, Buber challenges the reader: "But don't you know that God needs you—in the fullness of his eternity, you? How would man exist if God did not need him, and how would you exist? You need God in order to be, and God needs you—for that which is the meaning of your life" (K:130, S:82).

God is the basis of all reciprocity, and the dialectic of reciprocity undergirds the entire structure and message of *I and Thou.* Although paradoxes appear quite often, they are always a result of looking at persons—including God—in terms of their individual nature, feelings, character, and so forth. But to look at persons in this way is to abstract them from the context that alone can give them life. Persons are not primarily paradoxical individuals for Buber; they are beings who exist only by virtue of the relations that have created them. We exist as persons in mutual need with and of other persons. God needs us just as we need God. Buber's dialectic of identity is thoroughly reciprocal and transactional. All the contradictions and paradoxes that he affirms are ultimately revealed to be merely partial perspectives on relationships that are fundamentally reciprocal in character.

Paradoxical Existence

Nietzsche affirms manly instincts over against unhealthy instincts, and Buber calls for dialogical I-Thou relationships. The transformational version of the dialectic of existence that I discuss is found in Paul Tillich's *The Courage to Be,*[12] a series of lectures that explore the following proposition: "The courage to be is the ethical act in which man affirms his own being in spite of those elements of his existence which conflict with his essential self-affirmation"

---

12. Paul Tillich, *The Courage to Be* (New Haven: Yale University Press, 1952), originally given as the Terry Lectures at Yale University.

(3). At first glance, this seems to be an ethics of self-affirmation, somewhat reminiscent of Nietzsche. On closer inspection, however, we see that Tillich joins Buber in affirming the self's existence within community, that he paradoxically unites the individual and the community within faith, and, finally, that he pushes paradox even further with an affirmation of a radical faith that embraces anxiety.

Tillich refers to the relational aspect of human identity as the courage to be as a part. He attributes to "the polar structure of reality" the fact that greater self-relatedness makes a person more capable of such participation (90), which is necessary to be a person: "Only in a continuous encounter with other persons does the person become and remain a person. The place of this encounter is the community" (91). Participation in community is not understood by Tillich as an immediate and direct relation in which the individual has no choice. There are groups, of course, such as families and cultures, into which a person is simply born. But what Tillich has in mind is the courage to affirm oneself as a part of the community in which one participates. It is a conscious choice, an ethical act of will, by which a person acknowledges that individual existence is itself mediated through the community. There can be no life that is utterly solitary. When carried too far, this side of human existence results in collectivist societies in which the individual is understood as nothing more than a member of the group. Tillich discusses several examples: the Middle Ages, such "neocollectivist" movements as Nazism and Communism, and even what he calls "democratic conformism" (103).

The courage to be as a part both affirms and denies Buber's transactional I-Thou encounter. With Buber, Tillich acknowledges the priority of relation. Participation is prerequisite to becoming a person. This is no doubt why he treats the participatory pole of the structure of reality first: self-relatedness can be achieved only by a person who is already in community. But Tillich disagrees with Buber about the immediacy of relation. In his view, participation is always mediated: there can be no immediate relation with any Thou, for all relation occurs within the context of some sort of community. The religious implications of this difference are instructive. For Buber, the relation with the eternal Thou is realized by inference from the direct relations that we have with many other human Thous. It is affirmed as the immediate ground of all I-Thou relations, but Buber denies that we can encounter the eternal Thou directly. Tillich agrees that the courage to be as a part will not lead to a direct encounter with God, but it can open us to a mystical union with the ground of being.

However, the courage to be as a part is only one pole of Tillich's dialectic of identity. Equally important is the pole of self-relatedness, or individualization, "the self-affirmation of the individual self without regard to its participation in its world" (113), which is also called the courage to be as oneself. Tillich explores the courage to be as oneself as it emerged in the Enlightenment's embrace of "the individual self as the bearer of reason" (116), in Romanticism's courageous admission of personal guilt and even the presence of a "demonic depth" within the creative genius of the individual (122), and in existentialism, which is "the most radical form of the courage to be as oneself" (123).

According to Tillich, the great achievement of existentialism is the repudiation of essentialist philosophies that tend to underplay (by claiming to transcend) "the finitude, the estrangement, and the ambiguities of human existence" (125). Sartre's statement that "'the essence of man is his existence'" is praised as "the most despairing and the most courageous sentence in all Existentialist literature," for it proclaims that "there is no essential nature of man. . . . Man creates what he is." Thus "the courage to be as oneself is the courage to make of oneself what one wants to be" (149–50). Just as the courage to be as a part can be carried to an extreme where the self is lost in a collectivity, the existentialist courage to be as oneself, which includes the admirable courage to despair, can also go too far, and ultimately lose the world in which it exists and without which it cannot survive (154).

Like Nietzsche, Tillich believes that the polar opposition between participation and individualism is too radical to be reconciled in a dialectic of reciprocity. Against Nietzsche, however, Tillich maintains that the courage to be as oneself, if not held in a balance or at least a tension with the courage to be as a part, will ultimately destroy itself as a result of becoming totally alienated from its world, especially the social world in which it must live. Tillich's desire to hold participation and individualism together in their binary relationship is especially clear when he addresses the religious experience that corresponds to the courage to be as oneself: "The pole of individualization expresses itself in the religious experience as a personal encounter with God. And the courage derived from it is the courage of confidence in the personal reality which is manifest in the religious experience. In contradistinction to the mystical union one can call this relation a personal communion with the source of courage. Although the two types are in contrast, they do not exclude each other. For they are united by the polar interdependence of individualization and participation" (160).

Tillich goes on to criticize the Protestant tendency to identify faith with this experience of and belief in a personal God who gives courage to individuals. Faith should embrace both individualization and participation (172), both the encounter with God and mystical union with God. Indeed, it is faith alone that is really capable of uniting the two types of religious experience and the two types of human courage. It does this in a third form of courage, the transformational "courage to accept acceptance," which appears as the culmination of *The Courage to Be:* "Faith is the state of being grasped by the power of being-itself. The courage to be is an expression of faith and what 'faith' means must be understood through the courage to be. We have defined faith as the self-affirmation of being in spite of non-being. The power of this self-affirmation is the power of being which is effective in every act of courage. Faith is the experience of this power. But it is an experience which has a paradoxical character, the character of accepting acceptance" (172).

In this passage, Tillich relates faith to both its expression and to its source in being-itself, which is his preferred term for the Ultimate. A constant theme in his writings is that the word "God" is not adequate to the Ultimate, both because it has been so misused and abused and because positive and particularistic beliefs about God limit the Ultimate and thereby deny its unconditional ultimacy. Significantly, Tillich does continue to use the word God when referring to the theistic God of personal encounter as one aspect of the courage to be as oneself. He also frequently resorts to the paradoxical phrase "the God above the God of theism" (188, 189, 190) to express the relation of being-itself to the concepts of God found in particular religions (including Christianity). But this phrase is paradoxical only in the ironic sense that it appears to undercut precisely what it is affirming (or to affirm what it is questioning).

The positive and transformational paradox in Tillich's analysis emerges into full view in his discussion of the source and nature of faith as mature human identity: "Faith is the experience of this power [of being-itself]," Tillich writes (using the word "experience" in a receptive, rather than in Buber's objectifying, sense). We have already seen that neither mystical experience nor the experience of an encounter with God is adequate to faith, which paradoxically embraces them both. So how is this experience of faith an actual experience? According to the definition with which Tillich began, faith is the self's ethical act of affirmation rather than an experience of a power that transcends the self. In ordinary usage, ethical acts are performed rather than experienced, and transcendental powers may be experienced but lie beyond our powers of performance. If faith is an ethical act

that is the highest form of the courage to be, it is not really an experience
at all. It is the decision to accept the fact that one is accepted, an affirmation
of being in the face of nonbeing. This is emphasized in a passage near the
end of *The Courage to Be* in which Tillich denies that this Ultimate can ever
be a discrete object of faith:

> Absolute faith, or the state of being grasped by the God beyond
> God, is not a state which appears beside other states of the mind.
> It never is something separated and definite, an event which could
> be isolated and described. It is always a movement in, with, and
> under other states of mind. . . . It is not a place where one can live,
> it is without the safety of words and concepts, it is without a name,
> a church, a cult, a theology. But it is moving in the depth of all of
> them. It is the power of being, in which they participate and of which
> they are fragmentary expressions. (188–89)

We come at last to that aspect of *The Courage to Be* which sounds almost
as original and startling in Tillich's words as it did when Kierkegaard made
a similar proposal a century earlier: that anxiety is the concrete experience
and existential reality that completes the dialectic of identity by making
faith and conscious awareness of faith possible.[13] We have seen that Tillich
begins his essay with the proposition that "[t]he courage to be is the ethical
act in which man affirms his own being in spite of those elements of his
existence which conflict with his essential self-affirmation" (3). Anxiety is at
the core of all those elements in spite of which one must affirm one's own
being. Although the rhetoric implies an ethic of courageous self-affirmation,
courage could hardly exist in a reciprocal interdependence with anxiety.
But if Tillich identifies faith itself as a transformation of anxiety, then his
dialectic of existence goes beyond contradiction and reciprocity to paradox.

Paradoxical unity has already appeared in the courage to accept acceptance. This third type of courage, which Tillich identifies with faith, transcends and unites the courage to be as a part and the courage to be as
oneself. Mystical participation and individualistic encounter meet in faith.
They are no longer a simple binary opposition. But they are also not balanced or harmonized in a reciprocal fashion. They remain distinct from
and even in tension with one another, although they are now seen to be two

---

13. See Søren Kierkegaard, *The Concept of Anxiety,* trans. Reidar Thomte (Princeton:
Princeton University Press, 1980), 155–62. Kierkegaard and Tillich share a positive view
of anxiety but reach very different conclusions about how it leads to faith.

poles in a larger dynamic unity, the unity of faith. The claim is that these opposing poles simultaneously and paradoxically constitute a unity.

Just as there are three types of the courage to be and three corresponding types of religious experience, there are also three types of anxiety: fate, doubt, and guilt. Each represents one of the three ways in which nonbeing can and does threaten being. The anxiety of fate occurs when there is a threat to our simple ("ontic") self-affirmation or existence.[14] In its extreme form the anxiety of fate is the awareness of the possibility of death. Tillich introduces the anxiety of doubt as an anxiety of emptiness and meaninglessness (46), a threat to our spiritual self-affirmation and to our "ultimate concern," which is "a meaning which gives meaning to all meanings" (47). In its extreme form, the anxiety of doubt can become existential despair (48), which reminds us that Tillich's native German expresses despair (*Verzweiflung*) as an intensification of (the word for) doubt (*Zweifel*). Finally, the anxiety of guilt is produced by a threat to moral self-affirmation. In its extreme form, it is experienced as self-rejection or condemnation (52).

Tillich's discussion of the moral form of anxiety—the anxiety of guilt—shows how thoroughly he rejects a traditional Christian understanding of God. He clearly states that the anxiety of guilt occurs not in relation to judgment by God but in a situation of self-judgment (51). Moreover, Tillich denies that good and evil can be sharply distinguished from one another. Guilt arises not from the consciousness of having sinned, as in classical Christian understanding, but from an awareness of the "ambiguity between good and evil" that permeates all of personal life (52).

Tillich does not indicate that the three types of anxiety correspond to the types of the courage to be and religious experience. The anxieties of fate, doubt, and guilt can each beset the courage to be as a part, the courage to be as oneself, or the courage to accept acceptance; and all three forms of the courage to be can overcome any of the three forms of anxiety. For example, the courage to be as a part of a group can "take into" itself the anxiety of fate and personal death with the promise of a collective immortality, the

14. By "ontic," Tillich means "being in its simple existence," in contrast to the sort of philosophical analysis of being that is generally referred to as "ontological" (42). The difference here is between unreflective (ontic) consciousness of objects and (ontological) reflection upon the relation between those objects and our objective consciousness of them. This distinction between "ontic" and "ontological" had been discussed two years before Tillich published *The Courage to Be* by Martin Heidegger in *Hegels Begriff der Erfahrung,* published in *Holzwege* (Frankfurt: Vittorio Klostermann, 1950), 161–63, and translated as *Hegel's Concept of Experience* by Kenley Royce Dove (New York: Harper & Row, 1970), 105–8.

anxiety of doubt with "neocollectivist courage," and the anxiety of guilt with a blanket forgiveness for anything that is done in the interests of the group (100–102). However, Tillich does not claim that such participation can ever dispel totally the anxieties of fate, doubt, or guilt. In each case, the anxiety in question is simply "taken into" the particular form of the courage to be. Although Tillich had made himself a master of English style by the time he gave the Terry Lectures, it may be that "taken into" is his rendering of the German *aufgehoben*, a notoriously ambiguous word that means "taken up" in two contrary senses: to be taken away and thus to have perished, or to be taken up into and thus be preserved (as occurs when fruit is preserved). Tillich may be trading on this ambiguity, implying that the courage to be as a part takes the three forms of anxiety up into itself in such a way that they all both perish and are preserved at the same time.

This notion of transcendence as the paradox of simultaneously perishing and being preserved appears again in Tillich's discussion of the way in which faith unites participation and individualization: "If participation is dominant, the relation to being-itself has a mystical character, if individualization prevails the relation to being-itself has a personal character, if both poles are accepted and transcended the relation to being-itself has the character of faith" (156–57). Both poles must be accepted, while their merely contradictory relation is transcended. Faith is the dialectical culmination and paradoxical unity of the two opposing poles of participation and individualization. This is an excellent example of a paradoxical dialectic in which both poles are transformed by virtue of being *aufgehoben* in a higher unity: each must perish as simply the negation of the other in order that both may be preserved as aspects of a new unity. It is faith that accomplishes this transformation.[15]

To recapitulate: faith, which is the courage to accept acceptance, has been shown to take up into itself both the anxiety of guilt and the anxiety of fate. The courage to be as a part and the courage to be as oneself have been transformed into two types of the courage to accept acceptance. But the question still remains whether the pervasive anxiety of doubt in the modern world can thwart the unification of the two types of accepting

15. Although Tillich uses the language of "taking up" to describe the ways in which participation and faith work, he does not do so for individualization (120–21) or the types of anxiety. He even alters the third type of anxiety, ascribing that position to guilt throughout most of the book but to doubt in the final lecture. There is no indication that this change or the dialectical difference in how he treats participation and individualization has any systematic significance for him.

acceptance: "Is there a courage which can conquer the anxiety of meaninglessness and doubt?" (174)

Tillich rejects any leap into "dogmatic certitude" that claims to remove "the state of meaninglessness." He finds an answer instead in the "courage of despair," which affirms that "the acceptance of despair is in itself faith and on the boundary line of the courage to be. In this situation the meaning of life is reduced to despair about the meaning of life. But as long as this despair is an act of life it is positive in its negativity" (175–76). Tillich is fully aware of how paradoxical the positive negativity of his concept of faithful despair is. He points out its religious expression, namely, that one must have the courage to accept acceptance even when "in the state of despair there is nobody and nothing [i.e., no God and no Being] that accepts" (177). Meaninglessness prevails, and yet one can still experience the power of acceptance. Meaninglessness is deeper and more radical than any experience of mystical union or divine-human encounter. Indeed, the theistic claim for an encounter with God forgets that "the attack of doubt undercuts the subject-object structure" implicit in such claims (178).

Finally, then, Tillich's faith is an experience of anxiety that accepts radical despair but refuses to capitulate to it. The anxiety of fate, threatened by the power of nonbeing, is in fact the path to an awareness of being. The anxiety of guilt, threatened by the possibility of moral condemnation, is in fact the awareness of "the God above the [judging] God of theism" (189). And the anxiety of doubt, threatened by the specter of meaninglessness, is in fact the path to faith and the courage to accept acceptance. Tillich concludes his essay emphatically by stating: *The courage to be is rooted in the God who appears when God has disappeared in the anxiety of doubt*" (190). This is the faith that transforms anxiety even as it is validated by it.

•   •   •

Here, then, are three dialectics of identity: Nietzsche's theoretical opposition between individualistic manly instincts and the degenerative group influences of Christian and socialist thinking; Buber's reciprocity in I-Thou relations, which are said to be superior to I-It experiences, at least in spiritual and social transactions; and Tillich's paradoxical unity of individualization and participation within the transforming force of faith as the courage to accept acceptance in the face of despair. However close to one another Nietzsche, Buber, and Tillich may be as existentialist philosophers, this typological analysis shows that there are also dialectical differences that can help us to see how much they disagree on the nature of human selfhood.

Once again, a new aspect of each of the three types is revealed in this chapter. Whereas all the previous theoretical thinkers have been either objective (Skinner, Lévi-Strauss, and Benson) or subjective (Barthes admits his own solipsism), Nietzsche repudiates equally objectivist and subjectivist epistemologies. For him, the issue is not knowledge but will. This shows that his subjectivism is less a form of solipsism than an expression of his voluntarism. Buber has also deepened our understanding of his type, for he is the first of the transactional thinkers to develop the dialogical dimension of reciprocal human relations. Carr writes of the dialogue between the historian and the facts, but that is quite different from a dialogue in which two conscious persons participate as equals. Fromm implies a dialogical element in love, but never stipulates its necessity or character. Ellul and Douglas are even more indirect, if the concept of dialogue can be found in their pages at all. Tillich demonstrates the extent to which a dialectic of paradox can be worked out systematically. The works by Kuhn, Campbell, Niebuhr, and Kierkegaard are consistently but not systematically paradoxical. Tillich alone has worked out the dialectical development of his paradoxical understanding of the courage to be as participation, individualization, and faith. These three moments provide structure to his entire analysis, which would have displayed an even more careful structure if Tillich had correlated the three types of anxiety with them: the anxiety of fate with participation, the anxiety of guilt with individualism, and the anxiety of doubt with faith.

As in the preceding chapter, the topic of this chapter seems to put theoretical thinkers at a disadvantage. Human identity, like love, may be ill suited for a type of interpretation that never goes beyond contradiction and opposition. Nietzsche's insights into his opponents are brilliant, as his famous accusation of a "slave morality" at the heart of Christianity (a truth that is infrequently noted by Christians) attests. His call for a healthy relation with the senses and instincts, and for a rigorous overcoming of all self-indulgence, certainly needs to be heard in every age. But his inability to affirm the dependency and vulnerability that are a genuine part of every mature person leave both his psychological dialectic of identity and his new (a)morality sadly inadequate to the realities of actual human existence. Moreover, his attack upon reason and his extolling of the will combine to undermine all objective criteria in favor of (an albeit voluntaristic) subjectivism.

Buber seems to swing to the opposite extreme, for he cannot imagine an I apart from a Thou: we are utterly dependent upon relationships for our identity, and to ignore or deny that truth is to slip into the reifications of I-It experiences. Napoleon, for whom Nietzsche often expresses admiration,[16] is castigated as a "demonic Thou" by Buber. And yet Buber's relational self rings true. The very concept of a self that is really single, or utterly isolated, seems to be little more than an abstraction, and perhaps also a conceptual device for evading social and ethical responsibility. The power of relationships in shaping our identities is self-evident. As a dialectic of human identity, construed as a fundamentally social phenomenon, Buber's vision of reciprocity seems more than adequate to the subject matter.

Unless, of course, identity is rooted in what Tillich calls a "religious experience," perhaps an awareness of mystical unity with the One or an encounter with the Wholly Other, by which the individual self is utterly transformed. Such an experience, and the effects that follow from it, would transcend all preexisting relationships. Indeed, in a very real sense it would initiate a new relationship (with the One, or God) that would significantly preempt all others. That seems to be the key to the paradoxical dialectic of identity at the heart of Tillich's concept of faith as the courage to accept acceptance. Unfortunately, it is a message that is obscured by his inconsistent use of dialectical patterns of thinking. It appears that Buber, who thinks that such religious experience is merely an inference, a sense of the Eternal Thou that comes from many experiences of human Thous, has done a better job of stating his position on human identity.

16. See, for example, *Ecce Homo*.

6

Interpreting Theories of Interpretation

Like every theory of interpretation, the typology I am presenting here can serve as a vehicle for analyzing other theories of interpretation. Some readers, for whom that is its primary interest, may wonder why discussion of other theories constitutes only one chapter of this book. The simplest answer is that, while my commitment to this typology as a viable theory is substantial, my primary goal is to present it as a tool that others can appropriate, modify, and put to their own hermeneutical purposes. That is why I have presented the typology primarily through examples of its application to a variety of specific subjects. Illustrations demonstrate the heuristic potential of a tool better than abstract formulations.

A second reason for the decision not to devote the entire book to analysis of assorted theories of interpretation is that they constitute a highly unwieldy body of literature. Important contributions have emerged from literary theory, philosophy, theology, legal studies, history, sociology, anthropology, and the history and philosophy of science. Surveys and anthologies already offer excellent introductions to many of these areas;[1] but, as I stated in the Introduction, no survey could possibly do justice to them all. Since my intention is to present a tool for interpretation that is in principle applicable to any field or subject matter, a topic-oriented method of explication by illustration demonstrates the potential of the typology more forcefully than a broad survey of hermeneutical theories and debates could.

A third reason for the emphasis upon concrete illustration over abstract argument is the genesis of this project. I never set out to develop a theory of interpretation. Rather, I noticed that Kierkegaard's theory of stages sheds light on specific conflicts among interpretations of myth, history, and other topics. The path I am tracing in this book is more or less the same path that I have pursued in the decade since that first observation.

For these reasons, only this final chapter is devoted to theories that are explicitly about interpretation theory. From the abundance of recent theoretical approaches to interpretation, I have chosen to focus upon Michel Foucault's *Archaeology of Knowledge*. Foucault's influential works range among history, philosophy, critical theory, and political analysis of social institutions. A fine example of a transactional type of theory of interpretation is developed by E. D. Hirsch in *Validity in Interpretation* and *The Aims of Interpretation*. For the transformational type, I turn to the phenomenological position of Paul Ricoeur, as set out in a number of essays in *Hermeneutics and the Human Sciences*.

A Postmodern Protest

Whatever relation *The Archaeology of Knowledge*[2] bears to Michel Foucault's other work, it is a text that provides an excellent example of a postmodern theoretical type of interpretation. If a center can be discerned within its pages, it is Foucault's commitment to decentering. He describes his method as "a discourse about discourses, . . . trying to operate a decentering that

1. I shall mention just one, a collection of essays on ways of introducing undergraduates to the field of literary theory: *Teaching Contemporary Theory to Undergraduates,* ed. Dianne F. Sadoff and William E. Cain (New York: Modern Language Association, 1994).

2. Michel Foucault, *The Archaeology of Knowledge* and *The Discourse on Language* (New York: Pantheon Books, 1972). *The Archaeology of Knowledge* is translated by A. M. Sheridan Smith from *L'archéologie du savoir* (Paris: Éditions Gallimard, 1969), and *The Discourse on Language* (215–37 in the English edition) is translated by Rupert Swyer from *L'ordre du discours* (Paris: Éditions Gallimard, 1971).

leaves no privilege to any centre" (205). Foucault sees himself as a kindred spirit of Marx, Nietzsche, Freud, and de Saussure in their decenterings of, respectively, economics, philosophy, psychology, and linguistics. His target is the academic discipline of history, which he hopes to expose as a deceptive striving for a "total description [that] draws all phenomena around a single centre—a principle, a meaning, a spirit, a world-view, an overall shape" (10). His "new history" is not interested in the "meaning" of events, the "spirit" that drives nations or historical periods, the "world-view" of a society, or the "overall shape" of a culture. These are spurious centers used by traditional historians to promote the impression of a coherence and totality that are illusory.

Alleged centers such as a spirit or a worldview presuppose that history is the expression of a transcendental subject, whether human consciousness, the mind of God, or some other unified intelligence that transcends time and place. Foucault argues that any assumption of a meaning to be dug out of a historical text or statement is little more than "transcendental narcissism" (203), which is the imposition on history of a purpose and direction, as though it had the form of a conscious subject. He even criticizes his own earlier appeal to "an experience" in *Madness and Civilization* as "still close to admitting an anonymous and general subject of history."[3] The goal is to move beyond all centers to an understanding of history in terms of dispersion.

Dispersion in *The Archaeology of Knowledge* is closely related to the concept of discontinuity. Whereas traditional history seeks links and connections among the historical data, Foucault advocates the analysis of ruptures and discontinuities. Although he uses a variety of terms for such breaks—"thresholds," "displacements," "scales," "distributions," and "transformations"—all refer to radical disjunctions in the development of concepts, knowledge, and relations among different events. In place of the assumption that history unfolds as a linear (and perhaps even progressive) development, Foucault insists that fissure and contradiction are more indicative of its true nature.

A question arises from these preliminary remarks: if Foucault sees historical ruptures as transformations, would he not best be understood as a transformational interpreter? There are many reasons why this is not plausible, but the most obvious is the following: for Foucault, contradiction is not paradoxically affirmed and overcome by some sort of transformation; rather, he considers transformations to be the establishing of something

3. Ibid., 16. I am grateful to Allen Megill for his correction of "an experiment" in Sheridan Smith's translation. See *Prophets of Extremity: Nietzsche, Heidegger, Foucault, Derrida* (Berkeley and Los Angeles: University of California Press, 1985), 202.

new that stands in opposition to that which preceded it. The accent here is on rupture. Although he uses the term paradox frequently, he does not employ it to affirm the unity-within-contradiction of a dialectic of paradox. I shall return to this matter later.

Foucault's theory of interpretation can be described as a postmodern protest against the many modern concepts of continuity that have, in his view, governed most traditional interpretation: "And the great problem presented by [new] historical analyses is not how continuities are established, how a single pattern is formed and preserved, how for so many different, successive minds there is a single horizon . . . ; it is no longer one of lasting foundations, but one of transformations that serve as new foundations, the rebuilding of foundations" (5). Foucault further illustrates his interest in oppositions by a very structuralist inversion: whereas traditional history attempts to make the nonverbal ancient monuments studied by archaeologists speak as if they were written documents, recent history "aspires to the condition of archaeology" in that it "transforms *documents into monuments*" (7).

One result of this displacement (not development) in historical writing is that discontinuity, which was previously perceived as an obstacle to be overcome, is now embraced as "both an instrument and an object of research" (9). Another is that discontinuity challenges the traditional "sovereignty of consciousness" and "the founding function of the subject" (12, cf. 202). In other words, whereas earlier historians had assumed that their task was to understand the consciousness of historical individuals and groups, Foucault argues that their analyses were only an effort to justify their belief in the "synthetic" role of such a consciousness (14). The entire project was ideological—an unconscious apology for the hegemony of human consciousness. According to Foucault, human consciousness is just another spurious center. It lacks the power and authority that it claims, for all its thinking is subject to rules of which it is largely unaware. The rules vary from discourse to discourse: they can be economic (Marx), psychological (Nietzsche, Freud), or linguistic (de Saussure). *The Archaeology of Knowledge* is a manifesto calling for a new discourse of discontinuity in historical analysis.

Yet the new history is more than just a description of discontinuities; it also discerns new unities. On the one hand, it exposes such notions as tradition, spirit, the book, and the oeuvre as false unities that merely diversify and justify the claims for continuity (21–22); on the other, it engages in a search for unities that Foucault believes can be found by a *"pure description of discursive events,"* which involves describing "the material with which one is dealing . . . in its raw, neutral state" (27). Although this appears to be a claim for immediate experience of things or events as they are in themselves, Foucault explicitly rejects the attempt to describe "a group of characteristics that are presented, even in an unsystematic way, to immediate experience" (112). Indeed, much of his attack upon phenomenology is due to its claim to have direct access to the consciousness of putative historical or religious subjects. When Foucault writes of "this blank space from which I speak" (17), he does not refer to the immediate apprehension of the romantic imagination but to his own description of exterior surfaces and rules; the space from which he speaks is blank not because of its mystery or immediacy, but simply because it has been neglected by traditional thinkers.

Occasionally Foucault qualifies his rhetoric, stating that old unities are to be suspended rather than abolished. For example, if we focus only on the meaning intended by the author of a statement, we block the possibility of grasping the rules that govern the discourse within which the author's statement occurs. The suspension of such "accepted unities" as the author's intended meaning is therefore a necessary yet temporary method for opening a way to describe "other unities" such as those rules (28–29).

Those other unities are to be found within what Foucault calls "discursive formations" that are "systems of dispersion" (38). The grammatical paradox is intentional: discursive events present themselves as elements that are both organized systematically and dispersed. They can be systematically analyzed in terms of the rules that govern them, but they are dispersed in relation to the traditional categories used to classify them within the alleged continuity of a comprehensive history. Thus medicine must be described as such a discursive formation, not as an expression of the progressive history of science and ideas. Foucault's fourfold schema organizes each discursive formation in terms of how its rules give form to discursive objects, styles, concepts, and thematic or strategic choices (38).

These four elements, however, are not the unities sought by the new history. The new unities can be found only prior to the fourfold formation, in "the system that makes possible and governs that formation" (72). Foucault's conviction that rules constituting a systematic vertical "hierarchy of relations" do lie behind the actual discourse or text—and that those rules, rather than conscious choices by the author, are responsible for the form of the discourse—is clearly reflected in this representative example of his style:

> Behind the visible façade of the system, one posits the rich uncertainty of disorder; and beneath the thin surface of discourse, the whole mass of a largely silent development (*devenir*): a "presystematic" that

> is not of the order of the system; a "prediscursive" that belongs to an
> essential silence. Discourse and system produce each other—and
> conjointly—only at the crest of this immense reserve. . . . Behind the
> completed system, what is discovered by the analysis of formations is
> not the bubbling source of life itself, life in an as yet uncaptured
> state; it is an immense density of systematicities, a tight group of mul-
> tiple relations. Moreover, these relations cannot be the very web of
> the text—they are not by nature foreign to discourse. . . . One is not
> seeking, therefore, to pass from the text to thought, from talk to
> silence, from the exterior to the interior, from spatial dispersion to the
> pure recollection of the moment, from superficial multiplicity to
> profound unity. One remains within the dimension of discourse. (76)

Foucault's historical method is, then, an analysis of historical discourses,
a method to which he refers as "archaeological description." The most interesting and elusive category in this archaeological description is the archive,
the system by which statements are formed and transformed. It is "the law
of what can be said" and "that which, outside ourselves, delimits us"; the
archive regulates our statements; we can never step outside it to describe it
fully (129–30). Every person and every discourse can form statements only
on the basis of an archive, which is more than simply a collection of previous statements. The archive is an organized "positivity" that makes particular discursive formations possible. Foucault goes so far as to call such
a positivity "a *historical a priori*" (127), for it is made up of the rules and accu-
mulated practices that constitute the necessary conditions for a discourse
and give it unity through time.[4] However much we might like to think that
our statements are creatures of our own invention, Foucault insists that they
are primarily the products of those rules and practices that constitute the
positivity of the relevant archive. His new archaeological analysis "describes
discourses as practices specified in the element of the archive" (131).

The archive's primary role is to form statements, and these constitute the
new unity that Foucault explains in the greatest detail. A statement is "a
function of existence that properly belongs to signs and on the basis of
which one may decide, through analysis or intuition, whether or not they
'make sense,' according to what rule they follow one another or are jux-
taposed, of what they are the sign, and what sort of act is carried out by

---

4. Since a positivity is made up of rules and practices rather than specific content,
it constitutes the conditions for, but not a body of, knowledge that could qualify as a
science (181).

their formulation (oral or written). . . . [The statement] cuts across a domain of structures and possible unities, and . . . reveals them, with concrete contents, in time and space" (86–87).

This concept of the statement distinguishes it sharply from the sentence, which is a level of expression that invites interpretation of meanings that remain hidden or repressed (110). Analysis of the statements that make up a discourse neither hides meanings nor reveals what is beneath the surface. It simply analyzes the surface, the exterior presentation of signs, according to the rules of that discourse. Foucault calls this the "enunciative function" of a statement. Enunciative analysis operates on the premise that no statement ever says all that is to be said, but such analysis lets the omissions and gaps simply stand. It does not, like phenomenological interpretation, try to dig out or fill in meanings to overcome the unsaid or the repressed. It understands that discourse is "an asset that is, by nature, the object of a struggle, a political struggle" (120). Enunciative analysis is not interested in the subjectivity or mentality of the speaking subject; according to Foucault, its exteriority "may be paradoxical since its refers to no adverse form of interiority" (121).[5]

Foucault's discussion of the archive and the statement as key categories in archaeological description offers an opportunity to draw out more fully the typological character of his program. This task is made even easier by the fact that the program is primarily a protest. Foucault's efforts to distance himself from traditional history, the history of ideas, and all forms of phenomenology and philosophical hermeneutics demonstrate how strongly opposed he is to both transactional and transformational interpretation.

Foucault lists as the four principles of archaeological description the binary oppositions between: (1) documents that speak and mute monuments; (2) continuity and discontinuity; (3) the author of a statement or text and the rules that determine it; and (4) an interpretation of the inner meaning of statements and an analysis that reinscribes them in their exterior form but transposed according to the rules governing their discursive formation (138–40). Although he states that his rejection of the former of each of these oppositions is merely a suspension and a corrective, Foucault's rhetoric and his logic indicate that it is really much more. There is no

___

5. Enunciative analysis examines four aspects of the statement: how it (the statement as enunciative function) differentiates objects (the referential condition); how it establishes a position from which a statement can be made (the subject condition); how it coordinates the statement with other statements (the associated field condition); and the physical means (text, etc.) by which the statement is made (the material condition) (115).

attempt in *The Archaeology of Knowledge* to reappropriate any of the rejected older unities. Indeed, the nature of archaeological analysis precludes such a possibility: monuments, discontinuities, impersonal rules, and exterior reinscriptions completely displace documents, continuities, creative subjects, and inner meanings.

The extent to which Foucault's emphasis upon discontinuity and rupture is a rhetorical choice rather than a strict logical necessity is demonstrated when he turns to the questions of originality and contradiction. Surprisingly, Foucault comments that the older history of ideas tries "to rediscover the point of rupture" (142) in its effort to pinpoint the historical moment of origin of an idea, whereas his new archaeological description seeks out the regularities that every discovery shares with other enunciative, linguistic, and logical discursive formations. In other words, Foucault is pursuing connections and continuities, while the traditional historian of ideas seeks ruptures! This comes as quite a shock after more than a hundred pages of rhetoric claiming just the contrary. Of course the rhetoric is justified, for Foucault is deeply committed to a dialectic of contradiction. I mention this anomaly simply to demonstrate that his commitment does not follow from his so-called "pure description of discursive events." A dialectic of contradiction precedes and shapes Foucault's archaeological description, with the result that he stresses the discontinuities sought by his new method and the continuities prized by the old, rather than the reverse. His position is dictated from start to finish by a theoretical agenda.

The primary item on that agenda is subversion of the authority of the thinking, speaking, conscious subject. That is why documents must be transformed into monuments and intentions into discursive rules of formation. The authority of the creative subject is not simply revised or qualified; it is totally repudiated. With the demise of the creative subject as a topic for investigation, all the other rubrics that presupposed it also disappear: book, oeuvre, genre, community, tradition, historical period, and spirit. In *The Discourse on Language,* Foucault makes the point that our respect for authorship has undergone an interesting reversal in recent times. Whereas in the Middle Ages a scientific treatise was trusted only if it bore the name of a respected author, in the modern world the author's name has lost that status in science, which relies instead upon the authority of scientific method. In literature, however, just the opposite has happened: the author has moved from insignificance to preeminence (221–22). Foucault thinks that the shift of authority in science from personal reputation to methodological rigor should serve as a model for historical analysis. This entails a rejection of all "interpretation" (Foucault does not distinguish between the transactional and transformational types), for in all its forms it is simply a phenomenological analysis of inner meanings and hidden truths created to maintain the status of the interpreting subject.

Of special interest to transformational interpreters are Foucault's inner meanings and his theoretical paradoxes. Those paradoxes are really only simple oppositions, for they exploit oppositions and misdirections without ever overcoming or uniting them in a higher unity.[6] Foucault devotes an entire chapter to the analysis of selected contradictions that the history of ideas attempts to reconcile; in contrast, "archaeology describes the different *spaces of dissension*" (152). He is particularly interested in the "intrinsic contradictions" that occur within "a single positivity" or discursive formation (153). But he insists that the purpose of this archaeological analysis is "not to even out oppositions" but "to map" them—their origin, form, relations, and domain. Unlike transformational interpretation, archaeology simply lets stand all the irregularities, discontinuities, and contradictions.

In his discussion of comparisons Foucault reveals more concretely the extent to which archaeology is a meta-analysis, an analysis of the forms of analysis rather than a new analytical discourse on the same order as older discourses. Traditional modes of analysis constitute distinctive archives or positivities. Each has its own rules and practices, so comparison between them is difficult: it inevitably appears to reduce one to the other's terms. Thus medical discourse can be described in political terms, but the resulting analysis presents medicine as an expression or effect of politics. Archaeology works in the "spaces of dissension" between these and all other discourses. It operates by comparing and contrasting them, but not in order to explain one in terms of another: "If archaeology brings medical discourse closer to a number of practices, it is in order to discover far less 'immediate' relations than expression, but far more direct relations than those of a causality communicated through the consciousness of the speaking subjects. It wishes to show not how political practice has determined the meaning and form of medical discourse, but how and in what form it [political discourse] takes part in its [medical discourse's] conditions of emergence, insertion, and functioning" (163).

This passage can serve to clarify further the relation between objective and subjective theoretical interpretation. Foucault's archaeological discourse

---

6. Foucault comments that it is the history of ideas that "plays with paradox" (170), for it tries to find continuities where archaeology is content to find only discontinuities.

remains in the "spaces of dissension" between discourses, maintaining binary oppositions by a logic of neither/nor rather than a paradoxical both/and. In the terms I have been using, he would insist that his archaeological analysis is neither objective nor subjective, but that it works in the space between them, exploring and exploiting their conflict without attempting to alter or reconcile them at all. Thus he rejects the demands of objective rational discourse just as much as Barthes and Nietzsche do. All three treat objectivity as a form of false consciousness, for it betrays immediacy or the instincts, or it ignores the ideological character of traditional categories.

The attack on objectivity illuminates Foucault's relation to structuralism. Like Lévi-Strauss, he privileges formal analysis of rules and patterns over concrete analysis of specific content. But Foucault also employs diachronic analysis alongside synchronic patterns and, with his theory of decentering, undermines the objectivism upon which structuralism rests. The dissolution of the rational self is at most an implication of Lévi-Strauss's position, whereas it is the presupposition and goal that permeates Foucault's archaeological approach to knowledge. This inevitably raises the question of the status of his own analyses, for the criteria by which they are to be evaluated are never stated. Foucault vacillates between admitting and denying that he is simply creating new centers of meaning that might one day serve as objective criteria for an improved historical method. On balance, however, the denials seem to prevail, for Foucault energetically undercuts all centers, all conscious selves, and all criteria. In other words, despite the objective tone of so much of his writing, his theory has as its result a sort of solipsism-by-default. By trying to remain in the space of dissension between objective and subjective theoretical interpretations, Foucault rejects the objective centers that could help him stay there and slips into a subjective theoretical position in spite of himself.

This is certainly the protest of a postmodern theoretical thinker. Foucault's primary themes—decentering, discontinuities, subversion of consciousness and the interpreting subject, suspicion of the quest for hidden meanings and substantial truths, and the pervasive presumption of irreconcilable contradictions on both the substantial and the methodological planes—undermine not only objective theoretical concepts but also transactional and transformational interpretations. Yet representatives of those types have not suffered this and similar attacks in silence. I now turn to a transactional position that is explicitly presented as a response to recent developments in interpretation theory.

An Ethics of Interpretation

Whereas Foucault is primarily a political and historical thinker, the representative of transactional interpretation I have chosen for this chapter is a scholar of literature and literary theory who is also well read in philosophy: E. D. Hirsch. His hermeneutical position is a clear and forcefully argued defense of the paradigm that has dominated modern times—that understanding is the task of ascertaining the meaning intended by the original author or speaker. Just as Foucault casts his argument as a protest against that standard approach to historical interpretation, Hirsch opens his influential 1967 book, *Validity in Interpretation,* with a counterprotest against the "banishment of the author" by the "new" literary criticism of the previous four decades.[7]

Although Hirsch never, to my knowledge, describes the act of interpretation as a transaction between author and reader, his consistent emphasis upon the priority of the author's intention in the determination of meaning leaves no doubt about his view of the interpreter's primary responsibility: "[T]he root problem of interpretation is always the same—to guess what the author meant" (*VI,* 207). Moreover, "meaning is an affair of consciousness and not of physical signs or things. Consciousness is, in turn, an affair of persons, and in textual interpretation the persons involved are an author and a reader" *VI,* 23). Here three of the primary ways in which theoretical and transactional interpretation differ have already been signaled: the act of interpretation involves (1) conscious intentions (2) of persons (3) in which a reader is attempting to understand the meaning intended by the author. Texts are just meaningless sequences of signs on a page until they are "construed" as meaningful statements by an interpreter (*VI,* 13).

The defining characteristic of meaning for Hirsch is its determinacy or stability. This prerequisite for any knowledge in interpretation is the unifying theme of his work (*AI,* 1). If meaning is not based upon a determinate object, then the implication is unavoidable that it is merely a subjective mental process that will render communication between author and reader utterly unreliable (*VI,* 32). Hirsch grounds his position in the categories of philosophical phenomenology: the task of understanding is to grasp that

---

7. E. D. Hirsch Jr., *Validity in Interpretation* (New Haven: Yale University Press, 1967), 1; hereafter cited as *VI.* I also refer to Hirsch's later collection of essays, *The Aims of Interpretation* (Chicago: University of Chicago Press, 1976); hereafter cited as *AI.* Hirsch denies that there are "substantive revisions" of his position in the later book (*AI,* 7).

"object-directedness of consciousness [which] has been called 'intentionality'"
(*VI*, 38). This intentional object is, in the case of textual interpretation, a
verbal meaning that can be construed in substantially the same way by any
number of readers. It is the stable, determinate meaning originally intended
by the author of the text.

Although the meaning of an author's statement does not change, its
significance almost certainly will. The significance of a text will vary from
reader to reader and generation to generation; it is as "limitless" (*VI*, 63) as
the number of readers. This is because the significance, unlike the meaning, is determined by the interpreter's response to the meaning of the text
(*VI*, 39): "Significance is meaning-as-related-to-something-else" (*AI*, 80).
Ancient texts may be appropriated by modern readers in a psychological or
sociological way, but this does not justify claiming that such a modern reading articulates the meaning of the text, a reading that often could never
have occurred to the ancient author. All that the modern reading establishes is one of many possible claims for the significance of the text .

Central to Hirsch's analysis of interpretation as the discernment of the
author's intended meaning is the concept of genre. While others might
seek to establish the political or ideological context of a text, Hirsch believes
that the only context that counts for establishing the meaning of an utter-
ance is its genre: "All understanding of verbal meaning is necessarily genre-
bound" (*VI*, 76). Our conception of the type, or genre, of a text determines
how we approach it; we do not have the same expectations of poems, historical documents, and VCR manuals. Although our initial classification
in a particular genre determines the direction of interpretation, subsequent
reclassification is possible. The goal is to arrive at the author's intended
meaning, which requires knowing the "intrinsic genre" of the text, which is
*"that sense of the whole by means of which an interpreter can correctly understand
any part in its determinacy"* (*VI*, 86).

The concept of genre allows Hirsch to qualify his insistence upon a
strong identification of meaning with the author's conscious intention. The
implications of a text are certainly part of its meaning, but are not necessarily consciously intended by the author (*VI*, 64–65). Some texts, such as
the Bible and the Constitution, are even intended to have meanings that
go beyond those consciously thought by their authors (*VI*, 122). That seems
to imply that the intention of the text takes priority over the intention of
the text's author,[8] but Hirsch avoids this conclusion in two ways: by limiting

8. Hirsch occasionally speaks of texts as if they were conscious persons, but such

such situations to just one or two genres, such as bibles and constitutions, and by insisting that, even when the meaning of an actual statement is not consciously thought by the author, it is entailed within the genre intended by the author. Hirsch uses as an example a Freudian reading of *Hamlet* as an Oedipal drama, which he rejects, not just because Shakespeare knew nothing of Freud but because *Hamlet* is a different genre about a type of hero incompatible with one who would be conceivable in terms of Oedipal motivations (*VI,* 124–26). The "intrinsic genre" intended by Shakespeare for *Hamlet* precludes an Oedipal interpretation of meaning, although the Freudian reading may be a plausible claim for the play's significance.

Hirsch seems to qualify his identification of correct interpretation with the author's intended meaning again when he announces that "understanding is prior to and different from interpretation" (*VI,* 129).[9] Understanding is not simply passive, for it involves an "active construction of meaning" of the text, in "the text's own language," by the interpreter (*VI,* 134); yet it is silent and timeless in contrast with the garrulousness and historicity of interpretation (*VI,* 135, 137). Only one understanding or construction of the text's meaning can be correct (*VI,* 129), but many interpretations can translate that proper understanding into contemporary terms (*VI,* 136). This implies that interpretation no longer determines the stable meaning as distinct from the changing significance. In his effort to distinguish interpretation from understanding, Hirsch seems to have moved it into a limbo between understanding the meaning of the text in its own terms and criticizing the text's significance in contemporary terms, and he even concedes that "[a]ll textual commentary is a mixture of interpretation and criticism" (*VI,* 140).

A similar inconsistency appears in Hirsch's discussion of validation. On the one hand, his entire argument is based upon the need to establish interpretation as a discipline that can provide knowledge, so it must be able to demonstrate the objectivity of its claims. Yet Hirsch also admits that "the circularity of the interpretive process" can obscure the extent to which "certainty is always unattainable" (*VI,* 164). In later essays this tension between the inexorable ambiguity of the hermeneutical circle, which refers to the

---

instances seem to be figures of speech rather than changes in his position. Thus he writes of "texts that have only aesthetic aims" (*VI,* 155).

9. Hirsch is drawing upon and affirming a traditional distinction in hermeneutical theory between the art of understanding (*subtilitas intelligendi*), the art of explication or explanation (*subtilitas explicandi*), and the art of application (*subtilitas applicandi*). Hirsch's terms for these three arts are, respectively, "understanding," "interpretation," and "criticism."

way in which knowledge of the part and knowledge of the whole presuppose each other,[10] and the linear logic of validation, with its claim to objectivity, becomes acute. In order to protect the integrity of objective validation of interpretation from the encroachments of the hermeneutical circle, Hirsch ultimately proposes replacing the latter with Piaget's concept of a "corrigible schema" (*AI*, 32–34). What had been the ambiguous circularity and consequent uncertainty of all interpretation is now reconceived as the freedom of an interpreter to choose one from among the many possible approaches to interpretation. This freedom accounts for the unavoidably subjective aspect of interpretation without foreclosing the possibility of objective validation of one interpretation over others. It thus acknowledges the great variety in interpretation without forcing Hirsch to abandon his commitment to the author's intended meaning (or intrinsic genre) as "the only practical norm for a cognitive discipline of interpretation" (*AI*, 7).

The freedom to select one approach from many possibilities indicates the extent to which Hirsch is constructing an ethic of interpretation. This dimension is present in *Validity in Interpretation* and receives even greater emphasis in the later essays. In *Validity*, Hirsch argues against the notion that interpretation is determined by the text itself: "Any normative concept of interpretation implies a choice that is required not by the nature of written texts but rather by the goal that the interpreter sets himself. It is a weakness in many descriptions of the interpretive process that this act of choice is disregarded and the process described as though the object of interpretation were somehow determined by the ontological status of texts themselves" (*VI*, 24).

Hirsch argues that this stress on a free act of the will is required by the determinacy of meaning, for meaning that is unwilled is also indeterminate (*VI*, 47, 54). This is his voluntaristic way of stating the point made earlier about practical norms: if the interpreter does not choose to affirm the author's intended meaning as the true meaning of a text, no other hermeneutical procedure will provide a determinate meaning; there could be as many alleged meanings for a text as there are interpreters. The choice is a free one, and its consequences are substantial. The entire process of interpretation is a matter of goals and norms. Even genres, in Hirsch's view, have purposes (*VI*, 99).

In *The Aims of Interpretation,* Hirsch explicates his theory in even more

10. For example, a soliloquy by Hamlet must be understood within the context of the entire play and its dramatic genre, yet the entire play can be grasped only through study of its many parts, including that soliloquy.

strikingly ethical terms. Recalling his earlier observation that "the object of interpretation is no automatic given, but a task that the interpreter sets for himself," Hirsch adds that "[t]he choice of an interpretive norm . . . , being a choice, belongs to the domain of ethics" (*AI,* 7). He invokes "Schleiermacher's canon," namely, the "preference for original meaning over anachronistic meaning [that] is ultimately an ethical choice. I would confidently generalize from his example to assert that the normative dimension of interpretation is always in the last analysis an ethical dimension" (*AI,* 77).

In his eagerness to claim philosophical authorities for his position, Hirsch cites two ethical principles from Kant: the maxim that all persons should be valued as ends in themselves and not merely as means or instruments to be exploited, and the categorical imperative to act only according to maxims that one would want all others to observe toward oneself and toward one another. These Kantian principles of moral action are transposed by Hirsch into an "ethical imperative of speech": "[T]he ethics of language hold good in all uses of language, oral and written, in poetry as well as in philosophy. All are ethically governed by the intentions of the author. To treat an author's words as merely grist for one's own mill is ethically analogous to using another man merely for one's own purposes" (*AI,* 90–91). Words, like persons, are to be treated as "ends in themselves." As for Kant's categorical imperative, Hirsch assumes that theorists who disregard the author's intended meaning do not wish to be similarly disregarded by their own readers. But this inconsistency violates the categorical imperative and results in an unethical self-contradiction.

Yet Hirsch is not advocating a narrowly moralistic approach to texts. While rejecting any relativism that affirms diversity without further comment, he follows Matthew Arnold in calling for a balance or harmony of the moralistic and aesthetic attitudes in interpretation. Neither can suffice alone, which implies that a reciprocal relation between them will be the most satisfactory arrangement for both. Hirsch does not directly address the question of reciprocity or other dialectical ways of thinking, but he does affirm the Aristotelian "ideal of balance, governing culture, education, and criticism, [which] is at bottom an ethical ideal" (*AI,* 139).

Ethics provides the first and, for Hirsch, the most important of three dimensions in interpretation. There is also an analytical dimension, which turns not on personal choice but on impersonal logic, empirical description, and neutrality with respect to values. Hirsch believes that his distinction between meaning and significance is an example of analytical interpretation (*AI,* 78–79). The third dimension is the metaphysical, which Hirsch identifies with the appropriation of Heidegger's ontology for a theory of interpretation, presumably thinking of Gadamer's theory that language shapes the subject matter and thus also the interpretation.[11] He decries this on the grounds that it substitutes a spurious (linguistic) necessity for the ethical choice requisite to all interpretation, and also idealizes the ambiguous concept of a hermeneutical circle (*AI*, 81–85).

This criticism of metaphysical interpretation introduces a final and important aspect of Hirsch's argument: his ongoing polemic against other approaches. Unlike Foucault, who sometimes seems to lump all his opponents together under the rubric of "old history," Hirsch initially distinguishes sharply between two kinds of alternatives that are equally inadequate: aestheticism and historicism.

I use the term "aestheticism" for any interpretation based upon what Hirsch calls the principle of "semantic autonomy" (*VI*, 1). The alleged autonomy may belong to the actual text or discourse (e.g., Foucault's rules); or it may be ascribed to the subject matter discussed in the text (Gadamer and, as we shall see, Ricoeur). The movement to banish the author is present in both of these: whereas "New Critics" study "the poem itself" in its independence from whatever the poet may have meant, hermeneutical interpreters applaud Kant's claim to understand Plato better than he understood himself. Hirsch protests that Kant cannot possibly understand Plato's meaning better than Plato did, since the meaning of Plato's writings is identical with what Plato intended it to be. What Kant can understand better is the subject matter that Plato has, in Kant's view, inadequately grasped and expressed (*VI*, 19–20). But Plato's text cannot claim autonomy from Plato's intended meaning any more than the language (as in "discursive formations") of the text can. If the text were determined by impersonal or structural causes, the resulting autonomy it would have from its author would entail a corresponding loss of freedom for all interpreters, who would no longer have any choice in their goals and methods of interpretation.

Historicism at first appears to be asserting the opposite of semantic autonomy: that the text is, as it were, a captive of its own immediate historical context and can never be understood by anyone who does not participate in that context. Hirsch objects that this assumes a historical immediacy for the contemporaries of a text that they do not in fact have (*VI*, 43). To mention one of Hirsch's favorite analogies, historicists deny that an old slipper can ever fit the new Cinderella. To him, this denial is tantamount to admitting

    11. Hans-Georg Gadamer, *Truth and Method*, 2d rev. ed., trans. Joel Weinsheimer and Donald G. Marshall (New York: Crossroad, 1990), 381–405.

that there is nothing stable—no determinate slipper and not even a constant foot for Cinderella—that can constitute a meaning (*VI*, 46). He is particularly distressed by those theorists (Foucault and Derrrida are mentioned) who use the alleged inaccessibility of the author's intended meaning to justify the conclusion that "all textual commentary is therefore really fiction or poetry" (*AI*, 147).

In fact, however, aestheticism and historicism are guilty of exactly the same error: they both assume that there exists a decisive rupture between the author and the interpreter. Rather than a vehicle for communication between them, the allegedly autonomous text stands as an obstacle to mutual understanding. Indeed, the object of interpretation in all these cases is something other than the author's intended meaning: rules that govern the text, a subject matter that is revealed through the text, or the historical and cultural context that shapes the text. In each of these approaches, the fundamental assumption is that a discontinuity exists between the author and the interpreter, a discontinuity that is not mediated or moderated by the text. It is a discontinuity that would make Hirsch's ideal of interpretation impossible to achieve.

Perspectivism is the effort to validate all the discontinuities that occur in the process of interpretation. Hirsch repudiates the belief that there are a number of incompatible perspectives that are all equally true, for it contradicts his conviction that understanding is "a validating, self-correcting process" (*AI*, 34). Interpretation must not forget that it is producing secondary, rather than primary, sources. This distinction highlights Hirsch's criticism of so much recent theoretical work:

> [A] text cannot be *interpreted* from a perspective different from the original author's. Meaning is understood from the perspective that lends existence to meaning. Any other procedure is not interpretation but authorship.
>
> Every act of interpretation involves, therefore, at least two perspectives, that of the author and that of the interpreter. The perspectives are entertained both at once, as in normal binocular vision. Far from being an extraordinary or illusory feat, this entertaining of two perspectives at once is the ground of all human intercourse, and a universal fact of speech. (*AI*, 49)

This is perhaps as close as Hirsch comes to describing the event of interpretation in terms of a reciprocal relation or dialogue between author and reader, speaker and hearer. But it is evident that his entire program is a lucid expression of a transactional theory of interpretation, a theory based upon explicit commitments to an ethics of communication, the primacy of human intentions, the centrality of conscious choices, and an implicit dialectic of reciprocity.

Transforming Interpretation

The two most prolific and influential writers who have developed transformational theories of interpretation are Hans-Georg Gadamer and Paul Ricoeur. Since I have already discussed the paradoxical character of Gadamer's argument in *Truth and Method* elsewhere,[12] I focus here upon Ricoeur, who presents his own position as a revision of Gadamer's hermeneutical philosophy. In a series of essays originally published in French in the early 1970s, and later translated into English under the title *Hermeneutics and the Human Sciences*,[13] Ricoeur carefully articulates the major dimensions of his view of interpretation as transformation.

Starting with Schleiermacher's program in the early nineteenth century, hermeneutics embraced a tension between two directions: a critical quest for rules governing interpretation that are valid for all texts, and a romantic commitment to the author's creative genius as expressed in the meaning of the text. Schleiermacher labeled the critical direction "grammatical interpretation," which Ricoeur characterizes as objective, whereas the romantic direction leads to "technical interpretation" of "the subjectivity of the one who speaks" (47). Schleiermacher always considered technical interpretation the primary task of hermeneutics. In his later writings he referred to it more accurately as psychological interpretation, and it virtually eclipsed grammatical interpretation in his hermeneutical program.

This tension between objective and subjective interpretation provides the point of departure for Ricoeur's own theoretical contribution. He condemns the dominant version of this dichotomy—the opposition between

12. See my article, "Paradoxes in Interpretation: Kierkegaard and Gadamer," in *Kierkegaard in Post/Modernity*, ed. Martin J. Matustik and Merold Westphal (Bloomington: Indiana University Press, 1995), 125–41.

13. Paul Ricoeur, *Hermeneutics and the Human Sciences*, ed. and trans. John B. Thompson (Cambridge: Cambridge University Press, 1981).

(objective) explanation and (subjective) understanding[14]—as "disastrous" (43). Although it was discernible in an incipient form in Schleiermacher, Ricoeur lays the primary blame for its stranglehold on modern hermeneutics on Wilhelm Dilthey, a late-nineteenth-century philosopher who developed the psychological theory of interpretation to the point where the text came to be seen only as an expression of the author's creative intention, lacking any autonomy of its own (50–51; cf. 92). Ricoeur sees Gadamer as a much-needed corrective to Dilthey, thanks to his forceful argument in *Truth and Method* that the text belongs neither to the author nor to the reader (62).

According to Ricoeur, it is the image of the hermeneutical circle that can correct the disastrous dichotomy between explanation and interpretation. He demonstrates how this is so in a discussion of the paradoxical way in which discourse expresses an enduring meaning in a fleeting speech-event and also in its capacity for triple reference—to the reality described, to the speaker, and to the hearer—which provides Ricoeur with "the key to the hermeneutical circle" (168). Since all interpretation achieves its goal in an appropriation (or rejection) of meaning by the reader, a circular relation of objective analysis and subjective evaluation cannot be avoided. But Ricoeur insists that the circle does not represent a relation between the dual subjectivities of author and reader, or even the relation between the single subjectivity of a reader (who projects a meaning onto the text) and the text itself. The hermeneutical circle is not really psychological at all, but ontological: "The circle is between my mode of being—beyond the knowledge which I have of it—and the mode opened up and disclosed by the text as the world of the work" (178).

Ricoeur develops this ontological line of thinking in an essay on appropriation. Whereas appropriation by the reader of the meaning of a text has traditionally been understood as the acme of subjectivity in interpretation, Ricoeur counters that it is not subjective in the sense of something that is controlled by or merely a projection of the reading subject. Rather, to appropriate meaning is "to receive an enlarged self from the apprehension of proposed worlds which are the genuine object of interpretation" (182–83). No longer is the task of interpretation the discernment of the meaning intended by the author; but neither is it a meaning that arises in the response of the reader. The object of interpretation is a projection,

14. The dichotomy pits objective explanation against subjective understanding, comparable to Hirsch's distinction between interpretation and significance.

Ricoeur concedes, but it is the projection of the world revealed through the text rather than something imagined by the reader:

> If the reference of a text is the projection of a world, then it is not in the first instance the reader who projects himself. The reader is rather broadened in his capacity to project himself by receiving a new mode of being from the text itself.
>
>   Thus appropriation ceases to appear as a kind of possession, as a way of taking hold of. . . . It implies instead a moment of dispossession of the narcissistic *ego*. (192)

The dispossession of the ego is Ricoeur's hermeneutical expression for what Foucault calls the decentering and displacement of the subject, or self. But it is equally Ricoeur's affirmation of the objectivity of meaning (the intentional object), an affirmation that he shares with Hirsch over against Foucault. Ricoeur, like Hirsch, finds in Husserl a convincing argument that meaning is not a mental idea but "an ideal object that can be identified and reidentified, by different individuals in different periods, as being one and the same object" (184). To grasp such an objective meaning requires, in Ricoeur's view, a "relinquishment of the self" (183). He agrees with Foucault that the tyranny of the subject is subverted; against Foucault, however, he holds that this is accomplished by an affirmation rather than a denial of meaning.

Ricoeur's concept of appropriation as the reception of a possible mode of being or world from the text also supports his argument for "distanciation" as a necessary moment in the process of interpretation. Here he offers a corrective to Gadamer, who criticizes a methodological commitment to impartiality and personal distance from the meaning of a text and praises a hermeneutical pursuit of the truth revealed in a text. (Ricoeur is fond of commenting that the title of Gadamer's *Truth and Method* would be more accurate as *Truth or Method,* and that one of his own goals is to develop a genuine dialectic of truth *and* method.) On the basis of the object-orientation of interpretation, Ricoeur treats the debate over methodological impartiality as a red herring, since distanciation is unavoidable with any text. The methodological demand for distance is redundant, since every text "is much more than a particular case of intersubjective communication . . . it is communication in and through distance" (131).

The claim that all texts distanciate themselves is based upon several premises: that all language distanciates (134), that discourse is always a structured and objectified work (138), that writing distanciates a text further (than speaking) from the author's intended meaning (139), and that texts refer to a "being-in-the-world" that unfolds in front of them (141). It is this concept of the world of the text that is the key to Ricoeur's theory of interpretation. The world that is revealed in front of a text is already a distanciation "of the real from itself" (142). It is, like Gadamer's equally central concept of "the matter (*Sache*) of the text," a complex way of stating that the meaning of a text belongs neither to the author nor to the reader nor to the text as a linguistic structure. The meaning of a text is the world, or subject matter, to which the text refers. Since Ricoeur often asserts that this world is revealed "in front of the text," his statement that "to understand the text is *to understand oneself in front of the text*" (143) must mean that correct understanding can be achieved only as self-understanding within the world of the text. To understand the meaning of a text is to understand oneself in relation to whatever meaning is revealed in and through that text, which in turn requires openness to being transformed by that meaning.

A fifth and final premise of the self-distancing character of texts is that "understanding is as much disappropriation as appropriation" (144). This echoes the earlier point about the dispossession of the ego and the relinquishment of self; and it also points to one of Ricoeur's primary goals: to disprove the prevailing assumption that a sharp contradiction exists between the receptive stance of hermeneutics and the critical posture necessary to discern the ideological presuppositions and ramifications of a text (the "critique of ideology" advocated by Jürgen Habermas). Although Ricoeur recognizes that the hermeneutical and critical voices speak from such different places that no "super-system" encompassing both is possible (87), he does hope to help them achieve some degree of mutual recognition.

Ricoeur views this question of criticism as the one real difference between himself and Gadamer. He readily acknowledges that his own point of departure is Gadamer's concept of hermeneutical experience, a concept that already implies several ways of uniting the hermeneutical consciousness of belonging to a tradition of interpretation of an object with the critical consciousness of distance over against that same object (61). But he also feels that Gadamer's theory never realizes this possible union: "the hermeneutical experience itself discourages the recognition of any critical distance," just as the dichotomy between truth and method "prevents Gadamer from really recognising the [methodological] critical instance and hence rendering justice to the critique of ideology" (90). Ricoeur uses his concept of distanciation (as a necessary moment in all interpretation) to restore to the critical consciousness its rightful place within hermeneutical experience.

The basis for distanciation is, as we have seen, the objectivity of the meaning to be interpreted. In a passage that could have been written by Gadamer, Ricoeur demonstrates that his revision is actually just an extension of their common hermeneutical position:

> The relation to the world of the text takes the place of the relation to the subjectivity of the author, and at the same time the problem of the subjectivity of the reader is displaced. To understand is not to project oneself into the text but to expose oneself to it; it is to receive a self enlarged by the appropriation of the proposed worlds which interpretation unfolds. In sum, it is the matter of the text [Gadamer's term] which gives the reader his dimension of subjectivity; understanding is thus no longer a constitution of which the subject possesses the key. . . . Reading introduces me to imaginative variations of the *ego.* . . .
>
> In the idea of the "imaginative variation of the *ego,*" I see the most fundamental possibility for a critique of the illusions of the subject. (94)

Ricoeur's argument is quite ingenious: if interpretation involves an objectivity that displaces the subjectivities of author and reader, then the hermeneutic experience itself always includes an implicit, if not explicit, criticism of those subjectivities. This means that, with Gadamer, he affirms tradition, even while, against Gadamer, he also engages in criticism of inadequate (subjective) understandings of tradition. Ricoeur has crafted a position that is meant to correct Gadamer and answer Habermas's criticisms at the same time.

But does "a critique of the illusions of the subject" really constitute a criticism of a tradition of interpretation? Even when an interpreter realizes that previous readings have been shaped by false consciousness of one kind or another, does that automatically lead to an awareness of the complicity of the tradition in that false consciousness? Ricoeur thinks that it does. His effort to reconcile hermeneutics with Habermas's critique of ideology involves not only a revision of the former but also a challenge to the latter: how is it possible to criticize and reform the distorted understandings of the past "if not upon [the basis of] the creative renewal of cultural heritage?" Moreover, he continues, although a critical consciousness is certainly oriented more toward future change than is a hermeneutical rootedness in tradition, that very openness to criticism and reform is itself part of a tradition, the tradition of the Enlightenment, and also "the most impressive tradition, that of liberating acts, of the Exodus and the Resurrection" (99). So, although hermeneutics and critique of ideology should never be conflated, "nothing is more deceptive than the alleged antinomy between an ontology of prior understanding [hermeneutics] and an eschatology of freedom [critique of ideology]." To assert a contradiction between them is to reduce them both to mere ideologies (100).

Ricoeur's conviction that hermeneutics can work together with a traditional opponent (the critique of ideology) extends to scientific studies of human behavior (the "human sciences") in general and to structuralism in particular. In a pair of essays on the nature of a text, he attempts to negotiate a proper relation among these various approaches to understanding.

Whereas hermeneutics is reflection upon the interpretation of texts, understood as "any discourse fixed by writing" (145), the human sciences try to understand the meaning of human actions. Ricoeur argues that texts in fact provide a paradigm for meaningful actions, and he defends this position against possible objections. It may be that actions are passing events, whereas texts are fixed by writing, but actions are also inscribed, events that leave their mark on the world (205). Just as the meaning of texts becomes independent from the author's intended meaning, so do actions come to mean more than the actors intended by them (201, 207). As we have seen, texts project a world that goes beyond the dialogue between author and reader; likewise, "meaningful action is an action the *importance* of which goes 'beyond' its *relevance* to its initial situation" (207). In addition, texts can create an open-ended audience, as more readers offer diverse interpretations; and "human action is an open work, the meaning of which is 'in suspense'" (208).

The open-ended audience is related to Ricoeur's understanding of the place of determinacy in interpretation. Multiple readings of a text testify not to the indeterminacy of meaning but to "the nature of the object itself" (213). Ricoeur praises Hirsch's insight into the role of guessing in interpretation. However, he locates the stability of meaning not in the author's intention but in the object that is both understood (as in the human sciences) and appropriated in hermeneutical interpretation: "As the model of text-interpretation shows, interpretation has nothing to do with an *immediate* grasping of a foreign psychic life or with an *emotional* identification with a mental intention. Understanding is entirely *mediated* by the whole of explanatory procedures which precede it and accompany it. The counterpart of this personal appropriation is not something which can be *felt,* it is the dynamic meaning released by the explanation which we identified earlier with the reference of the text, i.e., its power of disclosing a world" (220).

This is Ricoeur's final answer to all those who, with Dilthey, assert a dichotomy between explanation and understanding or interpretation: there can be no understanding without prior and ongoing explanations that are in fact interpretations. Explanation and interpretive understanding presuppose each other in a circular and paradoxical way that supersedes their opposition.

•   •   •

As we have seen, structuralist analysis attempts to explain without interpreting. Foucault likewise attempts to understand a discourse in terms of the rules that govern it, without reference to the meanings intended by those who actually employ it. In Ricoeur's estimation, this methodological self-limitation suspends the text from its references and leaves it in a worldless limbo, related only to other texts within "the quasi-world of texts or *literature*" (148–49). Ricoeur thinks of this suspension as a refusal to see the outside of a text, in its relation to a world, in favor of examining only its inside (153). Curiously, Foucault reverses the spatial metaphors in his claim to study only the surfaces of discourses and not their deeper or internal meanings. Ricoeur characterizes the process of reading as a "recovery of meaning" that requires structuralist or semiotic analysis as a necessary stage on the path from naive to critical interpretation (161). A text is not simply a static object to be studied as an instance of rules and laws, although such study is valuable; a text is a dynamic opening of a path of thought for interpretation to pursue. A text is "the work of meaning upon itself"; put differently, all the interpretations of a text are "the work of the text upon itself. Appropriation loses its arbitrariness insofar as it is the recovery of that which is at work, in labour, within the text. What the interpreter says is a re-saying which reactivates what is said by the text." (164)

The concept of texts as the work of meaning upon itself shows how thoroughly transformational Ricoeur's approach to interpretation is. He insists that the object of interpretation is neither the author's intended meaning nor the reader's projected meaning: it is the meaning of the world that opens up in front of the work. The reader must open to this world just as the author presumably has in the act of writing, and such an opening requires a relinquishing of oneself, a willingness to be changed by the world before the text. At the very least, it entails a critique of the illusions of the old self, the self that the reader had been before the encounter with this new world of meaning. The mark of authentic interpretation in Ricoeur's scheme is indeed a transformation of the interpreter, whether as reader or as author.

His view is also transformational in that it tries to combine aspects of both the theoretical and the transactional types of interpretation. Ricoeur joins Foucault in rejecting Hirsch's insistence upon the author's intended meaning as the goal of all interpretation, but he is allied with Hirsch in affirming that meaning is in fact the proper object of interpretation, over against Foucault's "suspension" of meaning in favor of rules and regularities that determine the surfaces of texts.

Theoretical interpretation always operates within carefully prescribed parameters. The goal may be to discern structures in the text or to project meanings onto it, but it is never to find the meaning within the text. The criterion by which an interpretation is evaluated is its conformity to that methodological procedure. In contrast, transactional interpretation attempts to investigate the field of meaning intended by the author and expressed in the text. An interpretation that can support its claim to represent the author's intended meaning is thereby validated. Transformational interpretation also seeks a deeper meaning that is available only to those who open themselves to what the text reveals. This revelation, however, is not of the author's conscious or unconscious intention; it is of a world of meaning that is accessible only through the text.

Theoretical interpretation is methodologically either impersonal (when the goal is knowledge of [or according to] objective rules) or subpersonal (when the interpreter takes total control of the determination of meaning by rejecting objective criteria); transactional interpretation treats the interpersonal exchange between author and reader as the key to the determination of the author's meaning; and transformational interpretation sees both of the above as preliminary or ancillary operations in relation to the primary goal of interpretation, which is the apprehension of a transpersonal world of meaning revealed by the text.

Finally, the interrelations among the three types can be clarified by a return to their respective dialectical patterns of thinking. Foucault's privileging of discontinuities and contradictions, and his conviction that they can never be reconciled, is thoroughly theoretical. Hirsch is a consistently reciprocal thinker. Although he never addresses the question of dialectic directly, he is as uncomfortable with stark oppositions as with the collapse of important distinctions. His tendency is always to discern some way in which the two poles of a contradiction can reciprocally transact with one another without losing their distinctive identities. Ricoeur also often sounds somewhat reciprocal in his efforts to mediate between opposing positions, but his actual hermeneutical program is grounded in paradox. From the claim that interpreters are transformed by interpretation to the proposal that texts reveal a world of meaning—meaning that is independent of both author and reader yet can be known only thanks to their joint efforts—his penchant for unities-within-contradictions is apparent. Although he avoids the rhetoric of paradox (perhaps for fear of appearing to conflate distinctions that must be respected), Ricoeur's key concepts are a good example of a dialectic of paradox driving a transformational theory of interpretation.

As a theoretical thinker, Foucault is more difficult to classify than Barthes, whose lover speaks subjectively out of an Image-repertoire that sometimes seems external and objective in relation to him, and Nietzsche, whose attack upon reason is so constant and consistent. Foucault articulates what is entailed in the affirmation of contradiction without any paradoxical claim of unity. He tries to remain in the space between objective and subjective theoretical interpretations without privileging either one, and also without reconciling or paradoxically uniting them. But he cannot succeed, for he does not affirm any of those stable structures or centers of meaning that could support his own argument. Foucault remains trapped in a polemical limbo of his own creation, one that results in a subjective theoretical type of interpretation.

Hirsch has shown us something about transactional understanding that has only been glimpsed before: it is a profoundly ethical undertaking. Although the ethical dimension appeared in Buber's discussion of relationships and Fromm's view of love, Hirsch shows that it is a necessary part of interpretation theory and fundamental to all transactional understanding. Thus Ellul, Douglas, and Carr are also presenting an implicitly ethical interpretation of, respectively, science and technology, myth, and history. To think reciprocally is to insist upon such values as balance, harmony, mutual respect, the integrity of the other, and the affirmation of freedom and responsibility. Hirsch also illustrates another point that has remained implicit until now: not all objective meanings are objective in the theoretical sense. Objectivity (and subjectivity) exist within all three types of interpretation, although they are certainly construed differently by each of the three.

With Ricoeur we have arrived at last at what might be called a complete transformational type of understanding. Kuhn provided a first look at a circular hermeneutic; Campbell introduced us to the coincidence of opposites;

Niebuhr showed that paradoxical relations appear within the realm of historical meaning; Kierkegaard demonstrated the paradoxical character of a Christian understanding of love; and Tillich explored faith itself as a paradoxical union of anxiety and the courage to be. But Ricoeur alone among these transformational thinkers turned his attention to the affirmation of the other types. By his inclusion of semiotics on the one hand and critical theory on the other, Ricoeur shows that the intention of transformational interpretation is to take the theoretical and transactional types up into itself, to preserve their truth while eliminating their inadequacies, to transform them just as it does every transformational interpreter, whether author or reader.

Conclusion

It would be possible at this point to let the previous chapter on theories of interpretation serve as a conclusion to this book. Since it deals directly with the subject of hermeneutics, it provides a framework within which the character and contribution of my typology stand out clearly. For those whose primary interest is theory, it can provide a satisfactory closure to the project. There would seem to be little need for an actual conclusion to the entire book.

For others, however, theories of interpretation are intelligible only in relation to a concrete topic that illustrates their abstract concepts. As work on this book has progressed, I have often been asked what it is about. My answer, "It is about interpretation," almost always elicits the same response: "Interpretation of what?" "Well, interpretation of interpretation," I reply. "Oh," comes the somewhat bewildered response. "And also interpretations of myth and history and a few other topics," I add. Visible relief.

As important and fascinating as theory is, we must never lose sight of the transformational insight into the interdependence between the act of interpreting and the subject matter being interpreted. Theoretical thinkers often operate as though the actual content to be interpreted bears no relation to the method of interpretation. Transactional interpreters are more likely to equivocate, for they also affirm a method, but it is one that privileges the content intended by the original author. On this matter, I agree with the transformational thinkers about the priority and hegemony of the subject matter, the world revealed by the text. Every act of interpretation involves a complex web of relationships in which several parties participate. The word *text* designates a site where reader, author, and subject matter all have a voice. To determine the meaning of a text, however, it is primarily to the voice of the subject matter that we must listen.

In addition, it is useful to bring the six representatives of each type together in a way that has not been possible earlier in the book. Accordingly, I shall use this conclusion to revisit the major themes of the book by type rather than by topic, but I shall do so in relation to three subject matters that seem to me to determine the character of the three types of interpretation. Throughout the book I have described the types formally as characterized by contradictory, reciprocal, or paradoxical ways of thinking. Here I argue that those types both construct and are constructed by different subject matters, or worlds, as expressed in the three rubrics: theoretical knowledge, transactional relations, and transformational revelation.

Theoretical Knowledge

As noted in the Introduction, the word "theory" derives from the Greek *theōria* meaning official spectators. By extension, it also means the contemplation of an object. Theoretical interpreters approach whatever they wish to understand as observers, whether they are examining some aspect of external reality, as in objective theoretical interpretation, or are actually examining the observers themselves, as in subjective theoretical interpretation.

How is the approach of theoretical interpreters determined by the subject matter? Scientists will be quick to point out that the purpose of their methods and procedures is precisely to eliminate any influences from the scientist or any other source that might distort understanding of the subject matter under investigation. This is why B. F. Skinner calls for better "basic analysis" of causal relations in order to eliminate any appeal to personal desires, beliefs, and intentions. His primary reason for condemning the myths of freedom and dignity is that they undermine our will and capacity for a rigorously deterministic science of behavior. Claude Lévi-Strauss also considers his structuralist approach to analyzing cultural or mental products to constitute a scientific method, although one that provides a complementary alternative to standard scientific explanations (like Skinner's) that reduce or eliminate the mental dimension. He claims to be personally detached from his work, a mere crossroads where data and the structuralist categories of analysis meet. Lee Benson admits that there are several legitimate ways to interpret history, but his own interest is only in history as a discipline that provides reliable knowledge. Thus he echoes the same emphasis upon objectivity over subjective or personal intrusions that we find in Skinner and Lévi-Strauss. He also supports the commitment of objectivist historians to factual accuracy, a priority that entails a preoccupation with rigorous methods.

When the object under observation is the observing subject, the situation becomes more complicated, but the theoretical stance is still dominant. Roland Barthes presents the discourse of a lover as a form of introspection, a narrator's reflection upon himself both as a subject and as an object within a love relationship. The narrator/lover claims that his discourse is actually his subconscious repertory of images, expressed without any mediation. In other words, just as the scientific subject must not distort the object of objective theoretical interpretation, here, conversely, the immediacy of the subject's construction of self must not be distorted by the intrusion of any objective mediating factors. Friedrich Nietzsche's distrust of the abstractions of rational analysis leads him to a hermeneutics of suspicion with regard to all the claims of the conscious self. His passionate first-person style exemplifies his stated belief that reading is a matter of imposing one's own will upon the text, just as healthy living requires imposing one's will upon the world. Finally, the theoretical discourse of Michel Foucault attempts to be both objective and subjective. However, his claim to provide a pure description of discursive events and an archaeological analysis of different discourses is not supported by any articulation of objective methods of validation, so his attacks upon the conscious subject and his advocacy of decentering, dispersion, and discontinuity result finally in granting hegemony to the subject.

In both objective and subjective theoretical interpretation, then, the subject matter is defined in such a way as to determine the method of understanding. They share the assumption that objectivity and subjectivity are incompatible, and each is accordingly very suspicious of the other. Objectivists seek knowledge of external objects, and eschew any and all subjective influences upon that knowledge. For them, true knowledge results from disciplined observation of an object in its causal matrix. Subjectivists are also committed to disciplined observation and rigorous methods, but the object of their inquiry is the illusory or ideological character of objectivity, and their elimination of objective criteria leaves a vacuum that their subjective vision and passion quickly fill up. Thus self-knowledge implicitly becomes the subject matter, without, however, submitting to any objective methods of analysis. The irony of subjective theoretical interpretation is that it deconstructs the subjectivity of the conventional "objective" interpreter only to replace it with an even more subjective perspective of its own.

In transformational terms, all theoretical interpretation is the result of a one-dimensional opposition of subject and object, with the result that interpreters must choose one pole over the other, and the pole that they choose determines which sort of theoretical interpretation they will produce.

Transactional Relations

In a parallel way, the subject matter of transactional interpretation determines its methods and content. Interpersonal relations form the core of this subject matter, although, by extension or analogy, other sorts of relations can also be understood transactionally. Just as theoretical interpreters agree upon the binary opposition between knowers and what they know, transactional thinkers invariably look for ways to moderate opposed poles by seeing them in terms of their reciprocal relations.

The resulting tendency of transactional writers to protest against theoretical (mis)understandings is therefore not surprising. Jacques Ellul's denunciation of the effects of technique, particularly of the loss of personal choice and social equilibrium in favor of efficiency, can be seen in this light. A technical human being is indifferent to such relational matters as cultural and individual preferences, moral issues, and the vitality of communities. Ellul has shifted the focus of sociological method from demographic groups to individuals freely choosing their lives and relations. Mary Douglas's grid-group analysis is a more scientific approach to the dynamics of social control and individual choice, but she is no less committed than Ellul to showing that thinking, choosing, negotiating individuals possess the freedom and diversity that are denied by deterministic theories of social conditioning. She believes that a transactional relation exists between individuals and their social environments, each being influenced by the other. Human relations must be understood reciprocally. E. H. Carr could appear to be one of those determinists whom Douglas opposes, for he emphasizes the extent to which the work of historians is shaped by their cultures and times. But he also insists that individuals exercise discretion in their choice of methods, topics, and materials, and that the claim of objectivists to be mere reporters of the facts is spurious. Moreover, he urges us to understand that human relations and activities are best understood in terms of a dialectic of reciprocity.

The way in which the subject matter determines a transactional meaning to be interpreted is especially clear for the topic of love. Erich Fromm believes that, although we should strive for mastery of both the theory and the practice of loving, love never tries to master the beloved: it respects the integrity of every other person. Fromm endorses self-love when it manifests these characteristics, but not when it is merely selfishness or narcissistic manipulation of others. At the heart of Martin Buber's philosophy is the I-Thou relation. Individuals do not really exist as isolated individuals: everyone is born and develops in relationships, so the only alternative to an I-Thou relation is an I-It experience that is appropriate with objects but normally not with other persons. Individuality is a category of I-It experience, whereas genuine personality expresses the freedom of a person to enter into relation with the other, who can never become an object of experience. Although E. D. Hirsch does not discuss selfhood or relations, he views valid interpretation as the analysis of the consciously intended meaning of the author of a text. This is an ethical choice that must be made by anyone who wishes to establish the determinate meaning of a text, rather than simply the significance that a text has for later interpreters. Although Hirsch highlights the author alone, in fact his argument presupposes that the key to interpreting texts is an implicitly reciprocal relation between the author and the reader.

Transformational Revelation

If the subject matter that defines theoretical interpretation can be identified as the object to be known (whether something external or the observing self), and the subject matter determining basic transactional interpretation is the dynamic of relations among humans, then what is the subject matter that drives a transformational type of interpretation? I have defined transformational interpretation as a paradoxical mode of understanding, the affirmation of a unity-within-contradiction. A review of the six transformational texts will show that their common subject matter is the phenomenon of revelation, understood broadly as any encounter in which the interpreter is the surprised recipient of a new understanding of the subject matter, or world, of the text from that subject matter, or world, itself.

Thomas Kuhn argues that scientists can claim to be "objective" only by standing squarely within a paradigm that is limited to their scientific community. When a new paradigm displaces the old, it does so because a few scientists find themselves compelled to "convert" to it, to have faith in it before it is confirmed and articulated, and then others follow suit. The new paradigm has, as it were, revealed itself to them, and their perception has been changed by it in such a way that they will now work to find ways to validate and articulate it. His book is a transformational interpretation of science precisely because its focus is on the mystery of discovery. Less unpredictably, Joseph Campbell construes the discovery of mystic truths in a similarly paradoxical manner. All the symbols of contradiction that express the binary structure of ordinary existence unite in a mystical coincidence of opposites that is discernible only by someone who has also been transformed by a revelation of the transcendental identity of all beings with and within the One. Reinhold Niebuhr would have little use for this mystically monistic language, but he agrees that essential truths can be expressed only paradoxically, by deception and by statements that are intellectually absurd. To claim that two radically different realities (divine and human, justice and forgiveness) are also united as one is a foolish paradox that cannot be defended in rational terms. Such faith is either a response to revelation or it is sheer nonsense.

For Søren Kierkegaard, the Christian love of paradox becomes the paradox of love. Believing that God is love, he argues that all love must be as nonpreferential as God's love. Love of neighbor, which is thoroughly nonpreferential, is therefore the basis for love of every person, whether spouse or child or enemy. Even self-love is transformed into love of God and neighbor. For Kierkegaard, every love is clearly a relation that is with God first and with other humans second. But that means that love is fundamentally a revelation of God rather than a human relationship. Paul Tillich's thought also manifests a parodoxical dialectic in which, for example, the contrary religious experiences of a mystical participation in God versus an encounter with God are superseded by the experience of faith. Even more paradoxical is the claim that the God beyond God appears (is revealed) when God has disappeared in the anxiety of doubt. According to Paul Ricoeur, the hermeneutical problem is the widely assumed dichotomy between objective explanation and subjective interpretation or understanding. His solution to this dilemma is a paradoxical reinterpretation of the hermeneutical circle as the ontological relation between an interpreter and the world revealed in the text. Ricoeur insists that appropriation of that revealed world is to be understood not as a merely subjective reading but as the objective and paradoxically subjective work of the text upon itself.

Clearly, each of the three types of interpretation has distinctive strengths and very real limitations. Objective theoretical thinkers generally make the best "normal" scientists, but they do not do so well with the subjective aspects of either human relations or the appropriation of new "revealed" paradigms. Subjective theoretical interpreters are superb at exposing the self-deceptive discourses and ideological character of an established normal science, but, once their negative message has been delivered, they can offer nothing more without changing their approach and thereby adopting the very categories they had attacked. Transactional approaches to understanding construe everything in terms of relations, and therefore do well in situations where interaction and reconciliation are desirable. They provide a tempering influence, a voice for balance and harmony, even when they cloak what they advocate in the rhetoric of an attack upon theoretical thinking. Finally, transformational interpretation excels wherever the subject matter entails genuine novelty, something so new (at least to the interpreter) that its origins seem inexplicable and its truth can be grasped only paradoxically. The compelling power of this new revelation of a subject matter, or world, dominates transformational interpretation, just as theoretical explanation is shaped by the objective or subjective subject matter it seeks to grasp, and transactional understanding is a response to the reality of relations that can be discerned in every event of knowledge or revelation. For all interpreters, it is the subject matter they seek to understand that most decisively shapes how they proceed and what they produce.

Unfinished Agenda

Having arrived at the end of this book, I am aware that many of the topics I have contemplated treating do not appear within these pages. With a tool such as this typology, there is never any clear point of closure: the subjects to which it could be applied are virtually limitless. I have used it for years in a graduate seminar called Interpretation and Decision Making, and the students, most of whom hold management positions, often find it helpful for sorting out a variety of business and organizational issues. It could certainly be used to distinguish the key commitments dividing the theoretical psychoanalytic practice of Freudians from the transactional mode of Rogerian therapists and the transformational agenda of Jungians. My own background leads me to think about the question of theological method, where theoretical, transactional, and transformational paradigms also compete for influence. There is intense debate in America about religious cults, a subject that involves theories about both organization and religion. Whereas many theoretical thinkers invoke notions of deception and mind control, transactional interpreters look at the social dynamics within such groups, and an occasional transformational essay examines the spiritual appeal they have for those seeking truth.

Sometimes a particular book illustrates one of the three types so well that the prospect of a new topic arises, but the task of finding comparable works that represent the other two approaches to the same topic proves impossible within the time available. For example, I have found many excellent examples of feminist transactional interpretation, but only a few that are theoretical and almost none that seem to be thoroughly transformational. Given the fact that on most topics transformational readings are less well represented than the other two types, this is hardly surprising. But it does make finding appropriate books difficult. The opposite may be the case where Buddhist philosophy is concerned. Nagarjuna is one of the greatest philosophers ever to employ a dialectic of paradox. The difficulty with Buddhist thought may lie rather in finding adequate examples of transactional thinking.

Readers will, I hope, find the three types I have discussed useful as they pursue their own agendas in interpretation. To return to the question with which I started, this is not a book that summarizes all that we know about interpretation. It is, rather, an essay that is intended to facilitate and enrich the experience of interpretation for its readers. Opportunities to explore a variety of understandings surround us at every turn. Questions about whether a particular interpretation of a topic might be theoretical, transactional, or transformational appear constantly. Being able to identify its dialectical type, and those of its competitors, can make interpreting the character of many hermeneutical conflicts a more exciting and rewarding experience.

Index